Baedeker's

VIENNA

Imprint

Cover picture: The Vienna Philharmonic in the Musikvereinssaal

87 colour photographs
25 plans, 1 Underground map, 1 large city map

Conception and editorial work:
Redaktionskbüro Harenberg, Schwerte

English language: Alec Court

Text:
Dr Gerda Rob; Christa Sturm

General direction:
Dr Peter Baumgarten, Baedeker Stuttgart

English translation: Babel Translations Norwich

Cartography:
Ingenieurbüro für Kartographie Huber & Oberländer, Munich

Source of illustrations:
Albertina (1), Baedeker (1), Bildarchiv Preussischer Kultkurbesitz (1), dpa (23), Harenberg (4), Historia-Photo (8), Mauritius (1), Austrian Bundesktheaterverband (1), Naturhistorisches Museum (1), Prenzel (3), Rudolph (3), Uthoff (32)

Following the tradition established by Karl Baedeker in 1844, sights of particular interest and hotels of outstanding quality are distinguished by either one or two asterisks.

To make it easier to locate the various sights listed in the "A to Z" section of the Guide, their coordinates on the large city plan are shown in red at the head of each entry.

Only a selection of hotels, restaurants and shops can be given: no reflection is implied, therefore, on establishments not included.

In a time of rapid change it is difficult to ensure that all the information given is entirely accurate and up to date, and the possibility of error can never be entirely eliminated. Although the publishers can accept no responsibility for inaccuracies and omissions they are always grateful for corrections and suggestions for improvements.

4th edition

© Baedeker Stuttgart
Original German edition

© Jarrold and Sons Ltd
English language edition worldwide

© The Automobile Association 61010
United Kingdom and Ireland

US and Canadian Edition
Prentice Hall Press

Licensed user:
Mairs Geographischer Verlag GmbH & Co., Ostfildern-Kemnat bei Stuttgart

Reproductions:
Gölz Repro-Service GmbH, Ludwigsburg

The name *Baedeker* is a registered trademark

Printed in Italy by G. Canale & C. S.p.A. - Borgaro T.se - Torino

0–86145–204–6 UK
0–13–371303–2 US and Canada
3–87504–167–4 Germany

Contents

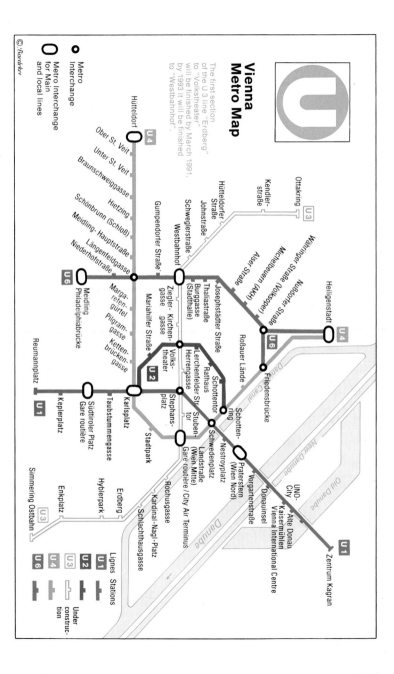

Vienna Metro Map

The first section of the U 3 line "Erdberg" to "Volkstheater" will be finished by March 1991. by 1993 it will be finished to "Westbahnhof".

● Metro
○ Interchange

○ Metro interchange for Main and local lines

© /Rarídkrr

Lignes	Stations
U6	
U4	
U3	Under construction
U2	
U1	

Preface

This Pocket Guide to Vienna is one of the new generation of Baedeker city guides.

Baedeker pocket guides, illustrated throughout in colour, are designed to meet the needs of the modern traveller. They are quick and easy to consult, with the principal sights described in alphabetical order and practical details about how to get there, opening times, etc., shown in the margin.

Each guide is divided into three parts. The first part gives a general account of the city, its history, population, culture and so on; in the second part the principal sights are described; and the third part contains a variety of practical information designed to help visitors to find their way about and make the most of their stay.

The new guides are abundantly illustrated and contain numbers of newly drawn plans. At the back of the book is a large city map, and each entry in the main part of the guide gives the coordinates of the square on the map in which the particular feature can be located. Users of this guide, therefore, will have no difficulty in finding what they want to see.

Facts and Figures

General

Vienna is both the capital of the Republic of Austria and one of neutral Austria's nine provinces. It is the seat of the Austrian President, the Federal Government, the supreme administrative governmental bodies and of local government for the province of Vienna.

Despite its peripheral location in present-day Austria, it is very much the political, economic, intellectual and cultural hub of the Republic.

Located in northern Austria, the city is encircled by the province of Lower Austria and, at an altitude of 558 ft (170 m), it lies on latitude 48°14'N and longitude 16°21'E.

Most of the city extends along the right bank of the Danube and it is bordered in the W by the Vienna Woods.

Situation

With a total area of 160 sq. miles (415 km²) Vienna falls within the middle range of European capitals. Within the 86 miles (133 km) of its borders, Vienna has 24,216 acres (9,800 ha) of agricultural land, 21,000 acres (8,500 ha) of gardens (of which 4,122 acres (1,668 ha) are open to the public), 1,656 acres (670 ha) of vineyards and 17,051 acres (6,900 ha) of woodland.

Area and population

Its population has declined in numbers since the First World War. In 1910 Vienna still had a population of 2·1 million but today it has only 1·5 million inhabitants with a density of 9,557 per sq. mile. The annual death rate of 24,000 is higher than the 15,000 annual birth rate and incomers (31,000) are less than the 32,000 who leave the city.

The city is divided into 23 Districts: I City Centre, II Leopoldstadt, III Landstrasse, IV Wieden, V Margareten, VI Mariahilf, VII Neubau, VIII Josefstadt, IX Alsergrund, X Favoriten, XI Simmering, XII Meidling, XIII Hietzing, XIV Penzing, XV Rudolfsheim-Fünfhaus, XVI Ottakring, XVII Hernals, XVIII Währing, XIX Döbling, XX Brigittenau, XXI Floridsdorf, XXII Donaustadt and XXIII Liesing.

City Districts (Stadtbezirke)

District I, the City Centre, corresponds to the historic city of Vienna. Districts III–IX, developed from outlying villages, are now termed "Inner Districts", while districts X–XIX, the former suburbs outside the Gürtel, the outer ring road, are the "Outer Districts". In a broader sense districts II and XX, together with the fringe districts XXI–XXIII, also belong to the Outer Districts. The smallest district (Josefstadt) covers an area of ¾ sq. mile (1·8 km²) while the largest (Donaustadt) is 40 sq. miles (102 km²) in extent. The most thinly populated district is the City Centre with 19,000 inhabitants and the most densely populated is Favoriten with 146,000.

◄ *Panoramic view of Vienna and its Cathedral*

Population and Religion

Administration

Both a district and a province, Vienna also plays a dual role in administrative terms. The District Council, consisting of 100 members elected for five years, is at the same time the Provincial Council and the elected Mayor heads both authorities. The Provincial Senate, the effective Government, is composed of the Mayor, two Deputy Mayors and 915 office-holding Councillors.

In order to decentralise the administration the 23 districts have their own representatives who elect one of their number to act on their behalf.

International organisations

Vienna is the headquarters of a great many international organisations: UNIDO (the United Nations Industrial Development Organisation), IAEA (the International Atomic Energy Agency), the UN High Commission for Refugees, ICEM (International Committee for European Migration) and OPEC (Organisation of Petroleum Exporting Countries). IAEA has 80 and UNIDO has 86 permanent delegations of member countries in the city.

In terms of foreign policy, Vienna has played some part as a mediator between East and West and was the venue for two top-level meetings of historic importance when President Kennedy met Nikita Kruschev, the Soviet Premier, in the city in 1961 and President Jimmy Carter met Leonid Brezhnev, the Soviet President, in 1979.

There are in Vienna plans to establish representation in the European Community.

Population and Religion

Population

In the Middle Ages Vienna, with a population of 20,000, was already one of the largest German-speaking cities. The influx into the city was at its height between 1880 and 1910 when the population figures soared from 592,000 to 2 million. The newcomers were mainly from Bohemia, Moravia, Hungary and Galicia and when, at the turn of the century, over 60% were non-German-speaking, Vienna became a gigantic melting-pot for ethnic and religious minorities.

After the Second World War those coming to settle in Vienna were chiefly refugees from Hungary and Czechoslovakia, most of whom have since become Austrian citizens. Since 1960 it has mainly been Yugoslav immigrant workers who have sought to settle permanently in Vienna.

Of Vienna's 113,500 registered foreigners and stateless persons the majority are Yugoslavs, Turks, Germans, Poles and North Americans. Among the smaller foreign groups there are many students from Arabic-speaking countries, from Africa and the Far East.

Religion

Seventy-four per cent of the Viennese are Roman Catholic, 7·5% Protestant and 0·5 Jewish. In addition there are congregations of the Old Catholic, Greek, Serbian, Russian and Bulgarian Orthodox Churches, and of the Armenian Church, Methodists and Mormons.

Vienna is also the seat of a Roman Catholic Archbishop.

The year 1979 saw the building of an Islamic centre and mosque for the city's 50,000 Muslims.

Transport

Vienna is situated at the intersection of important N–S and E–W routes, at a point where the Alpine Foreland merges with the Hungarian Plain. In the S, W and NW the encircling hills, with their woods and meadows, penetrate deep into the residential areas while the flat plain extends beyond the city in the E and NE.

Port

A 12½ mile (20 km) stretch of the Danube flows through E Vienna, splitting off Districts XXI and XXII from the rest of the city. This ranks as an international waterway and its banks are Federally administered.
The Altern, Lobau and Freudenau port installations are in the SE corner of the city and the commercial quay has its own customs house. Every year about 900,000 tons of cargo enter Vienna by the Danube and 460,000 tons are shipped out.
The passenger vessels of the DDSG (Danube Steamship Company) embark from Nussdorf and Reichsbrücke Station and carry almost one million passengers in a season.

Airport

Schwechat, Vienna's international airport, is 11¼ miles (17 km) from the city centre, to the E of the location of Schwechat itself. More than 37 airlines and 61 ancillary transport firms use the airport, carrying 3·8 million passengers annually.
Since 1977 there has been an Underground station at the airport, connected by fast trains with Wien-Rennweg and Wien-Nord.

Railway stations

European rail services from all points of the compass converge on Vienna, although not all at one central station.
Vienna has three main railway stations:
Westbahnhof (West Station) takes trains coming from W Austria and Western, Central and Northern Europe.
Südbahnhof (South Station) and Ostbahnhof (East Station) handle trains from S Austria, Italy, Yugoslavia, Greece, Warsaw and Moscow.
Trains from N Austria and Czechoslovakia arrive at Franz-Josefs-Bahnhof.
Vienna's railway stations sell 13 million tickets a year.

Urban rail transport

Commuters in particular are efficiently and speedily catered for by the rail network (117 miles (187 km)) operated by Austrian Railways within the city, with its 39 stations and 30 halts.
Tramways, S-bahn, Underground, Express railways and municipal buses serve a network of about 311 miles (500 km). Every year they carry more than 430 million passengers and cover over 56 million miles (90 million km).
In autumn 1982 the so-called basic network of the Underground which was started in 1969 had been completed with three routes (U1, U2 and U4). Further sections are under construction.
The "Silver Arrows" of the Underground reach top speeds of 50 m.p.h. (80 km p.h.) and run at an average speed (including stops) of 22 m.p.h. (35 km p.h.).
The Underground stations are closely supervised at night and are generally considered to be safe.

Schwechat, Vienna's international airport

Karlsplatz Station, part of Vienna's urban transport network

Vienna's first urban motorway is the partially completed "Gürtelautobahn", the ring road that runs round the S and SE part of the city, linking the S motorway with the roads running E and NE.

The W motorway (A1 – Westautobahn) from the W edge of the city leads to Salzburg and the Austrian border, while the S motorway (A2 – Südautobahn) departs in the direction of Wiener Neustadt and continues towards Graz. The A21 links the W and S motorways S of the city. The A4 leads in an easterly direction S of the Danube to Schwechat.

Other major roads (Bundesstrasse) out of Vienna:

Highway   1 – to Linz, Salzburg
          3 – to Krems, Wachau
          4 – to Horn, Lower Austria
          9 – to Hainburg
         10 – to Bruck/Leitha
         12 – to Mödling, Baden
         14 – to Klosterneuburg
         16 – to Eisenstadt, Burgenland
         17 – to Semmering, Steiermark
        230 – to Laxenburg

Roads

Culture

Vienna is one of the world's greatest metropolises from the cultural point of view and in terms of the number of international figures in the artistic world who gather there, particularly musicians. No other city has been the home of so many great composers nor of so many chamber ensembles, orchestras and choirs.

Many works of great value are on show in its more than 100 national and private museums and some 120 galleries while the Brueghel Collection, one of Europe's greatest collection of paintings, is here in Vienna, together with one of the world's most extensive collection of graphics and the largest number of Albrecht Dürer's drawings assembled in one place. The collection of incunabula in the National Library is the third largest in the world.

About 2·9 million visitors a year pass through the city's museums while the collections of the National Library attract 320,000 and over 2 million visit the Hofburg and Schönbrunn.

The University of Vienna, founded in 1365 as Alma Mater Rudolphina, is currently attended by 50,000 students, engaged on studies in all the classic faculties.

Of 15 Austrian Nobel prize-winners, 12 graduated from this University – in proportional terms in relation to the national population the highest figure in the world – and it enjoys an exemplary reputation in the fields of medicine, psychology, physics and technical studies.

Vienna also has a further 16,200 students at its universities for Technical, Veterinary and Agricultural studies and the study of Economics.

Universities

The Academy of Fine Art, the Academy of Diplomacy, the College of Applied Arts and the Academy of Music and Dramatic Art are all of international standing.

Academies and colleges

Artists who have lectured at the Academy include Arik Brauer, Wolfgang Hollegha, Markus Prachensky, Friedensreich Hundertwasser, Anton Lehmden, Josef Mikl and Arnulf Rainer, while at the Academy of Music celebrated musicians, singers and actors are on the teaching staff.

Academy of Science

The Austrian Academy of Science is located in Vienna. It has 26 institutes and 31 specialist commissions.
It is divided into two classes, that of philosophical and historical sciences and that of mathematical and natural sciences. Each class has 33 members as well as 60 correspondent members from abroad and 40 correspondent members within Austria.

Libraries

The foremost of the libraries in Vienna are the Austrian National Library with 10 important leading collections – encompassing 2·5 million volumes – and the University Library with about 2 million volumes. The most extensive specialist collection is that of the Technical University with 800,000 volumes (see Practical Information – Libraries).

Theatres, orchestras

Vienna's many theatres (see Practical Information – Theatres) can seat about 16,000 in total and their annual audience figures amount to close on 3·3 million.
The Burgtheater heads the dramatic league. The home of the great classics, it has become a byword among German-speaking peoples for the excellence of the German spoken on its stage.
The Vienna State Opera (Staatsoper) ranks among the three most important opera-houses in the world. It has international opera stars on its permanent staff and can call on the top names among performing artistes and conductors for guest performances. The Vienna Philharmonic gives its concerts in the Staatsoper and the Great Hall of the Musikverein, while the Vienna Symphonic performs in the Konzerthaus. The city has a further six orchestras, 28 chamber music ensembles and 20 choirs.
Over 700,000 a year enjoy the music on offer in Vienna's many concert halls (see Practical Information – Music).

Press

24 newspapers (6 daily, 18 weekly) are published in Vienna, as well as 1,412 periodicals and specialist publications.

Commerce and Industry

International status

The emergence of Austria as a small republic after the collapse of the Habsburg Empire in 1918, lost Vienna, in its peripheral location, much of its standing as a world power in commercial terms. Today Vienna owes its status as the place where commercially East meets West mainly to good bilateral trading relationships.
Many foreign and multi-national companies and banks are represented in Vienna as Austria's capital, and crucial decisions of far-reaching importance are taken here at the sessions of OPEC, the Organisation of the Petroleum Exporting Countries.

Centre of the
Austrian economy

Vienna is the hub of Austria's administration, commerce, industry and money market and the headquarters of 554

The Vienna Philharmonic performing in the Musikvereinssaal ▶

corporations, 150 co-operative societies and 27,150 registered firms.

Some 741,100 people work in Vienna (including 65,000 immigrants), 71,336 of them in the direct employ of the city.

Industrial tradition

For 200 years industry in Vienna has centred on the processing of imported and local raw materials. The sector with the greatest turnover is food and drink, followed by electrical industries, chemicals, mechanical engineering and steel construction, ironware and metal goods, as well as the clothing industry. Currently Viennese industry has a gross annual product valued at over 82 billion schillings.

The Viennese themselves are also skilled craftsmen when it comes to the production of fashion accessories, lace, petitpoint, luxury leather goods and gold and silverware.

Prominent Figures in Viennese History

Friedrich von Amerling
(14.4.1803–14.1.1887)

After studying at the Vienna Academy Amerling travelled across half Europe and it was Thomas Lawrence in London and Horace Vernet in Paris who had the decisive impact on his work. The son of a filigree-worker, Amerling became the portrait-painter most sought after by the nobility in his time. Amerling's most famous picture, "Emperor Francis I", hangs in the Marie-Antoinette Room at the Palace of Schönbrunn. Many of his other works are on show in the Historical Museum in the city of Vienna (see entry).

Ludwig van Beethoven
(16.12.1770–26.3.1827)

Beethoven, who was born in Bonn, was 22 years old when he came to Vienna where he remained until his death. His misanthropy was notorious. He stood aloof from society and never became a real Viennese although it was here that he found patrons and friends such as Archduke Rudolf and Princes Lichnowsky and Kinsky. Temperamentally never at his ease, he felt impelled frequently to move house. Of the many houses he lived in the most famous is No. 6 Probusgasse. Here he drafted in 1802, as his deafness worsened, his tragic "Heiligenstadt Testament".

The majority of Beethoven's works were composed in Vienna, all nine symphonies receiving their first performances here. The Ninth (Choral) Symphony was first performed in 1824 at a great concert in the Kärntnertor Theatre.

Johannes Brahms
(7.5.1833–3.4.1897)

Brahms settled in Vienna only in 1869 when the Gesellschaft der Musikfreunde invited him to become conductor of their concerts. Brahms's symphonies were originally offered to the public in Vienna, the Second and Third Symphonies receiving their first performances from the Vienna Philharmonic. His greatest success, however, came when his "German Requiem" was performed in the city. Brahms's work is considered to be the culmination of the Viennese Classical tradition in music.

He is buried in the central cemetery.

Ludwig van Beethoven

Johannes Brahms

Sigmund Freud

More a Spaniard than an Austrian, the Emperor Charles introduced strict Spanish Court ceremonial to Vienna. In 1713 he promulgated the Pragmatic Sanction under which his daughter Maria Theresa was allowed to succeed him.
Buildings erected in Vienna during the reign of Charles VI include the Karlskirche, the Court Library, the Winter Riding School, the Palace of Schönbrunn, Prince Eugene's Belvedere (see entries), numerous palaces for the nobility and several new churches for the religious Orders.

Charles VI (1.10.1685–20.10.1740)

Elisabeth, a Wittelsbach Princess, became Empress when she married Emperor Franz Joseph I in 1854. She also became Queen of Hungary in 1867. The marriage was basically intended to favour German interests in Austria. There were four children, Rudolf, the heir to the throne, and three daughters.
Elisabeth I, or Sissi as she was commonly known, was richly talented, artistic, sporting and capricious. Her aversion to strict Court etiquette drove her to spiritual loneliness. After her son, Crown Prince Rudolf, committed suicide in the hunting-lodge at Mayerling, she led a restless life, travelling constantly. In 1898 she was the victim of an attack by the anarchist Luccheni in Geneva.
The magnificent apartments of the Empress in the Hofburg and in the Palace of Schönbrunn are on show (see entry).

Elisabeth I (24.12.1837–10.9.1898)

J. B. Fischer von Erlach was born in Graz. After studies in Rome in the ambit of Bernini he became Imperial Court Building Superintendent. He is rated Austria's greatest Baroque architect.
He discovered a synthesis between Italian exuberance and Viennese charm, between French Early Classicism and Late Ancient style. His façades are not stiff or rigid; they are always dynamic.
Fischer von Erlach's masterpieces in Vienna are the Karlskirche, the Palace of Schönbrunn, the early parts of Prince Eugen's Winterpalais, Trautson and Neupauer Palaces, parts of the Schwarzenbergpalais and the Hofbibliothek which his son completed (see entry).

Johann Bernhard Fischer von Erlach (20.7.1656–5.4.1723)

17

Prominent Figures in Viennese History

Francis II (I)
(12.2.1768–2.3.1835)

With the Emperor Francis II the Holy Roman Empire of the German Nation came to an end. On account of the foundation of the Rhenish Confederation he abdicated as Roman Emperor in 1806 and from 1804 onwards he had assumed the title of Emperor Francis I of Austria.

The first Emperor of Austria participated in a variety of coalitions against France but gained no benefit. Finally Napoleon I moved into Schönbrunn, and in 1810 Francis I found himself obliged, for purely political reasons, to marry his daughter Marie Louise to the Corsican adventurer. The marriage took place in the Augustinekirche (see entry); Napoleon did not himself attend the ceremony.

Franz Joseph I (18.8.1830–
21.11.1916)

Franz Joseph I, Austria's penultimate Emperor and at the same time King of Hungary, came to the throne when 18 years old. He reigned for 68 years. In the course of his long reign there were military defeats in 1859 and 1866, the settlement of differences with Hungary, the formation of the Triple Alliance, the annexation of Bosnia and Herzogovina, and the outbreak of the First World War.

Vienna became bigger thanks to the Emperor's plans for enlarging the city, more beautiful when the Ringstrasse was laid out, and more important thanks to his support for the Arts. In his personal affairs the Emperor was dogged by misfortune; his brother Maximilian of Mexico was executed by a firing-squad in 1867, his son Crown Prince Rudolf committed suicide in 1889, Empress Elisabeth was stabbed to death in 1898, and Franz Ferdinand the heir to the throne was assassinated in 1914 in Sarajevo.

Sigmund Freud (6.5.1856–
23.9.1939)

Sigmund Freud revolutionised the realm of psychology. At a time when the monarchy was collapsing and all was in tumult, he analysed human failure and dreams, developing a method based on response to suppressed traumatic experiences.

The father of psychoanalysis was a professor at the University of Vienna. Taking into account the significance of the unconscious he influenced our understanding of the human mind, of the relationship between mind and body and psychiatry.

Freud's apartment, 19 Berggasse, has become a museum (see Practical Information – Museums).

Franz Grillparzer (15.1.1791–
21.1.1872)

Franz Grillparzer, Austria's most important playwright, came from an old-established Viennese bourgeois family. He was a civil servant, rising to the rank of Hofrat, going into the "Herrenhaus" (Upper Chamber) in 1871. Although essentially he had his roots in early-nineteenth-century middle-class culture he tried to lead the way towards a new style distinct from Romanticism. He became the classic author in the theatres of Vienna. In 1816 he made his début with "Die Ahnfrau" (The Ancestress) at the Burgtheater. In 1888 the rebuilt theatre opened with his "Esther". In 1955 a performance of his "Konig Ottokars Glück und Ende" (King Ottokar's Prosperity and Demise) was given to mark the opening of the reconstructed theatre.

Joseph Haydn (31.3.1732–
31.5.1809)

Joseph Haydn, the son of a wheelwright, began his career at the age of eight as a cathedral chorister in Vienna. He is considered the founder of the symphony and himself wrote more than one hundred works in the new style.

Joseph Haydn

Franz Grillparzer

Emperor Franz Joseph I

Even during his lifetime Haydn was recognised and famous. He served first as Musical Director to Prince Esterhazy, later scoring notable successes in Paris (Paris symphonies) and in London (London symphonies). He returned to Vienna in 1797. He was a successful man who composed two more of his finest oratories in his own house 19 Haydngasse (see entry). "The Creation" was first performed in Vienna in 1798 to be followed by "The Seasons" in 1801.

Lukas von Hildebrandt was the second outstanding architect of the Viennese High Baroque period. He was born in Genoa, settling in Vienna a decade after Fischer von Erlach. Though they were on good terms, great rivalry developed between these two gifted men as they strove to win the favour of patrons.

Johann Lukas von Hildebrandt (14.11.1668–16.11.1745)

An outward sign of the interplay between these two great talents is evident in various buildings which, reflecting the changing taste of their patrons, are partially by one and partially by the other.
Hildebrandt's masterpieces are his palaces for Prince Eugene, above all the Belvedere (see entry).

Hugo von Hofmannsthal, whose Jewish forebears came from Bohemia and Milan, was a genuine product of cosmopolitan Austria. He became famous as an author, writing plays and libretti for Richard Strauss's operas.

Hugo von Hofmannsthal (1.2.1874–15.7.1929)

His play "Der Schwierige" (The Bore) belongs to the repertoire of the Viennese theatre. His "Jedermann" (Everyman) is one of the great attractions of Salzburg.

Gustav Klimt belonged to that group of progressive artists who in 1897 broke away from the Künstlerhaus Verein and, as the "Secession", sought new developments.

Gustav Klimt (14.7.1862–6.2.1918)

As a painter Klimt is considered to be the main representative of the Viennese Jugendstil (Art Nouveau). He also had a major influence on the Wiener Werkstätte (Viennese Workshops). Several of his works of art are in the 19th and 20th c. Austrian Gallery in the Upper Belvedere (see Belvedere-Schlösser). His monumental "Beethoven Frieze" can be seen in the Secession building.

Prominent Figures in Viennese History

Franz Lehár
(30.4.1870–24.10.1948)

Franz Lehár was the outstanding personality in the second great age of operetta after 1900. Lehár, who was born in Hungary, was active in all centres of the monarchy as a military bandmaster.

"The Merry Widow" received its first performance in Vienna in 1905. It was followed by "The Count of Luxemburg" (1909), "Gypsy Love" (1910), "Frasquita" (1922) and "Paganini" (1925). After his 25th work for the stage he decided to write for the theatre in Berlin. He returned to Vienna only for his last two operettas "The World is Beautiful" and "Giuditta".

Maria Theresa
(13.5.1717–29.11.1780)

Charles VI's eldest daughter was the first woman to succeed to the throne of the Holy Roman Empire of the German Nation. This woman "with the heart of a king" had to defend her country against France, Prussia, Saxony and Bavaria. Despite three wars which were energetically waged she lost Silesia to Frederick the Great, King of Prussia.

Maria Theresa, who married Francis Stephen of Lorraine, was a thoroughgoing Baroque personality. She had 16 children and with immense energy and a vibrant passion for reform she reorganised the "House of Austria" and filled its empty treasury.

Wolfgang Amadeus Mozart
(27.1.1756–5.12.1791)

Wolfgang Amadeus Mozart was born in Salzburg where he became the Archbishop's Musical Director in 1769. He came to Vienna in 1781 and it was here that he wrote his great operas: "Il Seraglio" (Die Entführung aus dem Serail) first performed in 1782, "Marriage of Figaro" in 1786, "Così fan tutte" in 1790 and "The Magic Flute" in 1791. Only "Don Giovanni" and "La clementia di Tito" received their premières in Prague.

Mozart, who was adulated as a child, met with disappointments and successes in Vienna. The disappointments were mainly of a financial nature. Nine weeks after the first performance of "The Magic Flute" Mozart died; he was buried in an unmarked pauper's grave in St Marx's cemetery.

Johann Nestroy
(7.12.1801–25.5.1862)

Johann Nestroy, a raffish student, opera-singer, comic improviser and theatre manager, became famous for his farces. He portrayed the lowest social classes brilliantly and fought against the social ills of the time. He was, in many respects, at the opposite end of the scale to Ferdinand Raimund whose imaginary dream world he brought back to reality. His greatest success in Vienna was "Lumpazivagabundus".

Nikolaus Pacassi
(5.3.1716–11.11.1790)

Nikolaus Pacassi was Maria Theresa's Court Architect and her favourite. Overwhelmed with commissions he was the busiest architect of his age. Pacassi was responsible for completing the Palace of Schönbrunn, the reconstruction of the Theresianum and Hetzendorf Palace: he built the Gardekirche (see entry) and the Kärntnertor Theatre. Nearly all the major 18th c. public buildings in Vienna were reconstructed, enlarged or restored under his direction.

Ferdinand Raimund
(1.6.1790–5.9.1836)

Ferdinand Raimund, whose real name was Jakob Raimann, found scope for his dramatic and poetic talents in the Josefstädter Theatre in Vienna. He took the old Viennese fairy-tale and magical play and gave it a poetic form, thus founding a genuine folk drama. After Raimund had been bitten by a dog suspected of rabies he shot himself in a fit of depression.

Wolfgang Amadeus Mozart   Johann Nestroy

Ferdinand Raimund

The repertoire of the Burgtheater today includes some of his plays: "Der Verschwender" (The Spendthrift), "Der Bauer als Millionär" (The Peasant as a Millionaire) and "Alpenkönig und Menschenfeind" (King of the Mountains and Misanthropist).

France refused to let Prince Eugene join the French Army because of his diminutive stature. So he first became an Abbé, entering Austria's service as a soldier only in 1683. He rose to the rank of Field-Marshal, becoming Commander-in-Chief in the war against Turkey in 1697, President of the Court Council of War in 1703 and Viceroy in the Austrian Netherlands in 1714.

Eugene, Prince of Savoy
(18.10.1663–21.4.1736)

Among his triumphs are numbered victories over the Turks at Zenta, Peterwardein and Belgrade as well as successes in the War of the Spanish Succession. Prince Eugene was the Councillor of the Emperors Leopold I, Joseph I and Charles VI, and is considered to be the true creator of Austria's status as a Great Power. The Belvedere Palace provided a fitting surrounding for this great man (see entry).

A protégé of Gustav Klimt, Egon Schiele, a pupil of the Academy, specialised in life studies and drawings. At first an adherent of the Jugendstil, he later developed an entirely personal style and took his place at the head of Viennese Expressionistic avant-garde.

Egon Schiele
(12.6.1890–31.10.1918)

In his short life Schiele produced some 2,000 drawings and water-colours. His most important works are to be found in the Austrian Gallery in the Upper Belvedere (see entry) and in the Museum of the 20th Century (see entry).

Franz Schubert was born in Vienna. He was a composer who was able to express himself in a wide variety of musical forms. Beginning as an assistant to his father who was a schoolmaster, he became "the master of the 'Lieder'".

Franz Schubert
(31.1.1797–19.11.1828)

His life was short, but as well as suffering from poverty and anxiety he also enjoyed satisfying friendships, with authors such as Bauernfeld and Grillparzer and with the painter Moritz von Schwind. He wrote 600 "Lieder", 8 symphonies, 6 Masses, numerous pieces for piano and for chamber ensemble, overtures, operas, musical comedies and choruses.

The most impressive of his symphonies are "The Unfinished" and "The Great C Major". His song-cycles are in the repertoire of every major Lieder-singer.

Moritz von Schwind
(21.1.1804–8.2.1871)

Moritz von Schwind, a fresco-painter and pupil of the Viennese Academy, worked for a few years in Vienna but was disappointed by his lack of success. So in 1847 he went to Munich where he taught in the Academy.

Returning in 1863 to Vienna for a few years he painted the fresco-cycles in the State Opera. This theatre was bombed and gutted by fire in 1945, but the originals of Schwind's scenes from famous operas can still be seen in the foyer and the Loggia. Other frescoes by Schwind are to be found in the dome of the Austrian Gallery in the Upper Belvedere (see Belvedere-Schlösser).

Johann Strauss (Father)
(14.3.1804–25.9.1849)

As composer and conductor, Johann Strauss, together with his contemporary Josef Lanner, created the new form of the Viennese waltz in the second quarter of the 19th c. Strauss was first viola-player in Lanner's Quartet, formed his own dance band in 1825 and developed it into a large orchestra. He made concert tours to Germany, Paris and London. In 1835 he was appointed Musical Director of the Court.

The "Radetzky March" is probably his most popular composition.

Johann Strauss (Son)
(25.10.1825–3.6.1899)

Johann Strauss possessed exceptional charm, temperament and inventiveness. He was only 19 when, against his father's wish, he made his Viennese début with his own orchestra. Five years later he took over his father's famous orchestra and toured half Europe before going on to the USA.

He was called the "Waltz King" because he made the Viennese waltz world-famous. It was only later in life that he turned to operetta. He scored his first major success with "Die Fledermaus" (The Bat) in 1874, followed by "The Gypsy Baron" in 1885 and "Wiener Blut" (Viennese Blood) in 1899. Strauss composed his waltz "The Blue Danube" at 54 Praterstrasse. It is now the home of the Strauss Museum (see Practical Information – Museums).

Franz von Suppé
(18.4.1819–21.5.1895)

The history of Viennese operetta begins with Franz von Suppé, who was Musical Director at three Viennese theatres. Suppé began by composing comic operas including "Die Schöne Galathee" (Beautiful Galathea). Then, under Jacques Offenbach's influence, he wrote "Fatinitza", the first of his operettas to be performed in Vienna, and "Boccaccio" came just a little later. These are among the finest examples of classical operetta.

History of Vienna

5000 B.C.	First indications of human settlement.
2000 B.C.	Indo-Germanic settlements on the NW wooded slopes.
800 B.C.	Celts settle on what is now the site of the "Hoher Markt".
15 B.C.	The Celtic town of Pannonien is occupied by the Romans. "Vedunia" becomes the Roman "Vindobona".

Vindobona, a fortress with a garrison of 6,000 legionaries, expands, becoming a rectangular walled enclosure on the site of the present "Hoher Markt".	2nd c. A.D.
Vindobona is a city with a population of 20,000.	3rd c.
The Celts destroy the Roman city.	c. 400
Bajouarii found, around present-day Vienna, their first small settlements. The names of these end in -ing; among them are Penzing, Ottakring, Grinzing.	8th c.
Charlemagne founds the Carolingian province.	799
Austria under Babenberg rule.	976–1246
Emperor Conrad II is besieged in Vienna by the Hungarians.	1030
Emperor Henry VI holds a Council at Vienna.	1042
Babenbergs win suzerainty over Vienna.	c. 1135
The Wienerische Kirche (Viennese Church) is erected on the square in front of St Stephen's Cathedral.	1147
Duke Henry II, "Jasomirgott", Duke of Ostarichi, transfers his residence from Regensburg to Vienna. The first palace, Am Hof, is built.	1156
The city becomes larger, and the city wall is reconstructed.	c. 1180–98
Planning of the moat.	c. 1190
The Teutonic Order of Military Knights is summoned to Vienna.	c. 1198–1204
Coins are minted in Vienna.	1190
Consecration of the Schottenkirche (Scots Church).	1200
The Ducal Court moves into a new palace on the site of the present-day Stallburg.	1220
Vienna is granted the status of a city with the right to hold a market.	1221
For the first time Vienna becomes an Imperial Free City, a distinction it forfeits in 1239.	1237
The Babenberg line becomes extinct.	1246
Granting of the status of Imperial Free City.	1247
Rule of the Bohemian King Přemysl Ottokar II.	1251–76
Rudolf of Habsburg is elected King of Germany, taking the title of Rudolf I. He lays claim to Austria as a former Imperial part of the feudal empire. Přemysl Ottokar II refuses to do homage.	1273
Regency of King Rudolf I after the decisive defeat of Ottokar of Bohemia.	1278–82

History of Vienna

1365	Founding of the University of Vienna.
15th c.	Vienna's population grows to 40,000 in the course of this century.
1412	The city's privileges confirmed.
1438	Vienna becomes the seat of the Holy Roman Empire of the German Nation.
1485–90	The Hungarian King Matthias I Corvinus holds sway over Vienna for a short while.
1493–1519	Emperor Maximilian I expels the Hungarians from Vienna. Vienna sides with the Reformation.
1515	The double wedding between the children of Vladislav and the grandchildren of Maximilian constitutes the foundation of what will become the Danube monarchy.
1522	The failure of a popular uprising is followed by the Bloody Assizes of Wiener Neustadt.
1524	Execution of Caspar Tauber, the first martyr of the Wars of Religion.
1532–1672	The Turkish Siege leads to the erection of a massive circle of permanent defences.
1551	The Jesuits arrive in Vienna and spearhead the Counter-Reformation.
1577	Protestant services are forbidden: Vienna has become a Catholic city once again.
c. 1600–38	The "monastery offensive": many monasteries and churches are built by Franciscans, Dominicans, Capuchins, Barnabites, Discalced Carmelites and Servites.
1618–48	The Thirty Years War brings the Bohemians and the Swedes to the gates of Vienna (1645).
1629	Vienna is attacked by plague. The dread pestilence claims 30,000 victims in a very short period.
1683	Grand Vizier Kara Mustafa with 200,000 men lays siege to the city which is defended by no more than 20,000 under the leadership of Count Starhemberg. Vienna is delivered from the overwhelming Turkish army by a relieving force under the Polish King Sobieski.
1683–1736	Prince Eugene of Savoy, as Imperial Field-Marshal, gains victories over the Turks and French. This restores Austria to the status of a Great Power, and its capital gains lustre as "Vienna gloriosa".
1740–80	When Maria Theresa comes to the throne in 1740 160,000 people are resident within its fortifications. The Empress lays the foundations of present-day culture and institutes the system of central government.

The Palace of Schönbrunn is built.	1744–49
First population census: it reveals that Vienna has 175,000 inhabitants.	1754
Joseph II develops Vienna as a world city in accord with the concepts of Enlightened Absolutism, leading the capital into the Industrial Era.	1780–90
Pope Pius VI in Vienna.	1782
Reform of the city's government: appointment of a Chief Magistrate.	1783
Vienna has a population of 231,000.	1800
The French besiege Vienna.	1804
Under pressure from Napoleon, Francis II has to abdicate as Holy Roman Emperor. Henceforth he is simply Emperor of Austria.	1806
Napoleon takes up residence in the Palace of Schönbrunn. The siege of Vienna leads to the financial collapse of the State.	1809
The Congress of Vienna, renowned for its glittering festivities, debates under the presidency of Prince Metternich with a view to establishing a new order in Europe (the "Restoration") after Napoleon's defeat.	1814–15
Danube floods. Vienna's population has swollen to 318,000.	1830
Cholera epidemic	1831–32
Revolution in March against Prince Metternich's régime. Though the Revolution is put down by Prince zu Windischgrätz it leads to Metternich's retirement and the abdication of Emperor Ferdinand I.	1848
Franz Joseph I is Emperor of Austria.	1848–1916
Plan of the Ringstrasse area (partially opened in 1865) and razing of the fortifications.	1857
Building of the New Town Hall.	1872–73
The suburbs are incorporated in the city (11–19 Districts).	1890
Brigittenau becomes the 20th District.	1900
Collapse of the Dual Monarchy and abdication of the last Austrian Emperor, Charles I. Vienna becomes the Federal capital. Formerly the seat of government of a State with a population of 50 millions made up of 12 nationalities it becomes overnight simply the capital of a minor country with a population of 6·6 million. This diminution in size leads to immense political problems within the State. Vienna is surrounded by a belt of hideous modern blocks of flats which were built to relieve the social problems thrown up by this so-called "second foundation era".	1918

History of Vienna

1938	Vienna becomes an administrative region within the German Reich. The pan-Germanic interlude costs the lives of 200,000 Viennese inhabitants. Fifty-two air raids and 10 days of fighting in the city itself leave 21,000 houses destroyed and 86,000 dwellings uninhabitable. 120 bridges are blown up and 3,700 gas and water mains are smashed.
1945	The Red Army occupies the city.
1955	Austrian State Treaty. After 10 years of occupation the city, which had been divided up into zones administered by the victorious Allies, celebrates the freedom it gains thanks to the Treaty.
1956	Vienna becomes the seat of the Atomic Energy Authority.
1961	John F. Kennedy, President of the USA and Nikita Kruschev, Chairman of the Soviet Council of Ministers, meet here for the first time on 3 and 4 June 1961.
1967	Vienna becomes the seat of UNIDO.
1969	Construction of an Underground railway begins.
1979	Opening of UNO City. President Carter of the USA meets Leonid Brezhnev, President of the Presidium of the Supreme Soviet of the USSR.
1983	In the parliamentary elections the SPÖ loses its absolute majority. The Federal Chancellor, Bruno Kreisky, resigns; the new Chancellor is Fred Sinowatz (SPÖ). Vienna celebrates the "Turkish Year" (1683–1983), the 300-year existence of the Viennese Coffee House. – U.N. Conference on human rights in Vienna. – Pope John Paul II in Vienna on the occasion of the Austrian Catholic Conference.
1985	The 30th anniversary of the signing of the Austrian State Treaty is marked by a meeting of the Foreign Ministers of the countries which concluded it.
1987	The conference centre "Austria Center Vienna" is opened in April, increasing the conference facilities in the capital by almost 20%.

Vienna from A to Z

*Akademie der Bildenden Künste (museum)   C4

The Akademie der Bildenden Künste (The Academy of Fine Arts) is an institution of international importance for the training of painters, sculptors, graphic artists, stage-designers and architects. It also has a major print collection and impressive picture gallery.

Peter von Strudel, the founder of the Academy, started the first art school in his house called "Strudelhof" in 1692. He was inspired by Italian examples. In 1876 it transferred to new premises on the Schillerplatz; they were designed by Theophil Hansen in Italian Renaissance style. They were severely damaged in 1945, but have been restored.

Among former pupils of the Academy are such Viennese painters as Amerling, Waldmüller, Kupelweiser, Schwind, Schiele, Gütersloh, Fuchs, Hutter, Hausner and Lehmden.

Adolf Hitler applied for admission to the Academy in 1907, but he failed the entrance examination.

Location
3 Schillerplatz, I

Underground station
Karlsplatz (U1, U2, U4)

Bus
59A

Trams
1, 2, D, J, 62, 65

Before going up to the Print Room on the mezzanine, visitors should pause on the ground floor and take a look at the Aula, a classical hall for ceremonies with an arcaded gallery all round. On its ceiling is a painting by Anselm Feuerbach, "The Fall of the Titans".

The Print Room, adjacent to the Library on the mezzanine, has a collection of 30,000 drawings and water-colours, 25,000 engravings and etchings, unique Gothic architectural drawings from the Clerk of the Works' office at St Stephen's Cathedral, more than 300 nature studies by Friedrich Gauermann and 415 water-colours of flowers by the miniature-painter Michael Daffinger.

Print Room

Opening times
Mon. & Wed. 10 a.m.–noon;
Tues. & Thur.
2–6 p.m.; Feb., Easter, &
July–Oct., only by prior
arrangement.
Admission free

The Picture Gallery (west wing of the first floor) was originally intended as a "teaching aid" in order to train students in observation and feeling for style. However, the Academy was not only a school of art but also an institution and thus during the 18th c. the collection was increased by "accepted works". These were pictures which every student had to submit when applying to be a member of the Academy. In 1822 when the stock of pictures was increased by the acquisition of the collection of the late President of the Academy, Anton Graf Lamberg-Sprinzenstein, the first step towards the foundation of a gallery of international importance had finally been taken. Even today, when the collection is being increased by purchase and by gifts, the picture gallery of the Academy is characterised by the fact that at least one work of almost all the artists associated with it is included.

Picture Gallery

Opening times
Tues., Thur., Fri. 10 a.m.–
1 p.m., Wed. 10 a.m.–
1 p.m. & 3–6 p.m., Sat.,
Sun. 9 a.m.–1 p.m.

Rooms 1, 2 and 3 are used for administrative purposes.

Room 4: 15th and 16th c.; Dutch and German artists. Early Dutch art of the 15th c.; including Dierck Bouts's "Coronation of the Virgin"; altar-piece (c. 1500) by Hieronymus Bosch: the Last Judgment is flanked by Heaven and Hell.

An early work by Hans Baldung, known as Grien; "The Holy Family in the Open Air" and the "Holy Family", one of the major works of Lukas Cranach the Elder.

Room 5: 16th c. and Baroque; Italian and Spanish artists.
The Italian Renaissance is represented by the "Madonna and Child with Angels" (c. 1480) from Botticelli's workshop. Pictures of the Venetian School, among them Titian's "Tarquin and Lucretia".

Room 6: 17th c.; Flemish artists.
Works by Rubens, with the magnificent sketches for his ceiling-painting (subsequently destroyed by fire) for the Jesuit Church in Antwerp. Van Dyck, who worked as an independent artist in Rubens's studio, is represented by a self-portrait and the sketch of an "Assumption of the Virgin".

Rooms 7–9: 17th c. Dutch artists.
Typical pictures of the Haarlem School (Dirck Hals, Peter Codde, etc.). Portraits include Rembrandt's "Young Woman in an easy chair". Landscapes by Jan van Goyen, Jakob van Ruysdael and Cornelies Vroom.

Room 10: 18th c.
Works by Tiepolo, Magnasco and Pannini; eight Venetian "Vedutas" by Guardi. Austrian painting includes a portrait of the Empress Maria Theresa (1759) by Martin Van Meytens, a Director of the Academy, and works by Gran, Maulbertsch and Kremser-Schmidt.

Room 11: 19th and 20th c.; Austrian painters.
Works by Füger, Krafft, Maurer and Abel. Biedermeier painting is represented by Waldmüller, von Amerling and Danhauser; the "Pupils' Room" by the last named shows a classroom in the former academy building.

Room 12: Student collection and temporary exhibitions.
Works by Boeckl, Wotruba, Gütersloh, Pauser, Elsner, Hessing and by previous professors of the Academy, including Hundertwasser, Lehmden, Mikl and Rainer.

Albertina (art gallery) C4

Location
1 Augustinerstrasse, I

Underground station
Karlsplatz (U1, U2, U4)

Trams
1, 2, D, J (Ring), 62, 65, L

Opening times
Mon., Tues., Thur.
10 a.m.–4 p.m., Wed.
10 a.m.–6 p.m., Fri.
10 a.m.–2 p.m., Sat. &
Sun. 10 a.m.–1 p.m.
Closed on Sun July–Aug.

The Albertina possesses 45,000 drawings and water-colours, about 1½ million printed sheets of graphic material covering a period of half a millennium and 35,000 books – it is the world's most comprehensive collection of graphic material.
The collection was founded in 1768 by Maria Theresa's son-in-law, Duke Albert of Saxony-Tescha. Since 1795 it has been housed in the former Taroucca Palace. Between 1801 and 1804 the building was altered by Louis von Montoyer.
The Albertina as we know it today resulted from the amalgamation, after the First World War, of the collections of Duke Albert and the print room of the Imperial Library. The holdings are so rich and vast that normal exhibition is not possible. Instead only a portion of the collection can be shown at one time, and the displays are changed throughout the year. It is, however, between March and October that the choicest examples are on show:

The Albertina – the world's most important collection of graphic art

Dürer: "The Hare", "Madonna with all the Animals", "Praying Hands", and "The Large Piece of Turf". Raphael: "Madonna with the pomegranate". Rubens: The portraits of his family.
*For conservation reasons some parts of the collection are accessible only to researchers. There is, however, no catalogue.

The drawings are classified under national schools.   Drawings

German School after the 15th c. – 145 drawings by Dürer, who is more fully represented in the Albertina than anywhere else, works by Holbein the Elder, Baldung Grien, Cranach the Elder, Altdorfer, Kölderer, Menzel, Spitzweg, Feuerbach, Liebermann, Nolde and Kollwitz.

Austrian School, from the 18th c. onwards, including von Rottmayr, Troger, Kremser-Schmidt, Schwind, Daffinger, Amerling, Alt, Gauermann, Makart, Klimt, Schiele and Kubin.

Italian School, from the Early Renaissance onwards, including Pisanello, Fra Angelico, Lippi, Mantegna, Leonardo, Titian, 43 drawings by Raphael, Michelangelo, Tintoretto, Veronese, Guardi, Canaletto and Tiepolo.

Flemish School, from the 15th c. onwards, including drawings by Van Leyden, Brueghel the Elder, de Momper, Van Dyck and a collection of sketches by Rubens.

Dutch School, city schools from the 17th c. onwards, including drawings by Both, Asselijn, Van Goyen, Ruysdael, De

Hooch and 70 drawings from all Rembrandt's creative periods.

French School, from the 16th c. onwards, including examples of work by Clouet, Bellange, and Callot, choice drawings by Poussin and Lorrain, works by Watteau, Liotard and Fragonard, and by Picasso, Matisse and Chagall.

English School, from 1650 onwards, with drawings by Hogarth, Reynolds, Gainsborough and Romney.

The Special Collections, available only to experts, include architectural drawings (8,000 sheets), miniatures, views of Austria and Vienna, historic prints, illustrated books, Japanese woodcuts and posters and collections of sketch books (including those belonging to Waldmüller, Stifter, Gauermann, Schwind and Schiele).

Print Collection

The Print Collection (woodcuts, copperplate engravings, etchings, screen-prints, lithographs and metal cuts) includes the world's largest collection of 15th c. single-sheet xylographs, Dürer's woodcuts and copper engravings, Rembrandt's etchings, original work by Menzel, woodcuts by Munch, first impressions by Goya and works by Picasso and Chagall.

Film Museum

The Albertina also houses the Austrian Film Museum (film shows, but no exhibitions). Programmes can be found in the daily papers and weekly brochure of events.

Performances
Oct.–May, Mon.–Fri., 6 and
8 p.m.

Albrechtsrampe mit Danubius-Brunnen (fountain)   C4

Location
Albertinaplatz, I

Underground station
Karlsplatz (U1, U2, U4)

Trams
1, 2, D, J (Ring)

The ramp is now just the remains of the old, once-mighty Augustinian priory, on the site of some former city fortifications. The bastion was destroyed in 1858, and the ramp that remained was severely damaged by bombing in 1945. It was converted into open-air steps in 1952.

By the "ground floor" of what remains of the ramp stands the Danubius Fountain (also called the "Albrecht Fountain"). It, too, has survived only in a fragmentary state. The fountain was a gift to the city of Vienna from Franz Joseph I, and when it was unveiled in 1869, the allegorical figures of Danubius and Vindobona in the middle were surrounded by 10 more figures in alcoves. All of white Carrara marble, they personified the Rivers Theiss, Raab, Enns, Traun, Inn, Save, March, Salzach, Mur and Drau.

After severe war damage in 1945 the fountain had to be reduced to its middle section alone. The empty alcoves seem bare, giving a melancholy impression.

Amalienburg

See Hofburg

The square Am Hof dominated by the Baroque façade of its church

Am Hof (Church of the Seven Choirs of Angels and Square)

The square Am Hof (see entry below) is dominated by the remarkable Early Baroque W façade of the former Jesuit church dedicated to the Seven Choirs of Angels. In 1782 Pius VI, the only Pope ever to visit Vienna, pronounced his blessing "Urbi et Orbi" from the balcony above the entrance. It was from the same balcony that Emperor Francis II proclaimed the dissolution of the Holy Roman Empire of the German Nation in 1806.

The Gothic rectangular church was built in the 14th c., reconstructed in the Baroque style in the 17th c. and provided, probably by Carlo Carlone, with its façade which dominates the square in 1662.

Inside, the organ-casing is notable, as are the Maulbertsch frescoes (second side-chapel on the left), the Lady Chapel altar, and the ceiling-paintings by Andrea Pozzo in the Ignatius Chapel.

Am Hof (square)

Am Hof is the largest square in the city centre. But since the transfer of the Saturday Flea Market to the Naschmarkt (see entry) it has lost much of its colour and bustle.

The Romans set up camp on this site; remains of buildings may be seen at 9 Am Hof. The Babenbergs judged this the right place to build their first palace (1135–50), and Walther

Location
Vienna, I

Underground stations
Stephansplatz (U1)
Schottentor (U2)

Buses
1A, 2A, 3A

Trams
1, 2, D, T

Roman Camp
Open
Sat., Sun., public holidays
11 a.m.–1 p.m.

von der Vogelweide sang the glories of their glittering festivities there: "That is the wondrous court at Vienna" (plaque on wall of 2 Länderbank).

Later on the Mint of the ruling princes was erected here, replacing the Ducal Court.

In 1667 the Corinthian column with the bronze figure of the Virgin treading the serpent underfoot was erected in the middle of the square. The four putti symbolise the Virgin's protection against war, plague, hunger and heresy.

Fire Service Museum

Open
Sun. & public holidays
Admission free

The former Burghers' Armoury (10 Am Hof), built in the 16th c., later enlarged and extensively rebuilt in 1731–32, now houses the headquarters of the Vienna Fire Brigade and the Fire Service Museum. Among the more noteworthy houses around Am Hof are the Märkleinische Haus (No. 7), designed by Lucas von Hildebrandt and built between 1727 and 1730, the Urbanihaus (No. 12), a Baroque building with a Madonna relief, and No. 13 which dates from 1660. A tablet on this building commemorates the fact that Mozart made his first public appearance here in 1762.

Annakirche C4

Location
1 Annagasse, I

Underground station
Stephansplatz (U1)

The Church of St Anne in Annagasse was built in the 15th c. in the Gothic style. It was founded by Elisabeth Wartenauer, the wife of a burgher of Vienna. In the 17th c. the original church was rebuilt, and in 1715 it was refurbished in the Baroque style. It belonged successively to the Poor Clares and to the Jesuits, before being handed over in 1897 to the Oblates of St Francis of Assisi.

The church has a ceiling-painting and a picture above the High Altar, both by Daniel Gran. The 1505 wood-carving of Anne, above the first altar on the left, is ascribed to the Nuremberg Master, Veit Stoss.

Devotion to St Anne has deep roots in Vienna. The church has in its keeping as a precious relic the hand of the Saint in a rich Baroque setting.

Annagasse, which turns off right from Kärntnerstrasse (see entry), is a narrow thoroughfare which is a reminder of what Vienna looked like in the 18th c. The lane existed as early as the 14th c., when it was called "Pippingerstrasse", and there was a chapel already on the site now occupied by the Annakirche.

There are some fine old houses here: the 17th c. Esterhazy Palace (No. 2), Kremsmünsterhof (No. 4), Herzogenburgerhof (No. 6), Maibergerhof (No. 7), Deybel or Täuberlhof, which was a school for artists and engravers before the Academy of Fine Arts (see entry) was opened, Zum Blauen Karpfen (Blue Carp House, No. 14), now a hotel, and Zum Römischen Kaiser (the Roman Emperor, No. 16).

Augarten and Augartenpalais (park and mansion) A5

Location
1–3 Obere
Augartenstrasse, II

The Augarten is a 140 acre (52 ha) park between the Danube Canal and the Danube. In it still stand the ruins of the Alte Favorita, the Augarten Palace and Josephsstöckl.

The park was laid out as an Imperial pleasure garden in the 17th c., and reconstructed in 1712 to plans by Jean Trehet. In 1775, at the desire of Emperor Joseph II, it was opened to the people of Vienna "as a place dedicated to the enjoyment of all men".

The Alte Favorita, Leopold I's garden palace, was set on fire by the Turks in 1683. Joseph I had the Garden Pavilion erected on part of the ruins, and it was here that from 1782 the famous musical matinées took place, under the direction first of Mozart, then also of Beethoven.

The Augarten porcelain manufactory is at present housed in the former Garden Pavilion. It was founded in 1718 and has belonged to the city since 1924. Its traditional dinner-services, bearing the names Pacquier, Liechtenstein, Prince Eugene and Maria Theresa are known the world over. The most popular articles made for export are porcelain Lippizaner horses in the various haute école positions and Viennese types based on original models dating back to the era of Maria Theresa.

Augartenpalais

Since 1948 the Augarten Palace has been the boarding-school for the Vienna Boys' Choir (see entry for Wiener Sängerknaben).

A Privy Councillor had the proud mansion built towards the end of the 17th c., to plans produced by Johann Bernhard Fischer von Erlach. In 1780 it was purchased by Emperor Joseph II who, however, personally preferred to reside in the modest Kaiser-Joseph-Stöckl. The latter was built for him in 1781 by Isidor Carnevale. Nowadays this building houses the "transitional" members of the Vienna Boys' Choir, that is to say choristers who have to move on when their voices have broken.

In 1782 Pope Pius VI, stayed in Josephsstöckl.

Bus
5A

Trams
31, 32, N

---

*Augustinerkirche

C4

The Church of the Augustinians is externally without decoration, but it was once the scene of great weddings. In 1810 the Archduchess Marie Louise was married here to Napoleon I, who was so short of time that he had to be represented by a proxy. In 1854 Emperor Franz Joseph wedded Elisabeth (Sissi) of Bavaria here, and in 1881 the legendary and unfortunate Crown Prince Rudolf married Stefanie of Belgium.

The church was built for the Augustinian Canons. Between 1330 and 1339 Dietrich Ladtner von Pirn constructed an aisle-less oblong church in Gothic style. The aisle-less choir was added about 1400, and the tower was built on in 1652. The Chapel of St George dates from 1351, and the Loretto Chapel from 1724. The church was refurbished in Baroque style later, but all this was swept away in 1785 when J. F. Hetendorf von Hohenberg carried out a restoration, bringing back the Gothic style.

Walking round the church in a clockwise direction visitors will note – in addition to the features mentioned below – the icon to the left of the entrance, the chancel and the High Altar.

Location
3 Augustinerstrasse, I

Underground station
Stephansplatz (U1)

Bus
1A, 2A, 3A

Trams
1, 2, D, T (Ring)

Tour

Augustinerkirche

The Augustinerkirche – its unadorned exterior, its Gothic interior

The Loretto Chapel was once adorned with silver, but that had to be melted down during the Napoleonic Wars. The beautiful wrought-iron railing dates from the 18th c. In the Heart Vault the hearts of the Habsburgs are contained in small silver urns. The earliest is the heart of Matthias who died in 1619. Here rest the hearts of 9 emperors, 8 empresses, 1 king, 1 queen, 14 archdukes, 14 archduchesses and 2 dukes.

The Chapel of St George was built in the 14th c. by Duke Otto the Merry as a meeting-place for the knightly Order of St George. Later it was converted into a mortuary chapel, and the victor of Kolin, the Imperial Count Daun, lies buried here, as does Maria Theresa's Physician, Gerard van Swieten. The marble tomb of Leopold II (1799) is empty. The Emperor lies in the Imperial Vault in the Kapuzinerkirche (see entry).

The Christinendenkmal is a monument opposite the entrance. It is considered to be the most important piece of sculpture in the church. Antonio Canova's famous marble tomb for the Duchess of Saxony-Tescha, the daughter of Maria Theresa, dates from 1801 to 1805. Beneath the apex of the flat pyramid up against the surface of the wall, the spirit of blessedness bears the Archduchess's medallion. Her body, however, lies in the Imperial Vault in the Kapuzinerkirche (see entry).

The organ, like the pews, comes from the Schwarzspanier-kirche (The Black Spaniard Church) which was destroyed in a storm. This organ was used at the first performance of Bruckner's Mass in F minor. The organ was restored between 1974 and 1976.

Bäckerstrasse B5

In this street where bakers once lived and worked visitors will find old mansions and ancient doorways with coats of arms and signs on houses that have been handed down over the ages.

Among the more notable houses are:
No. 7 with a courtyard with Renaissance arcading and, on the first floor, a small collection of fine metalwork which the Viennese painter F. Amerling brought together.
No. 8 is the former Seilern Palace which was built in 1722 in J. L. von Hildebrandt's style.
No. 12 dates from the 15th and 16th c. and has a remarkable Renaissance oriel on its first floor. Once upon a time the house was called "Wo die Kuh am Brett spielt" (Where the cow plays chequers) and was painted all over.
No. 14 was built in 1558, and altered in 1700.

Location
Off Lueck, I

Underground
Stephansplatz (U1)

Buses
1A, 2A

*Baden (near Vienna) (spa)

Baden is a spa at the foot of the Valley of the Helenen. Its sulphur springs were known to the Romans as Aquae Pannonicae. Especially in the early 19th c. it was a popular resort for Viennese society. Here Mozart wrote his "Ave Verum" for the choirmaster of the parish church, and Beethoven spent 15 summers here at 10 Rathausgasse, working on his Ninth Symphony which he completed in 1823–24. Schubert, Liszt, Raimund, Stifter, Alt, Daffinger, Waldmüller and Schwind were frequent visitors to Baden. Lanner, Ziehrer and Strauss gave concerts in the Spa Gardens, and it was near here that Grillparzer composed "Das Goldene Vliess" (The Golden Fleece).
Today people go to Baden to bathe in the large hot baths in Helenenstrasse, to attend the open-air performances in the Summer Arena in the Spa Park and to gamble in the Casino.

Baden Railway
from Oper

Regional Railway
from Südbahnhof (R10)

Bus
from Westbahnhof
Bus Station

Distance
12½ miles (20 km) S

35

Interesting sights are a Trinity Column (1714) in the main square, the Town Hall (1815) and the "Imperial House" (1792), where the Emperor resided each summer from 1803 to 1834.

Basiliskenhaus (old house)   B5

Location
7 Schönlaterngasse, I

Underground station
Stephansplatz (U1)

The Basiliskenhaus, formerly also called the "House with the Red Cross", is known to have existed as early as 1212. It is one of the oldest houses in Vienna. It was damaged by bombing in 1944, and has been restored in 16th c. style.
There is a sandstone figure of a basilisk in a niche in the second storey of the façade. Legend has it that a monster, which had been disgorged by a hen, lived here in a fountain; its poison is supposed to have brought disease and death to many people until a brave man held a mirror up to the monster, which was so shocked at its appearance that it burst!

Beethoven-Denkmal (monument)   C5

Location
Beethovenplatz, I

Underground station
Stadtpark (U4)

The Beethoven Monument is the work of the Westphalian sculptor Kaspar von Zumbusch and dates from 1880. It stands in a little square in front of the Akademisches Gymnasium, founded by the Jesuits in 1552, and which is one of the oldest and best humanistic schools in Vienna; former pupils include Arthur Schnitzler and Peter Altenberg.
At the feet of the seated figure of the composer may be seen Prometheus in chains with the eagle pecking at his flesh. On the right stands Victory proffering a triumphal wreath, and all round are nine putti, representing Beethoven's nine symphonies. Formerly Beethoven's statue faced away from the River Wien, but since the little river was covered over it has faced the water.

**Belvedere-Schlösser (palaces)   C5

Location
Unteres Belvedere:
6 Rennweg, III
Oberes Belvedere:
27 Prinz-Eugen-Strasse, III

Underground stations
Karlsplatz (U1, U2, U4)
Taubstummengasse (U1)

Tram
D, 71

Opening times
for all museums Tues.–
Sun. 10 a.m.–4 p.m.
Son et Lumière in
summer daily 9.30 p.m.

There are two Baroque palaces built for Prince Eugene, the Unteres (Lower) Belvedere and the Oberes (Upper) Belvedere. They now house the three museums of the Austrian Gallery.
With the Château of Versailles in mind, Prince Eugene, who defeated the Turks, had a summer residence built on the abandoned slope of the Glacis by the Rennweg. Work began in 1700, and Lucas von Hildebrandt devoted 10 years to what was to be his masterpiece. In 1716 the Unteres Belvedere, where Prince Eugene actually lived, was completed. It was only in 1724 that the Oberes Belvedere with its reception-rooms was finished. It stands on higher ground. Montesquieu remarked, in connection with this building, that it was pleasant to be in a country where the lower orders were better housed than their master.
The two palaces are linked by a magnificent garden. Dominique Girard, a landscape-gardener from Paris, designed

them in accord with Hildebrandt's over-all concept of a terraced park laid out along an axis with cascades and symmetrical flights of stairs with hedges and paths forming the sides. The sculptures adorning the pools lead symbolically up from the bottom. At the foot we see the Underworld with Pluto and Proserpina in the bosquets, then Neptune and Thetis, the deities of water, in the area where the cascades play, together with Apollo and Hercules. From the terrace in front of the Oberes Belvedere there is a wonderful view down over the garden which drops away, and out over the towers of Vienna and heights of the Vienna Woods. S of the Oberes Belvedere is an Alpine Garden.

Alpine Garden

After the death of the Prince who remained a bachelor all his life, his heiress – "frightful Victoria", as the Viennese called her – sold off the entire property without a second thought. The Imperial Court acquired the buildings and the gardens in 1752. Franz Ferdinand, the heir to the throne, lived in the Belvedere between 1894 and 1914, and he was living here at the time of his tragic visit to Sarajevo.

Opening times
Daily 9 a.m.–4.30 or 6 p.m.

It was in the Marble Chamber of the Oberes Belvedere that, on 15 May 1955, the Foreign Ministers of France, Great Britain, the Soviet Union, the United States and Austria signed the Austrian State Treaty which restored Austria's independence.

A tablet in the curator's wing of the Upper Belvedere commemorates the death here of Anton Bruckner in 1896. The Emperor had placed the quarters at the disposal of the Court Organist and Composer as a mark of his respect.

The history of the palace is recounted in a Son et Lumière open-air presentation in the park in front of the Oberes Belvedere on summer evenings.

From the Upper Belvedere there is access to the Alpine Garden (see Botanical Gardens).

Museum mittelalterlicher österreichischer Kunst

The Museum of Austrian Art from the Middle Ages is housed in the Orangery of the Unteres Belvedere. The collection includes masterpieces of sculpture and panel-painting from the end of the 12th c. to the early 16th c., though there is some emphasis on 15th c. works. The oldest exhibit is the Romanesque Stammerberg Crucifix. It dates from the end of the 12th c. and is thought to be the oldest surviving example of Tyrolean wood-carving.

Location
Unteres Belvedere (entry through the Österreichisches Barockmuseum)

The collections of the museum are divided into five sections.

Section 1: Works by the "masters of the altar-pieces", including four stone figures by the Salzburg Master of Grosslobming (c. 1415–20) and a Madonna and Child on a throne (end of the 12th c. and the second oldest exhibit in the museum).

Section 2: The outstanding exhibits are the Crucifixion scenes, the so-called "Wiltener Crucifixion" and the centre panel of Conrad Laib's 1449 Crucifixion reredos.

Section 3: Here may be seen five pictures by the Tyrolean painter and carver Michael Pacher and seven pictures by

Rueland Frueauf the Elder. Among the works by Pacher owned by the museum are parts of the High Altar from the Franciscans' Church in Salzburg.

Section 4: Important exhibits include a pair of pictures: "Pietá" and "The Adoration of the Kings"; they once formed part of the original reredos in four sections of the Schottenkirche in Vienna and date from 1469.

Section 5: As well as Marx Reichlich's pictures of the Life of the Virgin and parts of the Waldauf reredos (from near Hall), the pictures by Urban Görtschacher, including an "Ecce Homo" of 1508, are especially noteworthy.

Österreichisches Barockmuseum

Location
Unteres Belvedere

The Austrian Baroque Museum has been housed since 1923 in Prince Eugene's residence, the Unteres Belvedere. It contains a collection of paintings and sculptures from the great age of the Baroque style in Austria.

The most important rooms in the museum are:
The Rottmayr Room (Room 3): Johann Michel Rottmayr painted figures like those of Rubens in bright, light colours. On show are two of his early works, "The Praising of the Name of Jesus" and "The Sacrifice of Iphigeneia". The picture "Susannah and the Elders" in the same room is by Martin Altomonte.

Kremser-Schmidt Collection (Room 5): Martin Johann Schmidt devoted himself almost exclusively to religious painting, but there are two of his secular paintings here. "Venus in Vulcan's Forge" and "The Judgement of Midas" were the two works he painted when he sought admission to the Viennese Academy.

Marble Hall (Room 8): This two-storey-high chamber with its extremely rich stucco decoration and its painted ceiling by M. Altomonte which depicts the Triumph of Prince Eugene,

Lower Belvedere
Austrian
Baroque Museum

1 Ticket Office
2 Portraits
3 Rottmayr, Altomonte
4 Gran, Troger; Giuliani
5 Kremser-Schmidt
6 Disciples of Troger and Maulbertsch
7 Marble Cabinet
8 Marble Hall: Figures by Donner
9 Baroque Sculpture

Ambraserhof

Entrance

10 Dormer Gallery
11 Maulbertsch Gallery
12 Funerary reliefs
13 Maria-Theresa Gallery
14 Grotesques
15 Maulbertsch Cabinet
16 Marble Gallery
17 Hall of Mirrors (Gold Cabinet)
18 Early Classicism

View from the Palace Gardens over the Lower Belvedere

the conqueror of the Turks, is the finest room in the Unteres Belvedere. In the middle stand the original figures made by George Raphael Donner for the Providentia Fountain in the Neuer Markt (see entry).

Donner Gallery (Room 10): In what used to be Prince Eugene's bedroom, with a painted ceiling by M. Altomonte, may be seen Donner's reliefs for the piscina at St Stephen's Cathedral, statuettes of Venus and Mercury, statues of Charles VI and of a nymph.

Maulbertsch Gallery (Room 11): Franz Anton Maulbertsch brought the Austrian Baroque tradition to its culmination. Some notion of the power of his monumental paintings is given by such works of his as the "Allegory of the Jesuits' Mission to the Whole World" and "Saint Narcissus".

Maulbertsch Cabinet (Room 15): Here hang some small-scale pictures and sketches by Maulbertsch.

Marble Gallery (Room 16): The former audience chamber portrays, like the Marble Hall, the Apotheosis of Prince Eugene. The life-size figures of Greek deities in the alcoves are the work of the Venetian artist Domenico Parodi.

Hall of Mirrors (Room 17) also called the Gold Chamber: This is a grandiose room with massive mirrors in golden frames which seem to make the room go on and on for ever. Here stands Balthasar Permoser's "Apotheosis of Prince Eugene", a marble sculpture carved in Dresden in 1721. It was commissioned by Prince Eugene himself.

Österreichische Galerie des 19. und 20. Jahrhunderts

Location
Oberes Belvedere

Opening times
Tues.–Thur., Sat.
10 a.m.–4 p.m., Fri.
10 a.m.–1 p.m., Sun.
9 a.m.–noon

This Gallery which is housed in the Upper Belvedere is devoted to Austrian art of the 19th and 20th c. It offers an excellent survey of Austrian artistic endeavour from the end of the Baroque era to the present day, taking in the art of the early 19th c., of the period when the Ringstrasse was being developed, and the so-called "Jugendstil", the characteristic Austrian version of Art Nouveau which developed at the end of the 19th c. The collection was started in 1916, and it has had its present form since 1953.

Ground Floor

On the ground floor (left of the vestibule) may be seen pictures by Friedrich Füger, the chief representative of Austrian Classicism, by the portrait-painter Johann Baptist Lampi and by Barbara and Peter Krafft.

First Floor

The 19th c. gallery is housed on the first floor. The most important rooms in the East Wing are: Room 1: Works by Moritz von Schwind (1804–71), including "Kaiser Max auf der Martinswand", "Party Game", "The Man cutting Bread", and "The Painter's Daughter". There are also landscapes by Friedrich Gauermann ("Althauser Lake" and "Landscape near Miesenbach") and by Stifter.

Room 2: Paintings of the Biedermeier period (1815–48). Most noteworthy are Rudolf von Alt's genre scenes and works by Peter Fend.

Upper Belvedere

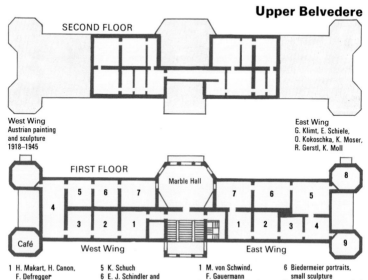

SECOND FLOOR

West Wing
Austrian painting
and sculpture
1918–1945

East Wing
G. Klimt, E. Schiele,
O. Kokoschka, K. Moser,
R. Gerstl, K. Moll

FIRST FLOOR

Marble Hall

Café   West Wing   East Wing

1 H. Makart, H. Canon,
F. Defregger
2 A. von Pettenkofen
3 A. Romako
4 H. Makart

5 K. Schuch
6 E. J. Schindler and
Impressionism
7 Th. Hörmann
O. Wisinger-Florian

1 M. von Schwind,
F. Gauermann
2 R. von Alt, P. Fendi, etc.
3–5 Waldmüller
Collection

6 Biedermeier portraits,
small sculpture
7 Nazarenes, history, paintings
8 Gold Cabinet
9 Palace Chapel

Rooms 3, 4 and 5: The Waldmüller Collection. Ferdinand George Waldmüller (1793–1865) was the most important Viennese master in the early 19th c. He painted portraits, landscapes, still-lifes and genre pictures. He was famous for his consummate skill in the handling of light. A Waldmüller canvas recently realised 4½ million Austrian schillings (about £135,000) at auction in the Dorotheum. The Gallery has examples of his work, including his "Corpus Christi morning", "The Monks' Soup" and "Perchtoldsdorf Peasant Wedding".

Room 6. Early 19th c. portraits. Friedrich von Amerling was the portrait-painter favoured by the nobility and the middle classes with a sense of their own importance. He painted such works as "Emperor Francis I", "Group Portrait of Rudolf von Arthaber with his children" and "Girl in a straw hat".

The most noteworthy rooms in the West Wing are:

Room 3: Anton Romako Room. This collection of pictures offers a cross-section of the production of this capricious artist (1832–89). It is devoted mainly to portraits and scenes of everyday life. The picture "Admiral Tegetthoff at the sea battle of Lissa" is particularly noteworthy.

Room 4. Hans Makart Room. As well as large formal pictures such as "The Triumph of Ariadne", "Modern Love" and "The Five Senses", the brilliant sketches, portraits and genre pictures by Hans Makart (1840–84) should also be looked at.

The 13 rooms on the second floor house the 20th c. Gallery. The most important artists represented are:

Second Floor

Gustav Klimt: On show are pictures and landscapes by the Master of the Vienna Secession (1862–1918). Among the most important works are "The Kiss", "The Picture of Fritza Riedler" and "Adele Block-Bauer sitting".

Egon Schiele: This artist (1890–1918) was not an adherent of the Vienna Secession and was in fact fully appreciated only after his death. His picture "The Family" is one of his major works, dating from the year he died.

Oskar Kokoschka: Works from all periods of this artist's life (1890–1980). One of the earliest paintings is "Child with the Hands of his Parents" and one of his last "Amor and Psyche".

Blutgasse (District)   B5

The Blutgasse District, just behind St Stephen's Cathedral (see entry) is one of the oldest and most interesting parts of the city. The medieval houses, forming a complex of seven old buildings (others in Fähnrichshof, houses Nos. 3–9), were restored and improved in 1965 in exemplary historical fashion. Where lovers of Schubert used to meet in the café whose name was altered to "Zur lustigen Blunze", there are now dwellings and artists' studios.

Location
Off Singerstrasse, I

Underground station
Stephansplatz (U1)

Bus
1A, 2A, 3A

The name "Blutgasse" (Blood Lane) is without historical warrant. According to legend, however, when the French Chivalric Order of the Knights Templar was dissolved here, so many Templars were slain that the narrow lane ran with their blood.

Böhmische Hofkanzlei
B4

Location
7 Wipplingerstrasse, I

Underground station
Stephansplatz (U1)

Bus
1A, 2A, 3A

The buildings of the former Bohemian Court Chancellery now serve as the seat of the Constitutional and Administrative Court.

The original building dates from 1710 to 1714. J. B. Fischer von Erlach designed this Baroque palace, and Lorenzo Mattielli was responsible for the many sculptures. In 1752 Maria Theresa commissioned Matthias Gerl to enlarge the building. The building was badly damaged in the war, and large-scale reconstruction was necessary (1946–51). A pedestrian passage was added in 1948.

Botanischer Garten (botanical gardens)
C5

Location
3 Mechelgasse, II

Underground station
Südtirolerplatz (U1)

Tram
71, D

Opening times
Mid April–mid Oct. daily
9 a.m.–dusk.

The chief attractions of the Botanical Gardens are its cacti and succulents and its orchids as well as the important collection of Australian plants housed in the Sundial House.

The garden, originally only for medicinal plants, was laid out by Maria Theresa in 1757 on the advice of her physician, G. van Swieten. There is a tradition that when one of the plants failed to bring the Empress any relief in an illness she ordered the physician and botanist Nikolas von Jacquin to forget about the medicinal plants and turn the place into a botanical garden.

Adjoining the Botanical Gardens on the S (entrance from Upper Belvedere) is a large Alpine Garden, with a comprehensive display of rare plants. (Open: Apr.–June, Mon.–Fri. 10 a.m.–6 p.m.; Sat., Sun. and public holidays 10 a.m.–7 p.m.; July–Sept., Mon.–Fri. 10 a.m.–4 p.m.; Sat., Sun. and public holidays 9 a.m.–4.30 p.m.)

Bundeskanzleramt
B4

Location
2 Ballhausplatz, I

Underground station
Volkstheater (U2)

Bus
2A

Trams
1, 2, D, J

The Office of the Federal Chancellor, the seat of the Austrian Government and of its Ministry of Foreign Affairs, is at 2 Ballhausplatz.

What was formerly the Privy Court Chancellery was erected here between 1717 and 1719 to plans by Lucas von Hildebrandt. It was enlarged by Nikolaus Pacassi in 1766 and made even bigger when the State Archive Building was added in 1902. It was damaged in the war, restoration being completed in 1950.

For more than 250 years Austrian history was made and suffered at Ballhausplatz. In 1814 and 1815 the Congress of Vienna met here for its deliberations after Napoleon's downfall. It was here, too, that the ultimatum to Serbia which led to

Oberes Belvedere, Prince Eugene's ceremonial palace ▶

The Office of the Federal Chancellor in Ballhausplatz

the outbreak of the First World War was conceived, and here, also, that Federal Chancellor Dollfuss was murdered in his office in 1934.

In 1938 Federal Chancellor von Schuschnigg concluded his famous farewell address with the words: "May God protect Austria." In 1940 Baldur von Schirach, Hitler's Governor in the Vienna District, moved into Ballhausplatz. The Federal Government has been housed here once more since 1945.

Bundessammlung alter Stilmöbel (period furniture museum)   C3

Location
88 Mariahilferstrasse, VII

Underground station
Mariahilferstrasse (U2)

S-Bahn station
Westbahnhof
6, 6D, S50

Trams
5, 6, 8, 9, 18, 52, 58

The Federal Furniture Collection contains precious furniture and tapestries from the former Imperial palaces. The Republic loans Imperial furnishings to official buildings where appropriate. The furnishings on show are divided into two sections. In the first part may be seen Court furniture from the Early Baroque era to the time of the Empire. The most important exhibit is the Schlosshofer Room which belonged to Prince Eugene of Savoy.

In the second section the 19th c. Imperial throne is on show, together with Joseph II's writing-desk and Francis I's bedroom.

Fifteen rooms have been set out in original early 19th c. style (with a music-room, a drawing-room, etc.).

Open: Tues.–Fri. 8 a.m.–4 p.m., Sat. 9 a.m.–noon. Guided tours every hour on the hour.

Burggarten (park)   C4

In 1809 Napoleon had the bastions of the Burg blown up which meant that at last there was room for an Imperial garden, generally called the "Promenade". Later the Neue Burg (see Hofburg) was erected on part of the site. The Burggarten has been open to the public since 1919. Attempts by young people to win the right to walk on the grass by organising sit-down strikes have so far been in vain.
In the park stand famous monuments to Mozart, Francis I and Franz Joseph I.

Mozart Memorial
The Mozart Memorial of 1896 is a master-work in marble by Victor Tilgner. The plinth is embellished with the various musical members of the Mozart family and with two reliefs from "Don Giovanni". The monument used to stand in Albertina-Platz, was seriously damaged in the last war, taken away and then, in 1953, after full restoration re-erected in the Burggarten.

Emperor Francis I Statue
The equestrian statue of the Emperor Francis I, by Moll, was erected in 1781 in the Paradiesgartel on the bastion. It was later moved to the present spot.

Franz Joseph I Memorial
During the Emperor's lifetime Vienna had no statue of Franz Joseph I, and then the Republic was not interested in erecting one. This memorial was erected as late as 1957, almost as an act of subversion. To general surprise, there were no unfortunate political consequences.

Location
Opernring/Burgring, I

Underground station
Mariahilferstrasse (U2)

Bus
3A, 57A

Trams
1, 2, 52, 58, D, J

**Burgtheater   B4

This theatre, "Die Burg" as the Viennese call it, is the stage with the richest traditions in the German-speaking lands. For a long time it was also the most important. The Classical style of the Burgtheater and the German spoken by the players exerted a decisive influence on the development of the German stage, and even now an engagement to play at the Burgtheater is still a high point in the artistic career of an actor or actress.
The theatre was built in 1751 with the agreement of the Empress Maria Theresa. It has had the status of a Court and national theatre since 1776. The theatre moved to new premises in 1888. These had been built on the Ring, to designs by C. von Hasenauer and Gottfried Semper.
When the Viennese voiced criticisms of the new theatre, Gottfried Semper retorted that "every theatre has to be rebuilt after 60 years or it is bound to burn down after that period". Right on time the Burgtheater was burned down in 57 years, when it caught fire in 1945. The auditorium was completely destroyed, and it was not until 15 October 1955 that the theatre could reopen with Grillparzer's "König Ottokars Glück und Ende" (King Ottokar's Prosperity and Demise).

Location
2 Dr-Karl-Lueger-Ring, I

Underground stations
Rathaus, Schottentor (U2)

Trams
1, 2, D, T (Ring), 37, 38, 40, 41, 42, 43, 44
Viewing
by arrangement
(tel. 51 44 40)

The "Burg" – the theatre with the richest German-speaking tradition

The building is 445 ft (136 m) long and the middle section is 320 ft (95 m) across. The height of the façade is 88 ft (27 m). In the auditorium there are seats for 1,310 and standing room for 210.

The exterior of the Burgtheater is impressive on account of the numerous decorative figures, colossal groups, scenes and busts by the sculptors Tilgner, Weyr and Kundmann. The interior has costly decoration in the French Baroque style. The staircase has frescoes by Gustav and Ernst Klimt and by Franz Matsch.

The theatre is open for ten months in the year. The price of seats is high. The stage has excellent technical facilities, but the scenery dock is situated away from the building, in the "Arsenal". This means that the scenery has to be transported to and from the theatre on a low-loader.

*Carnuntum (open-air museum)

Location
near Petronell
26 miles (42 km) E of
Vienna

S-Bahn
S7

The little market town of Petronell lies in part on the site once occupied by the Roman city of Carnuntum. This city which formed round the legionary camp a mile or so (2 km) away had in its prosperous days a population of 50,000 and was more important than Vindobona. It was in Carnuntum that Septimius Severus had himself proclaimed Emperor, and Diocletian convened an Imperial Conference here. In 375

The Burgtheater's staircases ▶

Danube

Bus
Bus route from Wien-Mitte
Bus Station

Carnuntum was successfully stormed by warriors belonging to the Quadi tribe. The remains of the Roman city un-
covered by excavation are now an open-air museum. The
foundations of houses may be seen, together with the ruins of
a palace, a 45 ft (14 m) high gate, the Heidentor (Pagans'
Gate), the so-called second amphitheatre with 1,300 seats
(2nd c.), and the remains of a hypocaust and bathhouse with
pavement mosaics.
Of the legionary camp there remain the ruins of a tower and
the foundations of the first amphitheatre (late 2nd c.). Open-
air performances are given here in summer.

Danube (Donau)   A6

The Danube, which is almost 330 yards (300 m) wide, flows
for 15 miles (24 km) through Vienna from NW to SE. In times
past this, the second largest river of Europe, brought great
problems to the city. The river meandered considerably –
every rise in its level caused catastrophic flooding and it often
formed new channels. Naturally the first efforts to control the
waters were concentrated on the channels nearest the city
and in 1598 the so-called "Danube Canal" was regulated. This
flowed for 10 miles (17 km) between Nussdorf and Prater-
spitz; it was navigable and commercially important. With the
introduction of larger vessels and with the growth of Vienna
along the right bank of the main river and its expansion on the
plain to the E it became necessary to regulate the main
stream. Between 1868 and 1876 the river was straightened
and provided on the E with a 550 yard (500 m) wide flood
channel. Further measures, begun in 1975 and now almost
finished, will complete the protection against flooding.
Parallel to the main river a relief channel, the "New Danube"
has been excavated in what had been a useful flood-plain,
forming an elongated island, called "Spaghetti Island" (see
Danube Island). The Danube is now in four parts; the main
stream, the New Danube, the Danube Canal and the Old
Danube, the last named being made up of the cut-off remains
of various arms of the old course of the river.
Below the Reichsbrücke the river is flanked by broad
meadows which have been converted into a park-like area in
the Prater and in the Lobau have been declared a nature
reserve. From here to the Czech border the Eastern National
Park is to be established. Within an over-all civic plan Vienna
will convert the Danube area into a scenically attractive
region.

Danube Island (Donauinsel)   A6

Location
Between Klosterneuburg
and the oil port Lobau

Vienna has to thank the scheme for the regulation of the
Danube for the creation of Danube Island which lies between
the relief channel, the New Danube, and the main river. The
island extends over 1,730 acres (700 ha) and includes woodland areas of grass, stretches of water and several kilometres
of bathing beaches. The island consists of three sections.

North Section

This is a paradise for yachtsmen and surfers, as the wind coming from the Vienna Woods blows most strongly here. There are surfing schools and yacht harbours; bicycles can be hired as can rowing, paddle and electric boats (motor boats are not permitted on the New Danube). There are good facilities for swimming and sunbathing and, as in the other parts of the island, restaurants and cafeterias.

S-Bahn station
Strandbäder (S1, S2, S3)

Bus
33B

Trams
31, 32

Ferry
DDSG landing-stage
Nussdorf

Central Section

As befits their function as a flood barrier, the banks of Danube Island are reinforced with boulders and concrete, but in a few places suitable for bathing a layer of fine gravel covers the stones and there are special areas with shallow water for children. Full-size football pitches, an 880 yard (800 m) long water ski lift and a water chute are available and there is a school for diving, sailing and canoeing. Further attractions include a roller-skating rink and a "fun" cycle area.

S-Bahn station
Strandbäder (S1, S2, S3)

Underground station
Donauinsel (U1)

Buses
80B, 91A, 18A

South Section

Here there are facilities for naturists and the handicapped. A 1,650 yard (1500 m) long cyclodrome provides a venue for cycle, roller-skating and wheelchair races. Sites are available for summer barbecues and anglers can find peaceful spots for their sport (a fishing permit is necessary) – some of the best fishing in Vienna is from the banks of the Danube. The "Toter Grund" (dead ground) with its pools and reeds is a protected area in this part of the island.

S-Bahn stations
Lobau, Stadtlauerbrücke
(S80)

Buses
18A, 80B, 91A

Tram
21

Ferries
at the Lindmayer and
Ronesch restaurants (R
bank), WALULISO (New
Danube); also for cyclists.

---

*Demel (café)   B4

Demel was once the Royal and Imperial pastry-cook's. Now it is the choicest and most expensive café in Vienna. All cooked dishes and cakes are prepared by hand to traditional recipes. In the kitchen machinery is hardly used at all. The waitresses, who are called "Demelinerinnen" (Demel's young ladies) in a famous song by G. Bronner and H. Qualtinger, still wear modest black dresses and address customers almost impersonally in a very formal language which is used only here. Here they say "Haben schon gewahlt . . . ?" (Has Madam already made her choice . . . ?).

Demel was founded in 1785 by a pastry-cook by the name of Ludwig Dehne, was acquired by Christoph Demel in 1857 and now belongs to a Swiss company.

About 60 years ago A. Kuh wrote an essay with the title "Demel and Lenin". His anxiety that Demel might fall a victim to democracy was without foundation. It was precisely in Demel that the Socialist politicians set up their exclusive Club 45.

Note that in Demel customers have to make their own choice at an enormous buffet. They then take a number, and waitresses bring to their table whatever has been selected.

Location
14 Kohlmarkt, I

Underground station
Stephansplatz (U1)

Bus
2A

Opening times
Mon.–Sat. 9 a.m.–7 p.m.,
Sun. 10 a.m.–7 p.m.

Demel's, formerly pastry-cooks to kings and emperors

Deutschmeisterdenkmal (monument)   B4

Location
Deutschmeisterplatz, I

Underground station
Schottenring (U2, U4)

Bus
40A

Trams
1, 2, D, T

In 1896, to celebrate and honour the second centenary of the Viennese garrison regiment, the K. und K. Hoch- und Deutsch-meister Nr. 4 (The Fourth Royal and Imperial High and German Masters), money was raised for a memorial. It was inaugurated in 1906.

Johann Benk made the bronze figures. Under an ensign bearing the standard of the regiment are gathered "Vindobona", and "Landshut Grenadier" and the "true comrade". Two reliefs recall the regiment's baptism of fire at Zenta in 1696 and the Battle of Kolin of 1757. In the course of the first 200 years (before the First World War, of course) the regiment lost 407 officers and 18,511 men.

On 1 November 1918 Egon Erwin Kisch formed the "Red Guard" in front of this memorial, and Franz Werfel, too, spoke at the mass meeting held at the same time.

Deutschordenshaus and Deutschordenskirche   B4

Location
7 Singerstrasse, I

Underground station
Stephansplatz (U1)

The buildings round two inner courtyards extend back as far as Stephansplatz (see entry) and Domherrenhof.

The Teutonic Order was called to Vienna by Duke Leopold VI at the beginning of the 13th c. The Order started constructing its premises, which probably included a chapel, a little later. In the 14th c. the Gothic church dedicated to St Elisabeth was incorporated into the buildings. In 1667 Carlo Carlone erected a new building which included a church. Between 1720 and 1725 this building was given the appearance which it has kept to the present day. The architect was Anton Erhard Martinelli. The church was remodelled between 1720 and 1722, to harmonise with the 14th c. Gothic work. It was restored in 1868 and 1947.

In the Middle Ages the Teutonic Order was devoted to colonial and military activity. Now it is a spiritual Order concerned with religious matters and also with service in hospitals and the care of the young and the old. Since 1923 the High Masters of the Order have always been priests of the Order.

Opening times
Daily 10 a.m.–noon; Tues., Wed., Fri., Sat. also 3–5 p.m.

The interior of the church is decorated with coats of arms and banners. Among the most precious objects are the Flemish reredos (1520) and the epitaph of Jobst Truchsess von Wetzhausen (1524).

Church

The Treasury of the Order is in four rooms. Room 1: Insignia of the Order and coins. The enthronement ring of High Master Hermann von Salza which is on show dates from the 13th c.

Treasury

Room 2: Chalices and other Mass vessels dating from the 14th to the 16th c. Also cutlery made of exotic materials.

Room 3: Art collection of the High Master Archduke Maximilian III (1602–18): silver and gold reliefs, ornaments, Oriental parade arms, clocks, astronomical equipment.

Room 4: Miniatures, rosaries, precious glasses, armour and 15th c. panel-paintings.

Dogenhof   B5

The Dogenhof (Doge's Palace) is a typical example of architectural taste at the end of the 19th c. It is inspired by the Ca d'Oro in Venice and is decorated with a stone lion of St Mark. Emperor Franz Joseph I wanted to designate for each of the various ethnic groups in the monarchy a specific part of Vienna and to let them create there an environment in which they would feel at home. Thus an Italian colony was supposed to grow up in Leopoldstadt. Not a lot came of the idea, and the Dogenhof stands now as a rather odd historical curiosity amid the other houses on Praterstrasse.

Location
70 Praterstrasse, II

Underground station
Nestroyplatz (U1)

Bus
5A

Trams
1, N

---

*Dominikanerkirche (officially the Rosary Basilica ad S. Mariam Rotundam)   B5

This church was promoted to the rank of a "minor basilica" in 1927, bearing the name "Rosary Basilica ad S. Mariam Rotundam".

The Dominicans were called to Vienna in 1226 and they consecrated their first church as early as 1237. After a series of fires work began on the construction of a Gothic church between 1283 and 1302. This suffered severe damage in the First Turkish Siege of 1529. The present church, the third, was built between 1631 and 1632. It is the most important Early Baroque church in Vienna. The frescoes, High Altar and the chapels are especially noteworthy.

Location
4 Postgasse, I

Underground stations
Stephansplatz, Schwedenplatz (U1)

Bus
1A

Trams
1, 2

51

Frescoes
The frescoes in the nave are by Matthias Rauchmiller (17th c.); those in the crossing are by Franz Geyling (1836), and those in the choir by Carpoforo Tencala (1676). All the wall- and ceiling-paintings in the side-chapels date from the 17th c.

High Altar
The subject of the picture above the High Altar, "The Virgin as Queen of the Rosary" by Leopold Kupelwieser (1839), refers to the institution of the Festival of the Rosary by Pope Gregory XIII.

Chapels
The chapels date from the 17th and 18th c. The oldest is the Thomas Aquinas Chapel with a painting above the altar dated 1638. The most important is the Vincent Chapel. Its altarpiece, "St Vincent raising a man from the dead", was painted by Françoise Roettiers in 1726.

*Dom- und Diözesanmuseum (museum)　　　　B5

Location
2 Rotenturmstrasse, I
(Entrance 6
Stephansplatz)

Underground station
Stephansplatz (U1)

Bus
1A

Opening times
Wed.–Sat. 10 a.m.–4 p.m.,
Sun. and public holidays
10 a.m.–1 p.m.

The Cathedral and Diocesan Museum stands in Zwettlerhof, adjacent to the Archbishop's Palace. Founded in 1932, it was remodelled in 1973 and extended in 1985. It displays religious art from the Middle Ages to the present day.

The Treasury contains the most valuable items from St Stephen's (see entry – Stephansdom), including two Syrian glass vessels of the 13th and early 14th c., the St Andrew's Cross reliquary and an important 14th c. reliquary which was refashioned in 1514. Mementoes of Duke Rudolph the Benefactor include the Chapter Seal, an antique medieval cameo and the portrait and funeral shroud of Duke Rudolf IV. Other valuable exhibits include a monstrance with a pattern of rays by Ignaz Würth (1784), enamelled 12th c. tablets with scenes from the Old Testament), a Carolingian 9th c. evangelistary with all its sides decorated with representations of the Evangelists, and the sword of St Ulrich (10th c.). Pre-eminent among the Gothic painted panels are the Upper St Veit Altar, based on a sketch by Dürer, and the "Man of Sorrows" by Lukas Cranach. Among Gothic sculptures are a relief of the "Descent from the Cross" and the Erlach and Therberg Madonnas (14th c.). The most valuable of the many 15th and 16th c. sculptures are the Madonna of the Shrine (early 15th c.) and the Anna Selbdritt group by Veit Stoss.
Pictures from the 16th, 17th, 18th and early 19th c. complete the exhibits. The most noteworthy Baroque works are by Paul Troger ("St Cassian"), A. Maulbertsch ("Golgotha"), Kremser-Schmidt ("St Sippe") and Jan von Hemessen ("Christ bearing the Cross").

*Donaupark and Donauturm (park)

Location
Danube/Old Danube, XXII

Underground station
Alte Donau (U1)

S-Bahn station
Strandbäder

The Danube Park occupies 250 acres (1 million m²) and is thus the second largest park in Vienna. It was laid out in 1964 in connection with the Vienna International Garden Show (WIG '64) at a cost of 7 million schillings (about £250,000).
The Danube Park Railway, a narrow-gauge line, runs round the gardens. There is an artificial lake (Lake Iris) on the bank of which stands a theatre which seats 4,000. A chair-lift follows a

triangular course between the Old and the New Danube, offering wonderful views of the entire park and the office towers of UNO-City (see entry) which is adjacent.

The Danube Tower is 825 ft (252 m) high, which makes it the tallest building in Vienna. It was opened in 1964. Its weight is 17,600 tons, and it is 100 ft (31 m) in diameter at the base. Two express lifts climb to 540 ft (165 m) in 45 seconds. They lead to the viewing-chamber and to the two revolving restaurants. The rates at which they revolve round the axis of the tower can both be regulated so that a cycle takes either 26, 39 or 52 minutes.

Buses
90A, 91A, 92A; 20B

Opening times
Tower: lift until 9.30 p.m.

Opening times
Restaurants:
11.30 a.m.–3 p.m. and
6–11 p.m.

Dorotheum   C4

The Dorotheum is one of the largest pawnbroking institutions in the world. The Viennese call it either "Tante Dorothee" or just "Pfandl" (The Pawn). It occupies a block of buildings erected by E. von Förster along the lines of a Baroque palace between 1898 and 1901.

There are 2,400 auctions a year, dealing with over 600,000 objects. In Vienna alone the Dorotheum has 16 branches. In the main building there are sections for furniture, carpets, pictures, small objects, furs, objets d'art, stamps, books and jewellery.

The four major art auctions, in March, June, September and November, attract experts from all over the world (see Practical Information – Auction Rooms).

The origins of the Dorotheum go back to 1707 when the Emperor Joseph I founded an office for pawnbroking. It was moved into the Dorothea Monastery which was empty at the time. These premises later underwent large-scale reconstruction.

Location
17 Dorotheergasse, I

Underground station
Stephansplatz (U1)

Bus
2A

Opening times
Regular auctions: see
Practical Information –
Viewing: Mon.–Fri.
10 a.m.–6 p.m., Sat.
9 a.m.–noon

Dreifaltigkeitskirche   B3

The Dreifaltigkeitskirche, dedicated to the Holy Trinity, is commonly called the "Alserkirche" in Vienna. It stands opposite the front of the General Hospital, and sick people and those on the way to recovery used to hang up thousands of votive tablets in the cloister and in the Antony Chapel.

The church which was completed in 1727 was taken over by the Minorites in 1784. In its exterior form it is an Early Baroque building with a façade flanked by twin towers and a high domed roof. Inside visitors find a cruciform plan with side-chapels to the left and right. Through the cloister on the right is the way to the Antony Chapel, and the church is the centre in Vienna of the devotion to St Antony.

The furnishing of the church dates primarily from the 18th and 19th c. An exception to this generalisation is the "Weeping Madonna" by the Spanish Baroque Master, Pedro de Mena y Mendrano. He carved this bust out of mahogany and pine in 1662–63; it may be seen in the Johann Nepomuk Chapel. There is a wooden Crucifix, larger than life-size, in the third chapel from the entry on the right; it dates from the 16th c. In 1827 the body of Beethoven was brought to this church. One year later, just a few weeks before his own death, Schubert wrote the hymn "Glaube, Liebe, Hoffnung" (Faith, Love and Hope) for the consecration of the church's bells.

Location
17 Alserstrasse, VIII

Underground station
Schottentor (U2)

Bus
13A

Trams
2, 5, 44

*Ephesos-Museum   C4

Location
Heldenplatz, Neue Burg, I

Underground station
Mariahilferstrasse (U2)

Trams
1, 2, D, J

Opening times
Mon. and Wed.–Fri.
10 a.m.–4 p.m.
Sat., Sun. 9 a.m.–4 p.m.

The Ephesos-Museum was opened in 1978 in the Neue Burg (see Hofburg); entrance behind the Prince Eugene Monument. It is the only museum between Istanbul and London which possesses a collection of finds from the ancient trading city on the coast of Asia Minor. Excavations by the Austrian Archaeological Institute which are still continuing have brought interesting finds to light, among them statues, architectural fragments, reliefs and bronzes. The exhibits from the Aegean island of Samothrace were dug up between 1873 and 1875. Particularly interesting is a model of Ephesus which fills an entire room and was made with countless little pieces of wood. The model cost 1·3 million schillings (about £40,000).

Sculpture Collection

Among the most remarkable exhibits in the Sculpture Collection are:
The bronze of an athlete (Roman copy of a Greek original, second half of the 4th c. B.C.).
Parthian Memorial, a nearly 130 ft (40 m) long frieze with life-size figures in relief commemorating Lucius Verus (who died in A.D. 169), who ruled with Emperor Marcus Aurelius. It was erected after the victorious conclusion of the war against the Parthians (161–165).
"Hercules fighting with the Centaurs", "Boy with a Goose" (Roman copy in marble of an Hellenistic original).

Architectural Remains

Among the architectural remains the following are especially interesting:
Fragments of the altar of a Shrine to Artemis (4th c. B.C.), of

Sightseeing in the Viennese "Fiaker" – a sight in itself

an octagon (second half of the 1st c. A.D.), of a so-called "Round House" (second half of the 1st c. A.D.) and of the Great Theatre (mid 1st c. A.D.) with erotic reliefs and a frieze of masks.

Exhibits from the island of Samothrace: Victory figures, pediment sculptures (from the Hellenistic Hieron), Ionic capitals (from the Ptolemaion), frieze of lotus fronds (from the Arsinoeion) and a gable-end from the Propylon.

Finds from Samothrace

Fähnrichshof

See Blutgasse

Fiakermuseum   B3

In the "Fiakerhaus", built 1952, the Viennese landau-drivers have set out in three rooms an exhibition tracing in prints, photographs, pictures and models, the 300-year history of their trade. The first licence for a carriage to ply for hire was granted in Vienna in 1693, 71 years later than in Paris. Towards the end of the 19th c. there were, however, 70 ranks. A hundred years ago a 3 mile (5 km) ride in a landau cost only about 1½ guilders. All the same, that provided a large enough income and Viennese landau-drivers paid for the Schrammel brothers to take music lessons, while the Fiaker Ball, with "Fiaker Milli" as queen of the dance was the high point of the carnival. Today there are only about three dozen "Fiaker". They ply for hire in Stephansplatz, in front of the Albertina in Augustinerstrasse and in Heldenplatz, taking visitors round the sights of the city centre. A few drivers still wear the traditional costume of Pepita trousers, a velvet jacket and a hard hat called a "Stösser".

The bronze in the garden of the Fiakerhaus is a reminder of the project to erect a "Fiaker Fountain" commemorating Vienna's landaus; it was finished at the beginning of the war but was never set up.

Location
12 Veronikagasse, XVII,
second floor

S-Bahn station
Alserstrasse (9, 9D)

Tram
2

Opening times
1st Wed. in month
8 a.m.–1 p.m.
Admission free

Figarohaus   B5

Figarohaus stands on Schulerstrasse which leads out of Stephansplatz (see entry). For three years, from 1784 to 1787, Mozart lived here with his wife and son in a typical Old Viennese house near St Stephen's Cathedral (see entry). These were his happiest years, and it is here that he wrote "The Marriage of Figaro". For a short while Beethoven was his pupil, and it was while he was resident here that Mozart was appointed Imperial Chamber Composer.

Mozart lived on the first floor of what was then called "Camesina House", and his rooms have been set out as a permanent memorial. Visitors can see the room (with a fine stucco ceiling) where Mozart worked, pictures and prints, figurines and the first German libretto of "The Marriage of Figaro".

Location
8 Schulerstrasse, I (Entrance
in Domgasse 5)

Underground station
Stephansplatz (U1)

Bus
1A

Opening times
Tues.–Sun.
10 a.m.–12.15 p.m.,
and 1–4 p.m.

---

*Franziskanerplatz   C5

Franziskanerplatz with the Franciscan monastery and church has 17th and 18th c. buildings all round and is one of the most attractive old squares in Vienna.

Location
Singerstrasse/
Weihburggasse, I

Freyung

Underground station
Stephansplatz (U1)

Bus
1A

The Moses Fountain, with its base like the jaws of a lion, used to stand in the courtyard of No. 6 Zum grünen Löwen (The Green Lion). Johann Martin Fischer designed the lead statue of Moses striking water from the rock. In 1798 it was placed on the base of the fountain which had been brought here.

The country coaches used to set out from the former Zum grünen Löwen in the days of Emperor Joseph. It was possible to travel 100 miles and more out of the city into the country by these coaches.

*Franziskanerkirche (officially St Jerome)

The Church of St Jerome at present standing on this idyllic old-world square is the only church in Vienna to possess a Renaissance façade. The interior is, however, decorated and fitted out in the Baroque style.

A 14th c. Poor Clares convent formerly occupied the site where this church was constructed between 1603 and 1611. Father Bonaventura Daum was responsible for the designs of the new building. The tower was added in 1614.

In the interior the High Altar by Andrea Pozzo dating from 1707 is particularly notable as is a venerated picture of the Madonna and Child from about 1550 which probably came from Grünberg in Bohemia. Behind the altar is the monks' choir which is reached by passing through the sacristy.

Also important are:

The Capristan Altar (second altar on the left) with a painting the "Martyrdom of St Capristan" by Franz Wagenschön. The Francis Altar (fourth altar on the left) with a picture of the church's Patron Saint by Johann George Schmidt. The Crucifixion Altar (third altar on the right) with a "Crucifixion" by Carlo Carlone (first half of the 18th c.).

The carved Baroque organ of 1643 is the oldest organ in Vienna. It has folding doors which are in part painted, in part carved, with the figures of saints on them.

According to legend, the Madonna on the reredos, popularly called the Madonna with the Axe, was being struck down by iconoclasts, but the axe remained firmly attached. Soldiers took this indestructible image of the Virgin with them on their campaign against the Turks and ascribed to it their victory at Pest in Hungary.

Freyung with the Austria-Brunnen   B4

Location
Vienna, I

Underground station
Schottentor (U2)

Bus
1A

Trams
1, 2, D, T (Ring)

The Freyung is a triangular space near the Schottenkloster (see entry – Schottenstift). The name Freyung ("free place") refers to the fact that, like St Stephen's (see entry – Stephansdom), it had the right of receiving and protecting any who were being pursued, except those who had shed blood. In olden days a Punch and Judy Show stood on Freyung, and later on there was a gallows where quick justice was meted out to traitors.

Mountebanks, hucksters and sweetmeat-sellers had their pitches here. It was only in the 17th and 18th c. that the buildings were erected which form the setting for Freyung today. From the 17th c. date Abensperg-Traun Palace (No. 2), which has the fountain with the sprite of the Danube in its courtyard, Harrach Palace (No. 3) and Kinsky Palace (No. 4).

In the middle of the square is the Austria Fountain which is a work of Ludwig Schwanthaler. It was cast by Ferdinand Miller in the Munich bronze-foundry and unveiled on Freyung in 1846. Its allegorical bronze figures represent Austria and the main rivers of the monarchy as it then existed, the Po, Elbe, Weischsel and Danube.

Austria Fountain

The Palais Ferstel, which Heinrich Ferstel, architect of the Votivkirche and the University, built in 1856–60 for the National Bank, has a distinct Italianate air. For years the building was neglected but has been restored exactly as it was in the elaborate "Ringstrasse" style as an exclusive venue for conferences and banquets.

In 1986 the Café Central was reopened in the Palais Ferstel. On entering the café from Herrengasse the visitor will find himself greeted by the writer Peter Altenberg – not, of course, in person but as a life-size model. Altenberg was a regular patron and often gave as his address "Vienna 1, Café Central".

Café Central
Open weekdays
10 a.m.–11.30 p.m.

Gardekirche "Zum gekreuzigten Heiland"

The Guards' Church dedicated to the Crucified Saviour stands on Rennweg, as do the Belvedere Palaces (see entry). It has been the Polish national church since 1897.

It was built during Maria Theresa's reign by Nikolaus Pacassi to serve as the church of the Imperial Hospital. In 1782 it was handed over to the Polish Life Guards. It was altered again between 1890 and 1898. The painting above the High Altar in the attractive central section of the building with its light Late Rococo decoration is by Peter Strudel and dates from 1712. Strudel was the founder of the Akademie der bildenden Künste (see entry).

Location
5a Rennweg, III

Underground station
Karlsplatz (U1, U2, U4)

Tram
71

Gartenpalais Liechtenstein

B4

The Summer Palace in Fürstengasse is accounted one of the most beautiful Baroque buildings in Vienna. The valuable Liechtenstein Picture Gallery was taken to Vaduz during the Second World War.

Domenico Martinelli put up the building between 1691 and 1711 for Johann Adam Andreas, Prince of Liechtenstein. The sculptural decoration is by Giovanni Giuliani, and the frescoes in the interior are by Andrea Pozzo, Antonio Belluci and Johann Michael Rottmayr. The ceremonial marble staircases are imposing.

Since 1979 the Museum of Modern Art has been here, as well as the former Hahn Collection and pictures on permanent loan from the Ludwig Collection (from Aachen).

Location
1 Fürstengasse, IX

Bus
40A

Tram
D

Museum of Modern Art

Highlights of this exhibition of international art from 1900 to the present day are the "modern classicists" – with works by Picasso, Kupka, Nolde, Schlemmer, Lipschitz, Kirchner, Pechstein, Klimt, Schiele and Kokoschka. Jawlensky and Marc represent the "Blue Rider" group. Non-figurative painters include Itten, Leger, etc. Abstract art is represented by Delaunay, Wotruba and others; works by Lehmden, Fuchs, Hutter and Hausner are examples of Surrealism.

Opening times
Daily (except Tues.)
10 a.m.–6 p.m.

Also to be seen are examples of "Nouveau Realisme", Pop art and Photo-realism.
A branch of the Museum of Modern Art is the Museum des 20. Jahrhunderts (see entry).

Geymüller-Schlössl (Sobek Collection) (museum)

Location
102 Potzleinsdorfer-
strasse, XVIII

Tram
41

Opening times
March–end Nov. Tues.–
Fri. 10 a.m.–3 p.m.
(notice required)

This small palace was built in 1808 for the banker J. Heinrich Geymüller. It is now the home of the Sobek Collection of old Viennese clocks, and is a separate department of the Austrian Museum of Applied Arts.
There are seven rooms decorated in the Empire and early 19th c. style. On show are 200 clocks – old Viennese pedestal clocks, case clocks and wall clocks. The oldest are Baroque clocks, but most of the exhibits come from the period 1780–1850.
Guided tours Sun. 11 a.m. and 3 p.m.

*Graben with Plague Pillar   B4

Location
Vienna, I

Underground station
Stephansplatz (U1)

Buses
1A, 2A, 3A

Graben, a wide-open space which is half street and half square, is the hub of the great city of Vienna. In 1950 it was the first place to have fluorescent lighting. In 1971 it became the first pedestrian zone, and soon afterwards cafés took over for the summer months what was formerly a major thoroughfare.
Graben was once the city moat round the Roman camp, then it became the flower and vegetable market, and from the 17th c. on it was the scene of Court festivities.

Plague Pillar

In the middle of Graben stands the famous Plague Pillar. This 70 ft (21 m) tall Baroque pillar (also called the "Trinity Pillar") owes its existence to a vow made by Emperor Leopold I. He swore that when the plague ceased he would pay for the erection of a pillar which would reach up to the heavens.
The plague of 1679 cost 75,000 Viennese their lives, other estimates even 150,000. The first plague pillar was erected in 1679, too. The construction of the definitive Plague Pillar was begun by Matthias Rauchmiller in 1681, continued after his death, which occurred in 1686, by J. B. Fischer von Erlach, and completed in 1693 by Locovico Burnacini. The figure of the Emperor kneeling in prayer is the work of Paul Strudel, that of the Trinity was modelled by Johann Kilian of Augsburg.
There are two old fountains, the Joseph Fountain and the Leopold Fountain. Both were altered many times. Lead figures were added by Johann Martin Fischer in 1804.
Of the numerous Baroque buildings that once surrounded Graben in the 18th c. only the Bartolotti-Partenfeld Palace (No. 11) remains.

Griechenbeisl (inn)   B5

Location
11 Fleischmarkt, I

This historic inn with the figure of "lieber Augustin" on the façade, was called "Zum roten Dach" (The Red Roof Inn) in the 15th c., becoming "Griechenbeisl" in the 18th c. Pilsner Urquell was first served here in 1852. Among the many

Griechenbeisl with "lieber Augustin" on its façade

famous persons to frequent the inn were Wagner, Strauss, Brahms, Waldmüller, Grillparzer and Nestroy.

It has been proved that Mark Twain wrote "The Million Pound Note" in a room at Griechenbeisl. The walls of the Mark Twain Room are completely covered with the autographs of famous artists.

There is no definite proof that it was in the seven little vaulted rooms which are full of all manner of curious objects that some anonymous ballad-singer wrote the mocking song "lieber Augustin" in 1679 while the plague was raging outside.

Underground stations
Stephansplatz,
Schwedenplatz (U1)

Bus
2A

*Grinzing

With its old houses and lanes, nestling in gardens and vineyards, the name "Grinzing" still is to many people all over the world synonymous with "Viennese Heurige".

The word "Heurige" has two meanings: wine made from grapes most recently gathered and thus new wine, but also the place where that wine is drunk. Places which are open have branches of fir over their entrances, and a sign is hung out. Genuine "Heurige" serve only their own wine, and they are open each year for only from three weeks to a maximum of six months. (Generally they use the self-service system.)

The big Heurige in Grinzing and the so-called "Nobel Heurige" are for the most part only pseudo-Heurige. They serve cold and hot meals, and their wines often come from Lower Austria.

Location
Vienna, XIX

Tram
38

Grinzing, synonymous with the "Viennese Heurige"

The little village of Grinzing is first mentioned in records in 1114. It was destroyed by the Turks in 1529 and there was a great fire in 1604. The village was destroyed again by the Turks in 1683 and in 1809 by the French. Nowadays there is another type of destruction, caused by the erection of buildings on the vineyards.

In order to counter this building it is possible for individuals to purchase 1 square yard (1 m²) of Grinzing with a vine. The vine is given a name-plaque, the purchaser receiving a certificate and declaration of ownership. Among owners of Grinzing vines are Kurt Waldheim, Jimmy Carter, Leonid Brezhnev, Leonard Bernstein and Sophia Loren.

Gumpoldskirchen

Location
Between Mödling and Baden

Südbahn station
Gumpoldskirchen (S1, R10)

Bus
From Wien-Mitte Bus Station

Distance
11½ miles (18 km) S

Amid the vineyards, at the foot of Anniger, lies Gumpoldskirchen, which is famous for its wine. There is evidence that wine has been made here for a thousand years, perhaps even for twice as long. Gumpoldskirchen wines – Zierfandler, Rotgipfler and Neuburger – were the first alcoholic beverages to take the air in the Zeppelin and graced the choice table on the occasion of the crowning of Queen Elizabeth II in London.

Visitors generally go to Gumpoldskirchen to drink the new wine in inns and pubs. The Renaissance Town Hall and the picturesque old houses of the burghers are also noteworthy.

Haarhof   B4

This tiny lane acquired its name which means "Hair Yard" because originally flax-sellers used to live here. The city ditch used to pass through here.
Since 1683 No. 1 has housed the Wine Cellar of the Dukes of Esterhazy.
No. 4 houses the collection of the Adler Heraldic and Genealogical Society. It has a collection of painted coats of arms, family trees and pedigrees, impressions of seals and some 80,000 family insignia.

Location
Naglergasse/
Wallnerstrasse, I

Underground station
Stephansplatz (U1)

Opening times
Adler Collection,
Wed. 5–7 p.m.

Haydn Museum   C3

Joseph Haydn acquired the single-storey house in the little street known as Steingasse (which later received the name Haydngasse) in 1793. He lived here until his death, and it was here he wrote his oratorios "The Creation" and "The Seasons". When he died in 1809 shortly after the second occupation of Vienna by the French, Napoleon ordered the posting of a Guard of Honour outside his house.
The museum here was opened in 1899. Among the objects on display are letters, manuscripts and personal possessions as well as two pianos and the deathmask of the composer.
Also in the house is a memorial room to Brahms, with mementoes and furniture from the composer's last home.

Location
19 Haydngasse, VI

Underground station
Pilgramgasse (U4)

Bus
57A

Trams
52, 58

Opening Times
Daily (except Mon.) 10 a.m.–
12.15 p.m. and 1–4.30 p.m.

Heeresgeschichtliches Museum   D5

The Museum of Army History is housed in the oldest building in Vienna to have been designed specifically as a museum. It contains valuable collections of militaria and historical relics concerned with the history of the army and of warfare in Austria from the outbreak of the Thirty Years War to the First World War.
It was Emperor Franz Joseph I who commissioned the museum, and Ludwig Förster and Theophil Hansen erected between 1850 and 1857 a building inspired by Byzantine architectural styles.

Ground Floor
On the ground floor are the Hall of the Field-Marshals, the Navy Room to the left, the Emperor Franz Joseph Room and the Heavy Artillery Room to the right.

The Hall of the Field-Marshals contains 36 life-size marble statues of Austrian rulers and military commanders.

The Navy Room has an impressive collection of model ships which recount the history of the Imperial (later the Royal and Imperial) Navy. The exhibits include a model of the "Novara" which circumnavigated the globe and a model of a longitudinal section (to a 1:25 scale) of the Austrian Navy's First World War battleship "Viribus Unitis" which was launched in 1911.

The Franz Joseph Room recalls the era of the Emperor with portraits, the insignia of the family Orders, pennants and

Location
Arsenalstrasse, Objekt 1, III

Underground station
Südtirolerplatz (U1)

S-Bahn station
Südbahnhof
(S1, S2, S3)

Buses
13A, 69A

Trams
D, O, 18

Opening times
Daily (except Fri.) 10 a.m.–
4 p.m.

Museum of Army History: the exterior and some of its exhibits

uniforms. In an adjoining room stands the motor car in which the heir to the throne, Archduke Franz Ferdinand, and his wife tragically lost their lives when attacked by an assassin in Sarajevo on 28 June 1914. Other mementoes are the Archduke's uniform, pictures and documents.

The Heavy Artillery Room has a display of the monarchy's heaviest guns from the period between 1859 and 1916. The most impressive is an M16 15 in (38 cm) motorised howitzer.

First Floor
The first floor houses the Commemorative Rooms; the Radetzky Room and the Archduke Charles Room are on the right, and on the left is the Prince Eugene Room and the Maria Theresa Room.

The Hall of Fame is a domed chamber with frescoes illustrating the most important military events in Austrian history.

The Radetzky Room is devoted to the period between Napoleon's downfall and the 1848 Revolutions and to the memory of Field-Marshal Radetzky. Relics of the Duke of Reichstadt, Napoleon's son, are displayed in a showcase.

The Archduke Charles Room recalls the Napoleonic era by means of pictures by Peter Krafft. There is a hot-air balloon (a "Montgolfière") which was captured from the French and a Russian officer's greatcoat which Napoleon is said to have worn when he was exiled to Elba.

The Prince Eugene Room has a display of weapons and armour from the period of the Thirty Years War and the wars against the Turks. There are also 15 battle scenes by the Court

Painter, Peeter Snayer. Mementoes of Prince Eugene include his breastplate, his Marshal's baton and his shroud.

The Maria Theresa Room illustrates the events of the War of the Spanish Succession and the last wars against the Turks. The Turkish Tent of State was probably captured at Peterwardein in 1716. The mortar did great service at the Siege of Belgrade in 1717. The central showcase shows the institution of the Order of Maria Theresa after the Battle of Kolin in 1757

The Artillery Halls, Objekte 2 and 17, contain the largest collection of guns in the world. Most of them date from the 16th and 18th c.

*Heiligenkreuz (monastery)

The prettiest route to Heiligenkreuz goes through the village of Perchtoldsdorf with its vineyards and Trinity Pillar by J. B. Fischer von Erlach on the Main Square, the friendly little town of Mödling and through the Hinterbrühl Valley (with an underground grotto by the lake and the historic Höldrichsmühle Inn).

The Cistercian Monastery of Heiligenkreuz was founded in the 12th c., and the main buildings date from the 17th c. The monastery church is Romanesque and has important stained glass dating from about 1300. The rich carving in the choir is by Giovanni Giulani (1707).

In the chapter-house may be seen the gravestone of Frederick II, the last Babenberg Duke. Visitors who take the conducted

Bus
From Wien-Mitte Bus Station (1092, 1093, 1094)

Distance
19¼ miles (34 km) SW

Heiligenkreuz: Trinity Pillar in the monastery courtyard

tour are also shown the Early Gothic cloister with more than 300 marble pillars.

In the Monastery Museum (West wing of the courtyard) illustrations dating from the 13th c. to the 16th c. are on show, together with about 150 clay models by the Venetian Baroque sculptor Giulani (1663–1744) who resided in the monastery as a "house guest" ("familaris") from 1711 until his death.

The hunting-lodge of Mayerling, today a Carmelite nunnery, lies 6 miles (10 km) away. In 1889 it was the scene of the tragedy when Crown Prince Rudolf and Mary Vetsera perished.

Heiligenkreuzerhof   B5

Location
5 Schönlaterngasse, I

Underground station
Stephansplatz (U1)

Bus
1A

The present Heiligenkreuzerhof complex, consisting of the abbey church, the prelacy, the counting-house and the courtyard, lies in the old and now totally refurbished Schönlaterngasse District (see entry). The Heiligenkreuzerhof was erected between 1659 and 1676 at the behest of the Abbots of the Monastery of Heiligenkreuz (see entry). Considerable alterations were made in 1746 when the complex took on the appearance it has at present. The counting-house was not built until 1754. The Baroque painter Martino Altomonte lived here in the monastery until his death in 1745. He spent his declining years here, paying rent and painting a fresco without payment, but he did dine at the Abbot's table.

The Bernhard Chapel near the prelacy is used for weddings and is one of the most beautiful of Vienna's churches. The picture above the High Altar, by Altomonte, dates from 1730.

*Heiligenstadt

Location
Vienna, XIX

Underground station
Heiligenstadt (U4)

S-Bahn station
Heiligenstadt (S9)

Tram
D, 37

Heiligenstadt, incorporated in Döbling in 1892, is the oldest and the prettiest of the Viennese wine-producing villages. Its narrow, winding streets have helped to keep it free from too much bustle. In the area around Probusgasse and Armbrustergasse it is still possible to see how the place used to look, with its vineyards and Empire and early 19th c. houses. St Jacob's Church (3 Pfarrplatz) was built in Romanesque times on Roman foundations; although frequently destroyed, altered and rebuilt, it is still worth seeing.

Beethoven stayed in Heiligenstadt on several occasions; in 1802 while working at 6 Probusgasse on his Second Symphony, he wrote his "Heiligenstadt Testament". In 1817 he was once more living in Heiligenstadt, this time at 2 Pfarrplatz, where he worked on his Pastoral Symphony.

*Historisches Museum der Stadt Wien (museum)   C4

Location
8 Karlsplatz, IV

Underground station
Karlsplatz (U1, U2, U4)

The Vienna City Historical Museum stands on Karlsplatz. The Vienna City Council decided to transfer it there from the New Town Hall on the occasion of the 80th birthday of Theodor Körner, the Federal President. It was opened in 1959, but Körner was no longer alive, having died in 1957.

From 1780 to the Present Day

SECOND FLOOR

Historical Museum of the City of Vienna

SECOND FLOOR
1 Pompeian Salon
2 First half of the 19th c.
3 Second half of the 19th c.
4 1848 Revolution
5 Grillparzer's Apartments
6 Theatre
7 Model of city as in 1898
8 Loos's living-room
9 Otto Wagner
10 Painting about 1900
11 First half of the 19th c.

From 1500 to 1780

FIRST FLOOR

FIRST FLOOR
1–4 History of the City from the 16th to the 18th c.: weapons, Turkish Siege; views of city, pictures, porcelain, etc.
5 Model of the Inner City in 1852–54
6–7 Castle of Laxenburg

Neolithic Period to 1500

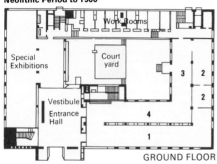

GROUND FLOOR

GROUND FLOOR
1 Prehistory, Roman period, Tribal Migrations
2–4 Middle Ages (maps of the city, views, architectural fragments from St Stephen's Cathedral, stained glass), Weapons and armour

Historisches Museum der Stadt Wien

Buses
4A, 59A

Trams
1, 2, D, J, 62, 65.

Opening times
Tues.–Sun. 9 a.m.–
4.30 p.m. (2nd floor:
closed noon–1.15 p.m.)

The exhibits on show in the museum display particularly clearly the history of the city of Vienna. All exhibits are numbered.

Ground Floor
Neolithic Period–Time of the Tribal Migrations. Finds from the Stone Age, Bronze and Iron Ages and the time of the Tribal Migrations. The most important exhibits are a painted Sequani gravestone (2nd c.; 1/28), a Roman altar (1/20) and an ancient treasury (1/12).

Middle Ages and Late Middle Ages. Views of the city and plans illustrating its development. The Albertinischer Plan (1/79) is considered to be the oldest plan of the city of Vienna. There are stone fragments and valuable architectural remains from St Stephen's Cathedral. These were removed during restoration and carefully preserved. Among them are an Early Gothic Anna Selbdritt (about 1320; 1/40), three larger-than-life-size pairs of Princes (about 1360–65; 1/43), Gothic stained glass from the Duke's Chapel (1/49) and the remains of an altar of lime wood (14th c.; 1/73).

Collection of weapons from armouries and arsenal. Among the exhibits are suits of armour, shields, spears and halberds, and also the oldest Italian horse-armour (1/82) and the funeral arms of Emperor Frederick III (1/77).

First Floor
History of Vienna in the 16th c. It was a warlike century, and so exhibits include weapons, armour, such as the gilt armour of Imperial Princes (2/30), ensigns, orders and battle pictures.

Counter-Reformation to the Great War against the Turks. The life of Vienna in the 17th c. is represented in portraits, medallions, coats of arms and etchings and engravings. An exceptional suit of armour (2/44) recalls the Thirty Years War, and the Turkish ensigns (2/81–83) are mementoes of Prince Eugene's victory over the Turks at Zenta.

The transition from Baroque to Classicism and City life in the 18th c. The views of Vienna by Delsenbach (2/108–110) are particularly interesting, as are the guild booths (2/132–137), the old house signs and traders' signs (2/162, 187–194) and the Baroque paintings, sculptures and prints (2/141 onwards).

Second Floor
Napoleonic Era. Medallions from the reign of Francis II (3/37).

The Caprara-Greymüller Empire Salon. This "Pompeian Salon" with its gold, white and pastel shades, tells us about the environment in which the nobility lived about 1800.

The Congress of Vienna, the early 19th c. (Biedermeier period), pre-1848 period and Revolution. There are a great number of paintings here with all the Viennese painters of the Biedermeier period represented (Fendi, Schindler, Danhauser, Gauermann, Rieter, Waldmüller and Amerling). There are displays of the fashions of the day (3/101), glass and porcelain (3/21), a survey of Viennese Biedermeier period social games (3/58), Lanner's giraffe piano (3/69) and Fanny Elssler's butterfly grand piano (3/81/2). The time of the Revolution is evoked in prints and paintings, and weapons of the National Guard are on show (3/103–123).

Foundation period (i.e. mid 19th c.). This is illustrated by portraits and relics, in handicrafts and busts. Theatrical life of the period is evoked, too.

Franz Grillparzer's Apartments. When the house at 21 Spiegelgasse was demolished, everything was brought here and the apartments were set up with careful attention to detail. The living-room of the architect Loos. This is one of the most outstanding examples of Viennese interior design from the early 20th c.

Jugendstil (Viennese Art Nouveau). The most important exhibits include paintings by Klimt (3/191–193) and Schiele (3/205–209) and designs by Kolo Moser (3/198, 225, 226/1, 228/10–12). There is also a sculpture by Rodin (3/231).

Vienna between the wars and during the Second World War. Documentation concerning the history of the period and modern art. There are works by Wotruba (3/237, 238) Kokoschka (3/240), Herbert Böckl (3/243–246), Rudolf Hausner (3/260) and Albert Paris Gütersloh (3/212).

History in pictures: mainly portraits of important personalities.

Hofburg (castle)   B/C4

The Imperial Castle in the inner city was for more than six centuries (up to 1918) the seat of the ruler of Austria, and for two and a half centuries (up to 1806) it was the seat of the German Emperor. It is now the official seat of the Austrian Head of State. The Federal President of Austria exercises his office and carries out representative functions in rooms once belonging to Maria Theresa.

The complex consists of ten major buildings, and in them may be seen a reflection of the 700-year-long architectural history of the Hofburg. Nearly every Austrian ruler since 1275 ordered additions or alterations to be made to the palace.

Location
1 Michaelerplatz, I,
Burgring.

Underground stations
Stephansplatz, (U1)
Mariahilferstrasse (U2).

Bus
2A

Trams
1, 2, D, J, 52, 58

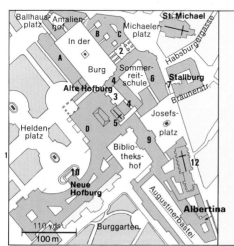

Hofburg at Vienna

A Leopoldine range
B Imperial Chancellery range
C Michaeler range
D Ceremonial Apartments range

1 Burg Gate, with Monument to Heroes
2 Entrance to State Apartments and Silberkammer
3 Schweizerhof (Entrance to Treasury)
4 Treasury
5 Castle Chapel
6 Winter Riding School
7 Entrance to Lippizaner Stables and New Gallery
8 Entrance to Spanish Riding School
9 National Library
10 Ephesos Museum
11 Museum of Ethnology
12 Augustinian Church

67

Accordingly in the Hofburg examples may be seen of architecture in a great variety of styles – Gothic, Renaissance, Baroque, Rococo, Classicism and the early 1870s.
Together with its squares and gardens the entire Hofburg complex occupies an area of some 59 acres (240,000 m^2). This "city within a city" comprises 18 ranges of buildings, 54 major staircases, 19 courtyards and 2,600 rooms. Some 5,000 people are employed here.

Alte Burg (Old Castle)

Schweizerhof or Schweizertrakt (the Swiss courtyard or range) is the name commonly given to the Alte Burg (Old Castle). There is evidence that it has been here since 1279. Ferdinand I had the buildings reconstructed in the style of a Renaissance castle between about 1547 and 1552.
The massive Schweizertor (Swiss Gate) dates from this period. All the emperors resided in the Burg from Ferdinand I's time until 1916.
Burgkapelle. The present castle chapel was constructed on the orders of Emperor Ferdinand III between 1447 and 1449. In the 17th and 18th c. there were alterations and additions in the Baroque style. More changes were made in the 19th c. when the interior was reconverted to the Gothic style in 1802.
Maria Theresa had the old wooden altars replaced by marble ones, but the present High Altar dates from 1802. The tabernacle contains Ferdinand II's miraculous cross; according to legend it inspired him with courage during the Wars of Religion.

Burgkapelle

Conducted tours
Tues. & Thurs.
2.30–3.30 p.m. except
July–mid Sept. and mid
Dec.–mid Jan.

The Burgkapelle is now a much-favoured and distinguished setting for weddings. The cynics say that the thirteen 500-year-old wooden statues of the "Helpers in time of need" – the 14th was removed to make space for the pulpit – are in their right place in a church used for marriages.
The boys' choir was originally founded to sing in the Burgkapelle used by the Imperial Court. The Vienna Boys' Choir (see entry Wiener Sängerknaben) developed from this. It now sings at Sunday Mass at 9.15 a.m. except July–mid Sept.
Innerer Burghof. The Inner Courtyard of the castle was used by the Emperor Maximilian II as a tilt-yard as early as 1545. Later it was the site of tourneys, festivities and executions. Today it is simply a park.
In 1846 a monument was erected to the memory of Emperor Francis II. On its plinth may be read a line from his will: "My life is for my peoples."

Stallburg (Mews)

Opening times
Visits to mews
See entry: Spanish Riding
School

In 1558 Emperor Ferdinand I ordered the construction of a Renaissance palace, one of the most important Renaissance buildings in Vienna, for the particular use of his son Maximilian. When Maximilian became Emperor and moved into the Hofburg, Maximilian's palace was converted into Court mews. Since the time of Charles VI the stables for the Lipizzaner horses (see entry) have occupied the ground floor.
The Neue Galerie (see entry) is on the second floor of the Stallburg.

Amalienburg

Following the example of his father, Maximilian II had a palace built for the particular use of his son. He was called Rudolf, hence the original name of Rudolfsburg. In the 18th c., however, the name was changed to Amalienburg when the

Heldenplatz: the Prince Eugene Monument

Michaelertrakt wall-fountain

Schweizertor on the Schweizerhof

Hofburg

Empress Wilhelmina Amalie lived here during her widowhood. The rooms later used by the Empress Elisabeth and Tsar Alexander I were furnished as State Apartments (Apartments 1322).

Leopoldinischertrakt

The Leopoldinischertrakt is a range of buildings built at the behest of Emperor Leopold I, Maria Theresa's grandfather. This Baroque range of buildings connects the Schweizerhof and the Amalienburg; they were erected between 1660 and 1680. They were occupied by Maria Theresa and her husband Francis Stephen of Lorraine; their apartments, together with those of Joseph II opposite them, now form part of the Presidential Chancellery. The Austrian President works in what was formerly Joseph II's study.

Reichskanzleitrakt

The Imperial Chancellery range constitutes the NE wing linking the Schweizerhof and the Amalienburg. It was designed by J. E. Fischer von Erlach who gave it its Baroque façade. The building was completed in 1730. Some of its rooms are set out as State Apartments (see entry for Schauräume 1–12).

Winterreitschule

Opening times
Displays and morning exercises see entry:
Spanish Riding School

The Winter Riding School, where the Spanish Riding School gives its equestrian displays, was the scene of numerous glittering events, especially during the Congress of Vienna in 1814 and 1815. This handsome white room was designed by J. E. Fischer von Erlach at the behest of Emperor Charles VI. The coffered ceiling spans an arena in which the horses exercise and which is 175 ft (55 m) long and 60 ft (18 m) wide. The gallery is borne on 46 pillars. The arena may be visited in July and August.

Michaelertrakt

The Michaeler range was the site of the Hofburg Theatre until 1888. After its demolition Emperor Franz Joseph I went back to the old plan drawn up by J. E. Fischer von Erlach and ordered the construction of a range of buildings linking the Reichskanzleitrakt and the Winterreitschule. This was done between 1889 and 1893. The grandiose Michaelertor (Michael Gate) which is flanked by figures of Hercules leads into the domed chamber. The figures in the niches symbolise the mottoes of various rulers: "Constantia et Fortitudine" (With Constance and Fortitude – Emperor Charles VI), "Justitia et Clementia" (Justice and Mercy – Maria Theresa), "Virtute et Exemplo" (By Might and Example – Joseph II) and "Viribus Unitis" (With all our Strength United – Franz Joseph I). In the hallway are the entrances to the Silver Room (see entry) and to the State Apartments (see entry).

Hoftafel und Festsaaltrakt

In 1804 Francis I ordered the reconstruction of the oldest part of the castle to provide a ceremonial suite in Classical style. The area of the chamber is 1,200 sq. yd (1,000 m^2). The magnificent coffered ceiling is supported on 24 Corinthian columns. It served as throne-room and ballroom. It was here that the Habsburgs formally renounced their rights to the throne in the event of a morganatic marriage (i.e. a marriage to a partner of lower social status). Nowadays the chamber is part of the Hofburg Congress Centre. Each year it provided the fitting setting for the Imperial Ball on New Year's Eve.

Heldenplatz

The Heldenplatz (Heroes' Square) was originally the parade-ground. After the erection of the two statues, one of Prince Eugene who defeated the Turks and the other to Archduke

Charles who won the Battle of Aspern, it was given the name Heldenplatz. Both statues are the work of A. Ferkorn.

The Outer Gate of the palace was built exclusively by soldiers, just as in Roman times. The plans were drawn up by Peter Nobile. It was inaugurated in 1824 on the anniversary of the Battle of Leipzig at which Napoleon was at last defeated. It was converted into a memorial to heroes in 1933.

Ausseres Burgtor

Plans for a vast Imperial Forum and a gigantic New Palace were drawn up by the architects Karl Hasenauer and Gottfried Semper. Emperor Franz Joseph I, however, gave his approval only to the building of a new wing to the palace, and the over-all plan was never carried out.

Neue Burg

Work on the interior of the Neue Burg went on until 1926. It has only once been the scene of historic events: it was here that Hitler proclaimed the annexation of Austria in 1938. Nowadays museums are housed here: Museum für Völkerkunde (see entry), Ephesos-Museum (see entry), Reading Room of the Nationalbibliothek (see entry), the Portrait Collection and Picture Archive (see Nationalbibliothek), the Sammlung alter Musikinstrumente (see entry) and the Waffensammlung (see entry).

Silberkammer

The so-called "Silver Chamber" has on display in six rooms the ceremonial and everyday tableware of the Imperial Court.

Location
Entry through Domed Chamber in Michaelertrakt (Michaelerplatz)

Opening times
Tues.–Fri. & Sun.
9 a.m.–1 p.m.

Room 1: East Asian porcelain; most of the exhibits belong to the 18th c.

Room 2: Formal service of the time of the Emperor Franz Joseph, now used at State receptions. Silver travelling service of the Empress Elisabeth Christine, wife of Charles VI (Paris 1717/18).

Room 3: Sèvres Services. There are three particularly fine 18th c. services of tableware in Sèvres porcelain, gift of the French Court. 18th c. cutlery (Vienna, Paris).

Room 4: Milanese table centre. It is nearly 10 ft (3 m) long and is made of meticulously carved and gilded bronze. Meissen service (c. 1775), Viennese Empire service (early 19th c.).

Room 5: The Ruby service. This is the most important of the services for Imperial grand occasions, with settings for 140 guests. It is decorated with silver which was given a gold hue by heat treatment. It was made by a Parisian goldsmith in the early 19th c. Smaller glass services (c. 1850), plates decorated with pictures and flowers (1800–30).

Room 6: 19th c. tableware. The most important exhibits are vases decorated with historical scenes and the "English service" which Queen Victoria gave to the Emperor Franz Joseph and a Romantic period service in Neo-Gothic style (Vienna 1821–24).

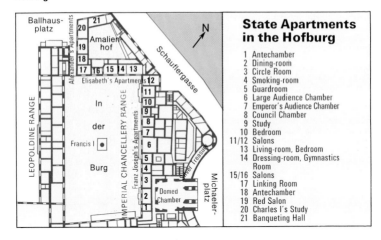

Ballhaus-platz
Alexander's Apartments
Amalien hof
Schauflergasse
N
Elisabeth's Apartments
LEOPOLDINE RANGE
IMPERIAL CHANCELLERY RANGE
Franz Joseph's Apartments
In der Burg
Francis I
Domed Chamber
Michaeler-platz
Imperial Treasury

1 Antechamber
2 Dining-room
3 Circle Room
4 Smoking-room
5 Guardroom
6 Large Audience Chamber
7 Emperor's Audience Chamber
8 Council Chamber
9 Study
10 Bedroom
11/12 Salons
13 Living-room, Bedroom
14 Dressing-room, Gymnastics Room
15/16 Salons
17 Linking Room
18 Antechamber
19 Red Salon
20 Charles I's Study
21 Banqueting Hall

Schauräume der Hofburg (Imperial Apartments)

Location
Entry through Domed Chamber in Michaelertrakt

Tours
Mon.–Sat. 8.30 a.m.–4 p.m.; Sun. 8.30 a.m.–12.30 p.m.

Franz Joseph's Apartments

The State Apartments open to the public in the Hofburg comprise the Franz Joseph Apartments in the Reichs-kanzleitrakt, together with Elisabeth and Alexander's apartments in the Amalienburg. It is not possible for visitors to see the living-quarters and ceremonial apartments of Empress Maria Theresa and of her son Emperor Joseph II (the Leopoldinischertrakt). This is because they are the official residence of the Austrian President. The furnishing of most rooms remains unaltered.

Dining-room: Here the Emperor used to take his meals with his Staff officers. The cartoons for the Gobelins tapestries from Oudenarde in Belgium were probably the work of the Flemish painter Peter Paul Rubens.

Circle Room: This was where the Court used to meet for conversation after meals. Rococo ceramic stove which was fuelled from the corridor. 17th c. Flemish tapestries with scenes from the life of the Emperor Augustus.

Smoking-room: The tapestries represent themes from Graeco-Roman history.

Guardroom: In the guardroom of the Imperial Life Guards the most interesting exhibit is the model of the old Hofburg.

Large Audience Chamber: This was the waiting-room for the audiences which took place twice a week. The Bohemian crystal candelabrum with 80 candles is especially fine.

The Emperor's Audience Chamber: On a lectern lies a list of people coming to an audience on 10 January 1910. It is said that audiences were conducted with everybody standing. Even the Emperor stood by his desk when he received those who came to an audience.

Council Chamber: It was in this room that the Emperor discussed matters with the Privy Councillors and his Ministers. It is furnished in Empire style. Francis Xavier Winterhalter's famous picture shows the Empress Elisabeth in a fine gown with jewelled stars in her hair.

Study: The rose-wood furniture is in the Louis XV style.

Bedroom: Franz Joseph I lived simply. He slept in a modest iron bed and took his bath in a wooden tub which was placed in the bedroom. (He died at Schönbrunn; see entry.)

Large Salon: This room has rose-wood furniture with bronze fittings. The sabre belonged to Field-Marshal Radetzky who was one of the small select band permitted to appear unannounced before the Emperor.

Small Salon: In the former breakfast-room may be seen one of the few portraits of Maximilian of Mexico, the Emperor's brother, and a bust of Admiral Tegetthof who brought back from Mexico the body of this unfortunate Prince.

Living-room: This is one of the prettiest rooms in the Hofburg. It served as living-room and bedroom, with its bureau, reading-desk, Neo-Gothic altar of Carrara marble and bed. The Spartan iron bed was pushed away during daytime.

Elisabeth's Apartments

Gymnastics Room: Elisabeth was fanatical about keeping slim and was a superb horsewoman. She, therefore, had gymnastic equipment fitted in her dressing-room which, moreover, she used regularly, much to the disgust of the Court.

Large Salon: Everything here is splendid. There is Louis XIV furniture, large Sèvres porcelain vases, Romantic landscape-paintings and Antonio Canova's marble statue of Napoleon's sister.

Small Salon: The showcases contain mementoes of the Empress who was assassinated in Geneva in 1898. There is a photograph of the gown she was wearing on the day she met her death.

Antechamber: The pictures are by Martin van Meytens, Maria Theresa's Court Painter (or from his studio); they portray her children. There is also a life-size statue of the 15-year-old Empress Elisabeth.

These take their name from Tsar Alexander I who occupied the rooms during the Congress of Vienna.

Alexander's Apartments

Linking Room: The busts are of the last Austrian emperor, Emperor Charles I, and of his consort, Empress Zita.

Red Salon: It is also called the "Boucher Salon" because the tapestries were worked to designs by François Boucher. They were presented to Emperor Joseph II by Marie-Antoinette. After 1916 it became Emperor Charles I's Audience Chamber.

Study: Charles I used to work beneath these 18th c. Brussels tapestries. It was at this desk that he drafted his abdication proclamation. The picture near the desk shows the Emperor in the uniform of an Imperial and Royal Field-Marshal.

Banqueting Hall. A special feature of the canopied "Highest Table" which is bedecked with gold and silver is the placing of all the cutlery on the right-hand side of the plate, in accordance with Spanish Court etiquette.

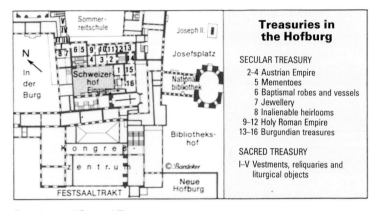

Treasuries in the Hofburg

SECULAR TREASURY
2–4 Austrian Empire
5 Mementoes
6 Baptismal robes and vessels
7 Jewellery
8 Inalienable heirlooms
9–12 Holy Roman Empire
13–16 Burgundian treasures

SACRED TREASURY
I–V Vestments, reliquaries and liturgical objects

Secular and Sacred Treasury

Opening times
Mon., Wed.–Fri. 10 a.m.–
6 p.m. Sat., Sun 9 a.m.–
6 p.m.

The Treasuries – reopened in 1987 after four years of restoration – contain in 21 rooms the Imperial regalia and relics of the Holy Roman Empire of the German Nation, coronation and chivalric insignia, badges of rank, secular and sacred treasures, and ornaments and mementoes formerly owned by the Habsburgs. It is all of incalculable artistic, historic and material value.

The origins of the Treasury go back to Ferdinand I's "Kunstkammer" (art chamber). From the 16th c. onwards all the emperors brought their treasures here and kept them in various rooms in the Hofburg. During Charles VI's reign the Treasury was moved to the ground floor of the palace. The iron door at the entrance bears the date 1712 and the Emperor's monogram. Secular and Sacred Treasuries are described together in the text. After leaving Room 8 of the Secular Treasury the visitor passes through the Robes Corridor into the 5 rooms housing the Sacred exhibits. Then, beginning with Room 9, the visitor returns to the Secular Treasury.

Secular Treasury

The Secular Treasury is housed in 16 rooms, with the collections organised on a thematic basis.

Room 1: Insignia of hereditary fealty. This applied to the Habsburg monarchs who as rulers of Austria had the rank of Archduke until 1804, whereas in the Holy Roman Empire they ruled as Emperors and Kings. The Imperial orb (second half of the 15th c.) was borne by the Emperor Matthias. The sceptre (mid 14th c.) belonged to Charles IV, and the sword of investiture, used at fealty ceremonies, belonged to Maximilian I.

Room 2: The Habsburgs, who remained Holy Roman Emperors until 1806, had their own private insignia made, since the insignia of the Empire were kept in Nuremberg from 1424. On view are the Imperial Crown ("Kaiserliche Hauskrone") of Rudolf II, made by the Court Jeweller Jan Vermeyen (1598–1602) together with the orb and sceptre made in Prague (1612–15).

The Crown of the Holy Roman Empire and the Imperial Cross

Room 3: In 1804, with the rise of Napoleon, the Holy Roman Empire came to an end and Francis II proclaimed the hereditary Austrian Empire. Exhibited is his gold-embroidered mantel with an ermine collar which he wore in 1830 when his son was crowned King of Hungary. Also on view are civil orders; the Hungarian Order of St Stephen (1764), the Austrian Order of Leopold (1808) and the Order of the Iron Crown (1815).

Room 4: The Congress of Vienna awarded Austria the Lombardo-Venetian kingdom. The coronation regalia and sword are exhibited, together with a herald's tabard of this kingdom.

Room 5: Mementoes of Marie Louise, daughter of Emperor Francis I and consort of Napoleon I. These include a silver jewel box, a silver-gilt trivet presented by the City of Milan on the birth of her son (King of Rome, Duke of Reichsstadt), a silver-gilt cradle given by the City of Paris on the same occasion. There are also mementoes of the Emperor Maximilian of Mexico.

Room 6: Baptismal robes and vessels. Among the exhibits are the baptismal robes given by Maria Theresa. It is said that the Empress herself undertook some of the embroidery. There is also a gold christening flagon and spoon (1571) and a little gold jug from the Prague Court workshop.

Room 7: Jewellery. Only very little of the Imperial jewellery was preserved. On 1 November 1918 the Senior Chamberlain, Count Berchtold, took the Habsburgs private jewellery out of the country at the command of Charles I. On view are the Colombian emerald (2,680 carats), hollowed out to form a salt-cellar and polished (1641) and the hyacinth "la bella" (416 carats), set as a double eagle into enamel, flanked by an opal and an amethyst. There is also the "Golden Rose", a Papal decoration given in 1819 to Carolina Augusta, fourth wife of Frances I, two Turkish sabres used by Charles VI and Maria Theresa at the Hungarian coronation and the crown of Stephen Bocskay who became King of Hungary in 1605.

Room 8: Inalienable heirlooms. Two items left by King Ferdinand I (1564) were considered so valuable that the Habsburgs raised them to the status of inalienable heirlooms. They are an agate dish of the 4th c., the largest of its kind that is known and which was once considered to be the vessel of the Holy Grail, and the 96 in. (243 m) long narwhal's horn which in the Middle Ages was believed to be the horn of the legendary unicorn, a symbol of Christ.

Room 9: Holy Roman Empire. The presence of the regalia of the Electoral Prince of Bohemia is explained by the fact that from the 14th c. the elected king was also King of Bohemia and, therefore, the duties of the electoral office were delegated to a deputy at the coronation festivities. Also on show are pictures and documents of the coronation of Joseph II (1764).

Room 10: Holy Roman Empire. Garments which formed part of the Imperial regalia from the 13th c. came into the possession of the Hohenstaufens; they were presumably used at the coronation of Frederick II and were assigned in 1246 to the Imperial Treasury. They include the coronation mantel of King Roger II, made 1133–34, an indigo tunic of the same period, a white robe of 1181 which corrésponded to the outer garment of the Byzantine emperor and which was later worn as an alb, red silk stockings of the last Norman king, William II, sumptuous shoes and gloves and a gold-woven sword belt from Sicily. Two items were added in the 14th c. – the eagle dalmatic which was worn instead of the blue tunic and a stole.

Room 11: Imperial Jewels and Coronation Insignia of the Holy Roman Empire. On view are the Imperial Crown (2nd half of 10th c.), the Sacred Lance, the Processional Cross and the Imperial Cross (1024–25), the orb (end of 12th c.), the Gothic sceptre, the Aspergillum used for sprinkling holy water on the altar and the Imperial Cross (renewed c. 1200). Also exhibited are the Imperial Gospel, a Carolingian purple codex (end of 8th c.), on which the new ruler took the oath and the sword (first half 10th c.) formerly a relic of Charles the Great with which kings were girded at their coronation.

Room 12: Here can be seen the sacred relics belonging to the Imperial Treasury.

Rooms 13–16: Treasures of the Burgundians. These comprise the treasures of the Order of the Golden Fleece and the inheritance of Maria of Burgundy who married the future Emperor Maximilian. On show are the insignia of the Order, coats of arms and Mass vessels (between 1425 and 1475) as well as the Cross (about 1400) of the Order of the Golden Fleece on which the oath was taken and Philip the Good's Court cup (c. 1453–67).

Sacred Treasury

The five rooms of the Sacred Treasury exhibit liturgical objects, reliquaries and robes which were used at the Imperial Court.

Room 1: 18th c. robes and the silver-gilt replica of the Am Hof Maria Column (see Am Hof).

Room 2: Medieval objects and the reliquary cross of the Hungarian King Ludwig the Great (between 1370 and 1382). St Stephen's purse, the oldest item in the Sacred Treasury (late 11th or early 12th c.), a Gothic goblet belonging to the Emperor Frederick III (1438). Also to be seen is a collection of reliquaries and small altars of ebony with silver or gold decoration (late 16th–early 17th c.).

Room 3: As well as cut gem stones, Augsburg silver work and rock-crystal there are valuable carvings including crucifixes (Giambologna, Guglielmo della Porta), a Crucifixion group (Geremias Geisebrunn), an ebony tempietto (Christoph Angermair).

Room 4: Among the most impressive items are the reliquary which holds the nail which is said to have pierced the right hand of Christ, two reliquary altars (1660–80) which belonged to the Emperor Leopold I and the monstrance containing the fragments of the Cross, which were preserved in a miraculous fashion in 1668 when the Hofburg caught fire.

Room 5: 18th and 19th c. works including 22 reliquary busts, some of them very large and made of silver, rosaries and a tempietto with one of St Peter's teeth.

---

*Hoher Markt with Ankeruhr and Roman Ruins   B4/5

The oldest square in Vienna is found on the edge of the textile district (called "Fetzenviertel" by the Viennese, meaning "the rag district"). It is rich with memories that go back to the very start of the city's history. The Romans called it the "old forum"; here stood the palace of the Commander of the Roman fortress of Vindobona, and it is here that Emperor Marcus Aurelius died. In the Middle Ages executions were carried out here. It was the Reuthof of the Babenbergers, the fish market and the trading site favoured by the cloth-sellers. After the destruction resulting from the events of 1945 nearly all the houses in the Hoher Markt had to be rebuilt. The focal point of the square is the Espousals Fountain (sometimes called Joseph's Fountain) which depicts the espousal of Joseph and Mary. The statue is by Antonio Corradini. Originally it was erected by J. B. Fischer von Erlach who used wood. In 1792 it was restored by his son J. E. Fischer who replaced the wood with white marble. It was paid for by Leopold I.

Location
Hoher Markt/
Rotenturmstrasse-
Wipplingerstrasse

Underground stations
Stephansplatz,
Schwedenplatz (U1, U4)

Buses
2A, 3A

Trams
1, 2 (quayside)

Ankeruhr

On the E side of the square it is impossible not to see the splendid clock of the Anker Insurance Company on the archway spanning Rotgasse. Every hour historical figures solemnly go past in order from 1 to 12 – Emperor Marcus Aurelius (1), Charlemagne (2), Duke Leopold IV and Theodora of Byzantium (3), the poet Walter von der Vogelweide (4), King Rudolf I with his consort, Anna of Hohenburg (5), Master Hans Puchsbaum (6), Emperor Maximilian I (7), Mayor A. von Liebenberg (8), Count Rüdiger von Starhemberg (9), Prince Eugene (10), Empress Maria Theresa with Emperor Francis I (11) and

Opening times
The figures go past at noon

The Anker clock – historical figures pass across on the hour

Joseph Haydn (12). At noon all the figures form up and process, accompanied by music.

This remarkable clock was built by the painter Franz von Matsch at the beginning of the First World War. It is dedicated to "the people of Vienna".

Roman Remains

Opening times
Daily (except Mon.)
10 a.m.–12.15 p.m.,
1–4.30 p.m.

A stairway by house No. 3 leads down to underground ruins dating from the Roman period. It is possible to see the footings of walls of houses for officers in the neighbourhood of the barracks of Vindobona (2nd and 3rd c.). There are also remains of a Germanic house (4th c.), as well as casts of reliefs, stamped tiles, remnants of a palisade and, in showcases, various remains.

*Hotel Sacher   C4

Location
1 Philharmonikerstrasse, I

Underground stations
Stephansplatz (U1),
Karlsplatz (U1, U2, U4)

Trams
1, 2, D, J (Ring)

Vienna's most famous old-world hotel still preserves its style and quality, with silk tablecloths, Biedermeier furniture from the mid 19th c. and valuable pictures.

Eduard Sacher had the hotel built in 1876. But his cigar-smoking wife Anna Sacher became more famous than he did. She used to allow unlimited credit to the scions of rich parents – the so-called "Sacher lads" – until they came into their inheritances. She also organised those discreet little "séparées" which have survived at any rate in literature in Arthur Schnitzler's "Abschiedssouper" (The Farewell Supper). Now the famous "separate rooms" have become little dining-rooms.

Roman ruins at the Hoher Markt

A hint: for genuine Sacher "Torte", the only ones that are genuine as was made clear in a long-drawn-out court case, it is necessary to go to a tiny shop round the corner in Kärntnerstrasse. They come in all sizes and all sorts of packages. The "Torte" were invented by a predecessor of Sacher during the Congress of Vienna

*Hundertwasser Haus   B/C5/6

This fantastic building was the creation of Friedensreich Hundertwasser. It was built between 1983 and 1985 by the local authority as part of a housing project, but most of the residents are artists. There are 50 apartments of various sizes in this striking building which has become the subject of much comment and which attracts 1,500 sightseers every day. There is a terrace café, a doctor's surgery and a store. Each apartment has its own colour and round the whole edifice runs a 3 mile (5 km) long ceramic band, joining the apartments and at the same time separating them by an individual colour.

In general Hundertwasser follows the principle of "the tolerance of irregularity", so that all corners are rounded, the windows are of different sizes; internally bathrooms are irregularly tiled, corridor floors uneven and the walls wavy (on the lowest storey the wall provides a surface on which children can scribble and paint). The façades of the complex imitate those of the aristocratic palaces and houses on the Grand Canal in Venice. In addition a piece of the old house was incorporated into the façade so that the "spirit of the old house resettles in the new one" and places it under its protection.

Location
Kegelgasse/Löwengasse III

Underground and S-Bahn station
Wien-mitte/Landstrasse (U4, S7)

Bus
75A

Tram
O

79

Josefsplatz, Vienna's finest Late Baroque square

Two golden "onion towers" surmount the building which, according to Hundertwasser, raises the occupier to the status of a king. Lively elements are the coloured crooked pillars, the fountain and the figural decoration, all copies of originals. Art or kitsch – the viewer must decide for himself!

*Josefsplatz   C4

Location
Augustinerstrasse, I

Underground station
Stephansplatz (U1)

Bus
2A

The Josefsplatz is deservedly called the finest square in Vienna. It is 200 years old, was built in a unified Late Baroque style and creates a fine impression. Round it stands the Öster-reichische National Bibliothek (see entry), the Winterreit-schule (see Hofburg), the Palais Pálffy (see entry) and the Palais Pallavicini. The Palais Pallavicini (No. 5 – now a club and conference centre) is a noble Classical building with a magnificent portal supported on caryatides and figures on the metopes dating from 1786 by F. A. Zauner. The Palais itself was built by Ferdinand von Hohenberg in 1783–84.

The memorial in the middle of the square shows Maria Theresa's son, Joseph II; it is by A. Zauner and dates from 1795 to 1806. The reformer, clad in the garb of a Roman emperor, is shown blessing his people. The reliefs on the memorial celebrate Joseph's services to Austrian commerce and recall the many journeys he made abroad in order to benefit his people. The memorial became the spot where Viennese people loyal to the Imperial principle gathered in 1848 while the Revolution was in progress. It was their homage to an Emperor who had died half a century earlier.

Josefstädter Bezirksmuseum (Regional Museum)   B3

Up until 1963 rolls, croissants and bread were baked in the Old Bakehouse. Since 1965 it has been in part an offshoot of the Josefstadt Regional Museum with displays illustrating the crafts and trades of the area and, in part, a unique gastronomical business.

All sorts of objects connected with baking are on show – dough-troughs, weights, measures and the old baking-ovens. These all date from 1701. It was at that period that a well-to-do baker built for himself one of the finest Baroque houses in Vienna.

The bakery has been restored meticulously to its original form, and a café has been installed here. The wine bar was once the flour store, and the "snug" was the coachman's room.

A tip – the "Millirahmstrudel" taste best when they have just come out of the ovens at midday.

Location
34 Langegasse, VIII

Underground station
Lerchenfelderstrasse (U2)

Bus
13A

Opening times
Tues.–Sat. noon to midnight, Sun. 2 p.m. to midnight

*Josephinum (anatomia plastica)   B4

The Institute of the History of Medicine and the Pharmacognostic Institute for Medicine are housed in the palatial Late Baroque building designed by Isidor Canevale.

The world-famous collection of anatomical and obstetric models (anatomia plastica) in wax was commissioned by Joseph II from Tuscan sculptors. These lifelike and for the most part coloured wax figures and models provide an unusual but fascinating collection for the study of the human body. There is an experimental apothecary's collection which is protected for its historical significance and also a great collection of drugs and remedies.

The Josephinum was founded during the reign of Joseph II for the training of doctors and surgeons for the army. The buildings were remodelled in 1822. It was elevated to the status of a military academy in 1854, which was, however, taken away again in 1872. In the Court of Honour there is a fountain with the figure of Hygeia; the lead statue is by J. M. Fischer and dates from 1787.

Location
25 Währingerstrasse/
3 Van-Swieten-Gasse, IX

Underground station
Schottentor (U2)

Trams
37, 38, 40, 41, 42

Opening times
Mon.–Fri. 11 a.m.–3 p.m.

Judenplatz with Jordanhof   B5

The Judenplatz (Jews' Square) was the centre of Vienna's ghetto from 1294 to 1421. Here stood the rabbi's house, the school and the synagogue. The synagogue was demolished in 1421, materials from it being used to build the Old University.

One of the most remarkable houses in the square is Hans "Zum grossen Jordan". Its relief depicting the Baptism of Christ dates from the 16th c. It serves as a reminder of the burning to death of Jews on the Gänseweide in 1421.

The house was built in the 15th c. In 1560 a descendant of the original owner Jörg Jordan sold the house to the Jesuits, but it has been in private ownership since 1684.

Other remarkable houses are No. 8 (the Tailors' Guild House)

Location
Jordangasse/Drahtgasse, I

Underground station
Schwedenplatz (U1, U4)

Bus
2A

Trams
1, 2 (Quayside)

Kahlenberg – the capital city's own mountain summit

and the Böhmische Hofkanzlei (see entry) in Wipplinger-strasse whose rear façade bounds the Judenplatz on one side. From the W corner of the square Drahtgasse leads through to Am Hof (see entry).

*Kahlenberg

Location
Vienna, XIX

Underground station
Heiligenstadt (U4)

Bus
38A

Kahlenberg stands 1,585 ft (484 m) high. It is, so to speak, Vienna's own "mountain" and virtually the last part of the Vienna Woods to the E. There is a magnificent view from the terrace. Near by are the vineyards of Grinzing (see entry) and Nussdorf, and farther off, beyond the city and the Marchfeld, the Little Carpathians and the Schneeberg region.

On the summit of Kahlenberg stands a television tower and the Stephanie Observatory (125 steps to top; entrance fee). It was from up here that in 1683 the relieving army of the Polish Prince Sobieski brought aid at the 11th hour to the city of Vienna which was being besieged and almost overrun by the Turks for a second time. The event is commemorated by the Sobieski Chapel in the little Church of St Joseph.

Poets and composers have always had a soft spot for Kahlenberg. The fact that it was once called "Sow Hill", presumably on account of the numbers of wild boar in the dense oak woods, was forgotten long ago. Grillparzer wrote: "If you have seen the land all around from the top of Kahlenberg, you will understand what I have written and what I am."

**Kapuzinerkirche   C4

The Capuchin Church dedicated to Our Lady of the Angels is, as befits a Mendicant Order vowed to poverty, modest, sober and almost totally lacking in ornamentation. Nothing visible reminds us that it was founded by an empress (Empress Anna) in 1618.

The most precious work of art in the church is a "Pietà" by the altar in the right-hand transept. It is by Peter von Strudel, the Founder of the Academy of Fine Arts.

On the left-hand side of the church is the entrance to the Imperial Vault

Location
Neuer Markt, I

Underground station
Stephansplatz (U1)

**Imperial Vault (also called Capuchin Vault)

Beneath the Church of the Capuchins is the Habsburg family vault where 138 members of the House lie buried. Since 1633 all the Austrian Emperors have been buried here, with just a few exceptions. (Ferdinand II was buried at Graz, Frederick III in St Stephen's Cathedral (see entry – Stephansdom), and Charles I, the last Emperor, at Funchal in Madeira where he had gone as an exile.) The coffins contain only the embalmed bodies without the internal organs (see entry – Stephansdom) and the hearts (see entry – Augustinerkirche).

Opening times
Daily 9.30 a.m.–4 p.m.

The nine vaults are arranged in chronological order which makes it easy to trace the evolution of taste. Unfortunately the bronze caskets dating from the 17th and 18th c. have been attacked by decay, which necessitates extremely expensive conservation work.

Founder's Vault: Emperor Matthias, who died in 1619, and Empress Anna, who died in 1618, are considered to be the inaugurators of the family vault. Originally they were laid to rest in the Monastery of St Dorothea, and their bodies were the first to be transferred to the Imperial Vault in 1633.

Leopoldine Vault: It is also called the Angel Vault for among the 16 bronze caskets are 12 in which children were laid to rest. Ferdinand III, who died in 1657, is also buried here. Balthasar Ferdinand Moll's casket for Elenore of Pfalz-Neuburg who died in 1720 made such a favourable impres-

Entrance

Imperial (or Capuchin) Vault

1 FOUNDERS' VAULT (1622–33) – Emperor Matthias I (d. 1619), Empress Anna (d. 1618)
2 LEOPOLDINE VAULT (1657 and 1701) – 16 sarcophagi, 12 for children
3 CAROLINE VAULT (1720) – 7 sarcophagi
4 MARIA THERESA VAULT (1754) – double sarcophagus for Empress Maria Theresa (d. 1780) and Francis of Lorraine (d. 1765)
5 FRANCIS II VAULT (1824)
6 FERDINAND VAULT (1842)
7 TUSCAN VAULT (1842)
8 NEW VAULT (1960-62) - 26 sarcophagi
9 FRANZ JOSEPH VAULT (1909) – Franz Joseph I d. 1916, Empress Elisabeth (d. 1898)
10 Chapel: In the chapel is a memorial tablet to Emperor Charles I (d. 1922)

Capuchin Vault: the tomb of Emperor Franz Joseph

sion on the Emperor that Moll, a Professor at the Academy for Fine Art, spent half the time of his remaining years working on sarcophagi.

Caroline Vault: Johann Lucas von Hildebrandt designed the sarcophagi for Leopold I (d. 1704) and for Joseph I (d. 1711). B. F. Moll designed the sarcophagus of Charles VI (d. 1740); a magnificent work of art it rests on four lions and is decorated with the coats of arms of the Holy Roman Empire, Bohemia, Hungary and Castile.

Maria Theresa Vault: Jean-Nicholas Jadot de Ville Issey designed the domed chamber dominated by Moll's masterly double sarcophagus in the Rococo style for Maria Theresa, who died in 1780, and for Francis I, who died in 1765. The sarcophagus takes the form of a bed of state; at the head of the Imperial couple an angel of fame with trumpet and a crown of stars proclaims the triumph of faith. On the sides are numerous reliefs depicting scenes from Maria Theresa's life. It is also ornamented with four mourning figures and the crowns of Austria, Hungary, Bohemia and Jerusalem.
B. F. Moll is also responsible for several Rococo sarcophagi for the children of the Imperial couple, though not for the excessively simple copper coffin for Emperor Joseph II who died in 1790.
In a niche in the Maria Theresa Vault is found the coffin of the Countess Karoline Fuchs-Mollart who died in 1754. She was responsible for the upbringing of Maria Theresa and is the only person buried here who was not a member of the Imperial House.

Francis II Vault: the last Emperor of the Holy Roman Empire, Francis II who died in 1835, lies here with the graves of his four consorts all round. The Classical copper coffin is the work of Peter Nobile.

Ferdinand Vault. Ferdinand I, the Kindly, who died in 1875, whose coffin stands on a pedestal, shares this chamber with 37 other members of the Habsburg family who are placed in niches in the walls.

Tuscan Vault: This vault for members of the Tuscan collateral branch of the Habsburg House is at present being altered.

New Vault: It was created between 1960 and 1962 under the direction of Professor Schwanzer. In the sarcophagi lie Emperor Maximilian of Mexico who was executed in 1867 and Marie Louise, Napoleon's wife who died in 1847. The body of their son, the Duke of Reichstadt, was transferred to Paris where it was buried in the Invalides on the orders of Adolf Hitler as a gesture intended to win the good will of the French.

Franz Joseph Vault: Emperor Franz Joseph who died in 1916 was the last Habsburg to be buried in the vault. He was predeceased by the Empress Elisabeth who was murdered in Geneva in 1898 and by his son, Crown Prince Rudolf, who committed suicide in the hunting-lodge at Mayerling in 1889.

Chapel: There is a memorial tablet to Emperor Charles I, the last Emperor of Austria. He died in exile on the Portuguese island of Madeira in 1922.

Karlskirche C4

The church dedicated to St Charles Borromeo was designed by J. B. Fischer von Erlach and his son. It is Vienna's most important religious building in the Baroque style. Emperor Charles VI vowed he would build it when the plague was raging in 1713, and in 1737 the church was dedicated to St Charles Borromeo, one of the saints invoked during plagues. In 1738 it was handed over to the Knights of Malta, and in 1783 it was declared an Imperial prebend.

The vast Baroque building is some 262 ft (80 m) long and 200 ft (60 m) wide. The dome rises to a height of 235 ft (72 m). It cost 304,000 guilders to build. All countries owing allegiance to the Crown had to contribute to the cost, as did Hamburg which also had to contribute to the cost as a fine for the deliberate destruction of the chapel of the Austrian Embassy.

There is much to be seen in the church with its tall oval central area, two major side-chapels and four smaller chapels in the corners.

Porch. The relief on the metope over the portal portrays the plague being overcome. The Latin inscription means: "I fulfil my vow in the presence of those who fear the Lord."

Location
Karlsplatz, I

Underground station
Karlsplatz (U1, U2, U4)

Bus
59A, 4A

Trams
1, 2, D, J

Perambulation

85

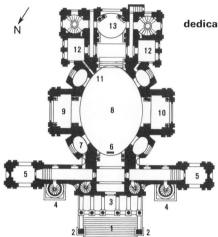

Karlskirche
dedicated to St Charles Borromeo

1 Stairway
2 Angel with bronze crosses
3 Porch in form of Greek portico with reliefs on the metopes
4 Triumphal pillars with spiral bands in relief
5 Campanile
6 Organ. Fresco ceiling above the organ-case by J. M. Rottmayr: it shows St Cecilia with the angels
7 Baptistery with stone dome
8 Dome with frescoes of the Apotheosis of St Charles Borromeo by J. M. Rottmayr (1725–30)
9 Reredos of the Assumption of the Virgin, by Sebastiani Ricci
10 Reredos of St Elisabeth of Thuringia by Daniel Gran (1736–37)
11 Pulpit
12 Vestries
13 High Altar by L. Mattielli

Karlskirche, looking towards the High Altar

Triumphal Pillars. These are based on Trajan's Column at Rome. Their spiralling bands in relief depict scenes from the life of St Charles Borromeo. The pillars, which are 110 ft (33 m) high, are surmounted by the Imperial Crown over the lanterns.

Organ. M. Rottmayr painted the fresco on the organ-case. It depicts St Cecilia with angels making music.

Dome Frescoes. The light interior is dominated by Rottmayr's frescoes in the dome. They represent the apotheosis of St Charles and the petition that plague may be averted. On the left an angel with a flaming torch sets fire to Luther's Bible which has fallen to the ground.

Noteworthy Reredoses: "Jesus and the Roman Captain" and "Healing of a man sick of the palsy" by Daniel Gran; "Raising of the Young Man" by M. Altomonte; "St Luke" by van Schuppen.
The painting of the Assumption of the Virgin on the left of the High Altar is by Sebastiani Ricci, and that of St Elisabeth of Thuringia to the right of the High Altar is by Daniel Gran.
High Altar. The subject is the ascent into Heaven of St Charles Borromeo. The sculptural decoration with clouds behind the High Altar is based on designs by J. B. Fischer von Erlach.

Karlsplatz   C4

Karlsplatz, where important tram and underground routes converge, is one of the busiest squares in central Vienna. In 1977–78 the square was newly laid out and the striking station building of Otto Wagner was re-erected. One of Wagner's 1901 pavilions, decorated with marble and gold leaf, now serves as an entrance to the U-Bahn station and also for minor temporary exhibitions of the Historical Museum (see entry); the other one becomes a café in summer.
In the gardens in the southern part of Karlsplatz stand monuments to Johannes Brahms (1908), to Josef Ressel (1862), the inventor of the ship's screw, and to Josef Madersperger (1933), the inventor of the sewing machine. On the N side of the square stand the Kunstlerhaus and the Musikverein building (see entries), on the S side are the Karlskirche (see entry) and the Technical University, a building erected 1816–18 with an upper storey added later. On the E side stands the Historisches Museum (see entry) and on the W the Secession Building (see entry).

Location
1st district

Underground station
Karlsplatz (U1, U2, U4)

Buses
4A, 59A

Trams
1, 2, D, J

*Kärntnerstrasse   C4

Vienna's most elegant shopping street leads from Stephansplatz (see entry) to Karlsplatz. Since 1973 it has been a pedestrian precinct up as far as Walfischgasse, with lime trees, and pavement cafés, with mountebanks and buskers. The modern-style street lights and idiosyncratic fountains have given rise to much debate. Beneath the junction of Kärntnerstrasse and the Ring lies the "Operngasse", with shops, snack bars and the central Tourist Information Office.

Location
Stephansplatz
Opernkreuzung, I

Underground stations
Karlsplatz (U1, U2, U4),
Stephansplatz (U1)

Trams
1, 2, D, J

Kärntnerstrasse is first mentioned in documents as early as
1257 under the name of "Strata Carinthianorum". Most of the
houses date from the 18th c. and the most interesting façades
are those of Nos 4, 16 and 17. Only the Maltese Church still
has a few features dating back to 1265. Inside there are
numerous coats of arms of Knights of Malta as well as the
1806 stucco monument with Turkish figures on either hand to
the memory of Jean de la Valette, the Grand Master who
defended Malta against the Turks in 1565.

Kleiner Bischofshof   B5

The former Small Bishop's Palace which later became the
"Haus zum roten Kreuz" (House with the Red Cross) dates, in
part, from the 15th c. Matthias Gerl gave it a new façade in
1761. The Madonna relief in a pretty Rococo frame with Turkish trophies on the wall is especially noteworthy.
It was here that Franz Georg Kolschitzky died in 1694. According to the history of the city, he had set up the first Viennese
coffee house here.

Location
6 Domgasse, I

Underground station
Stephansplatz (U1)

Klosterneuburg (monastery)

Klosterneuburg stands on the NE edge of the Vienna Woods
and is separated from the Danube by a broad grassy island. It
attracts many visitors mainly on account of its monastery
which was founded by the Augustinian Canons. There is an
extensive range of buildings high up above the Danube. It
originated as a monastery founded by the Babenberg Margrave Leopold III ("The Pious") in the 12th c. In 1730 Emperor
Charles VI embarked on a programme of large-scale new
building, but this was stopped again in 1755. Work was only
completed in 1842, and then on a reduced scale.
The buildings of the monastery comprise the monastery
church with Romanesque features and which was refurbished in Baroque style in the 17th c., the Leopold Chapel, a
Romanesque-Gothic Cloister, the Leopold Courtyard and the
monastery wine-vaults.
The famous "Verdun Altar" in the Leopold Chapel is especially noteworthy. It is made up of 51 enamelled panels by the
goldsmith Nikolaus of Verdun and dates from 1181. This
reredos for a funerary chapel is among the finest examples of
High Medieval goldsmith's and enameller's work.
Cloisters and Freisinger Chapel, and the monastery lapidarium. Entry is through the Leopold Chapel to the beautiful
Gothic Cloisters, the 600-year-old Freisinger Chapel and the
monastery lapidarium. In the latter is preserved, with other
examples of Romanesque and Gothic sculpture, the sandstone "Klosterneuburg Madonna", a life-size figure dating
from about 1310.
New Building. The new monastery building erected during
Charles VI's reign has two copper domes,
one of which is surmounted by the German Imperial Crown,
the other by the Lower Austrian Archducal Bonnet. Among
the features shown by guides when a conducted tour is taken

Underground station
Heiligenstadt (U4) thence by
bus

Distance
7½ miles (12 km) N, on the
Danube

Tours
Mon.–Sat. 9 a.m.–noon and
1–5 p.m., Sat., Sun. and
public holidays 1.30 p.m.–
dusk (according to
demand).

◄ *Klosterneuburg: 12th c. monastery founded by Margrave Leopold III*

Museum of Art History

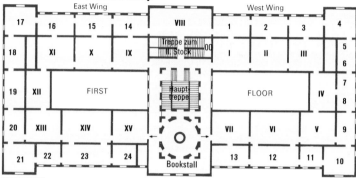

FIRST FLOOR
Picture Gallery
East Wing
Rooms

West Wing
Rooms

VIII 15th–16th c. Dutch	15 Dürer	I Raphael, Correggio	4 Bassano

East Wing
Rooms
VIII 15th–16th c. Dutch
IX 16th c. Dutch
X P. Brueghel the Elder
XI 17th c. Flemish
XII Van Dyck
XIII Rubens
XIV Rubens
XV 17th–18th c. Dutch
Cabinets
14 Bosch, Mor

15 Dürer
16 Altdorfer, Huber
17 Cranach
18 Holbein the Younger, Clouet
19 Mannerists
20 Rubens
21 Teniers the Younger
22 Hals, Van Goyen
23 Rembrandt
24 Ruysdael, Vermeer

West Wing
Rooms
I Raphael, Correggio
II Titian
III Veronese, Bordone
IV Tintoretto
V Caravaggio, Ribera
VI Reni, Fetti, Giordano
VII Crespi, Tiepolo
Cabinets
1 Mantegna, Vivarini
2 Bellini, Titian
3 Dossi, Savoldo

4 Bassano
5 Schiavone
6 Moretto, Marino
7 De Predis, Luini
8 Barocci, dell'Abate
9 Bronzino, Coello
10 Velázquez, Murillo
11 Poussin, Cortone
12 Fetti, Strozzi, Cavallino
13 Guardi, Canaletto

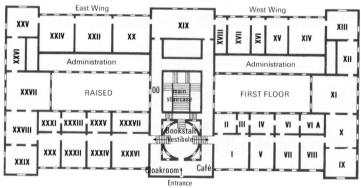

RAISED FIRST FLOOR
East Wing
Sculpture and Applied Arts Collection
Middle Ages
Rooms XXXIV–XXXVII
Renaissance
Rooms XXVIII–XXXII

Mannerism
Rooms XXIV–XXVII
Baroque and Rococo
Rooms XIX–XXII

West Wing
Egyptian
Oriental
Collection
Rooms I–VIII

Antiquities
Rooms IX–XVIII

are the Baroque main staircase, the Marble Hall with frescoes by Daniel Gran, the Imperial Apartment, the Tapestry Room and the Treasury.
Monastery Museum. The Museum has a rich collection including a Habsburg genealogy, the Albrechts Altar which was given in 1438 and valuable medieval pictures.
The monastery also possesses vineyards and famous winevaults. In the monastery cooperage may be seen the "Thousand bucket barrel" dating from 1704. Each year on St Leopold's Day, 15 November, there is a great barrel-rolling carnival.

Kunstgewerbemuseum

See Österreichisches Museum für angewandte Kunst.

**Kunsthistorisches Museum   C4

The Museum of Art History was founded when it was realised that Vienna had no counterpart of the great art galleries of London and Amsterdam, particularly since the Imperial collections in Prince Eugene's former summer mansion had become far too large for those premises.
Karl Hasenauer and Gottfried Semper were charged with the task of drawing up plans for two splendid museums, the Kunsthistorisches Museum and the Naturhistorisches Museum (see entry), its counterpart in the life sciences. Between 1872 and 1891 they erected the vast pair of buildings which form the left- and right-hand sides of Maria-Theresien-Platz. Though the State was close to bankruptcy, the architects were under instructions not to make economies, and they were able to use expensive materials and commission highly rated artists with the decoration of the interior.
Among those who worked on the embellishment of the Museum's interior were Viktor Tilgner, Hans Makart, Michael Munkacsy, the brothers Ernst and Gustav Klimt and Franz Matsch.

The Künsthistorisches Museum's collections are divided into 10 departments. The main building houses the following:
The Egyptian-Oriental Collection; the Collection of Antiquities; the Sculpture and Applied Arts Collection; the Collection of Paintings with the so-called "secondary galleries", and the Collection of Medals, Coins and Tokens.
The following collections belonging to the Kunsthistorisches Museum are found elsewhere:
The Neue Galerie (New Gallery) in der Stallburg (see entry).
The Treasure in the Hofburg (see entry).
The Sammlung alter Musikinstrumente (collection of old instruments; see entry).
The Waffensammlung (collection of weapons; see entry).
The Ephesos-Museum (see entry).
The Wagenburg (Mews) in Schönbrunn (see entry).

A tour of the main building of the Kunsthistorisches involves climbing four flights of stairs, walking 2½ miles (4 km) of corridors and visiting 51 rooms. It is generally advisable to follow the order given here.

Location
Maria-Theresien-Platz, I

Underground station
Mariahilferstrasse (U3)

Buses
2A, 3A, 57A

Trams
1, 2, D, J, 52, 58

Opening times
Tues.–Fri. 10 a.m.–6 p.m.,
Sat.–Sun. 9 a.m.–6 p.m.
Evening illumination (parts of collection alternately)
Tues, Fri. 6–10 p.m.

Note: visitors without a lot of time at their disposal should note that the Egyptian-Oriental Collection and the Picture Galleries are the most highly rated departments of the Museum.

Egyptian-Oriental Collection
(Raised First Floor)

Room I: Exhibits illustrating the cult of the dead. Large stone sarcophagi (600–100 B.C.); painted wooden coffins (1100–100 B.C.); mummies with painted wrappings, etc.

Room II: Oriental Collection. Glazed tile relief with representation of a pacing lion from Ischtartor in Babylon (c. 580 B.C.); tiles and tablets, stone inscriptions, reliefs and bronzes from southern Arabia (1st c. B.C.), etc.

Room III: Cult of animals. Mummified sacred animals; figures of animal gods; Apis stele from Sakkara, etc.

Room IV: Everyday objects including furniture, clothes, jewellery, tools for working with stone and wood representation of the development of old Egyptian writing, etc.

Room V: Ptolemaic Age. Two copies of colossal statues of rulers (2nd c. B.C.). Sphinxes, statues, reliefs, bronzes; two seated statues of the lion-headed goddess Mut, etc.

Room VI: Pre- and early history of Egypt (5000–2635 B.C.). Stone and earthenware vessels; Nubia and its connection with Egyptian culture; Hyksos as a foreign ruler in Egypt (1650–1550 B.C.); Austrian excavations in Tel el Dab'a, etc.

Room VIA: Old Kingdom. Cult chamber of Prince Kaninisut from Giza (about 2400 B.C., 2nd Dynasty).

Room VII: New Kingdom (1550–1080 B.C.). Statues of gods, kings and citizens; grave steles, memorials, reliefs and vessels. Middle Kingdom (2134–1650 B.C.). Statues and parts of statues of kings and citizens; steles, small stone vessels, etc.

Room VIII: Old Kingdom (2635–2155 B.C.). Statues, architectural relics and vessels from private tombs of the 4th–6th Dynasty (about 2500–2150 B.C.) in Giza. Of especial interest and one of the finest examples extant is the "head of a man" (about 2450 B.C.) sculpted from the finest limestone.

Antiquities
(Raised First Floor)

Room IX: Art from Cyprus. Bronze Age pottery and sepulchral reliefs from Palmyra.

Room X: Greek and Roman sculpture, including the precious bronze statue "The Youth of Helenenburg" (second half of the 5th c.) and a head of Artemis (2nd c. B.C., possibly a copy).

Room XI: Later Greek and Roman sculpture and a magnificent Roman mosaic pavement (2nd c.).

Room XII: Greek bronzes and Minoan statuettes from Crete (end of 2nd millennium B.C.).

Room XIII: Etruscan art, including the clay statue of Athena from Rocca d'Aspromonte (5th c. B.C.).

Room XIV: Pottery decorated with pictures and reliefs, Tanagara figures and an especially precious Ptolemaic cameo with the portraits of a Ptolemaic king and his consort (Showcase 14).

Room XV: Roman art, portraits of Emperors, ceremonial utensil, miniature sculptures and cameos, including the world-famous "Gemma Augustea" (1st c. B.C.).

Room XVI: Art of Late Antiquity, individual finds from Austrian excavations, including marble portrait heads from Ephesus.

The Kunsthistorisches Museum: view of exterior

Room XVII: Textiles from Egypt and Early Christian handi-crafts, including the Siebenburg golden treasure from Szilagysomlyo.

Room XVIII: Byzantine and Old Bulgarian work, including silver treasures from Galicia and Bukovina. The prime exhibit is the treasure from Nagyszentmiklós with 23 gold vessels.

The sequence of the rooms is clear from the plan.

Sculpture and Applied Arts Collection
(Raised Ground Floor)

Room XXXVI: High and late Middle Ages. Ivory carving, rock-crystal vessels and two famous chalices, one from Wilten Abbey at Innsbruck, the other from St Peter's at Salzburg.

Rooms XXXVII and XXXV: Clocks, scientific instruments and automata of the 16th and 17th c.

Room XXXIV: Late Medieval German sculpture. Fine Nurem-berg vessels, including the so-called Dürer and Maximilian cups. Gothic sculpture including the famous "Krumau Madonna".

Room XXXII: Florentine Early Renaissance. Many reliefs and busts from Donatello's and Della Robbia's workshops; Setti-gnano's "Laughing Boy" and Laurana's "Portrait of a Young Lady".

Room XXXI: 16th and 17th c. small bronzes, ivory work, rock-crystal and carved stone vessels.

Room XXX: Upper Italian Renaissance. Busts, plaques and bronzes by Antico (Venus Felix), Moderno and Riccio.

Room XXIX: Italian vessels of rock-crystal, lapis lazuli, etc.; valuable 16th c. cameos; Spanish gold work.

Room XXVIII: German Renaissance. Wooden statuettes; inlay work and carving.

Room XXVII: 16th c. Italian bronzes. Many impressive works by Giambologna and Benvenuto Cellini's famous salt cellar.

Room XXVI: French 16th c. Mannerism with elegant vessels and Limoges display pieces.

Room XXV: German 16th c. Mannerism. Items from Archduke Ferdinand II's collection; rare Venetian jewellery; Tyrolean pottery, etc.

Room XXIV: Collection of carved stone vessels from the time of Rudolf II; fine gold and silver work, jewellery and cameoes of the 16th and 17th c.; so-called Florentine mosaic.

Room XXII: High Baroque. Mainly miniature work, ebony statuettes, bronze busts and figurative reliefs made from Kehlheim stone.

Room XX: Austrian High Baroque and Rococo. Notable are the bust of Marie-Antoinette, Marie Theresa's gold breakfast service and the toilet set of her husband, Francis II.

Room XIX: 17th c. carvings in crystal and quartz. The tapestries on the walls are frequently changed as they are sensitive to light and dust.

Picture Gallery
(First Floor)

The world-famous Picture Gallery is housed in 15 rooms and 24 cabinets. It is a good idea to go round rooms VIII to XV and rooms I to VII, turning off to see the cabinets on either side.

Room VIII: Early Netherlandish painting of the 15th and 16th c. Works by Rogier van der Weyden, Hans Memling, Joos van Cleeves and two portraits by Jan van Eyck.

The Peter Paul Rubens Collection

Room IX: 16th c. Netherlandish painting. Genre pictures by Pieter Aertsen and a series depicting the Seasons by Lucas van Valckenborch.

Room X: A definitive collection of works by Pieter Brueghel the Elder, with about one third of the surviving works of the Master, including "The Seasons" and "The Peasant Wedding".

Room XI: 17th c. Flemish masters. Still-lifes by Frans Snyderss and Jacob Jordaens.

Room XII: Paintings by Rubens's pupil and collaborator Sir Anthony van Dyck, with his "Picture of a young general".

Rooms XIII and XIV: Peter Paul Rubens Collection. More than 30 of his works hang here, including many of his masterpieces.

Room XV: Dutch 17th and 18th c. painting, with pictures by Rembrandt and landscapes by Ruysdael.

The most important cabinets in this part of the gallery are:
Cabinet 15, with eight major works by Dürer.
Cabinet 18, with portraits by Hans Holbein the Younger.
Cabinet 20, with more paintings by Rubens.
Cabinet 23, with self-portraits by Rembrandt and landscapes by Ruysdael.
Cabinet 24, works by Vermeer.

Rooms I to VII are devoted to Italian, Spanish and French painting.

Room I: Works by Raphael, Parmigianino and Correggio.

Room II: Titian's masterpieces and later works, including "Ecce Homo" and "Danaë".

Room III: Representative works by Paolo Veronese – "Death of Lucretia", "Judith with the head of Holofernes", etc., and large pictures of Old and New Testament subjects.

Room IV: Venetian Mannerism, represented primarily by Tintoretto, including his painting "Susanna in the Bath".

Room V: 17th c. chiaroscuro paintings. The major work here is the famous "Madonna of the Rosary" by Michelangelo Caravaggio.

Room VI: Christian themes from the Counter-Reformation era. Notable is the famous "Baptism of Christ" by Guido Reni.

Room VII: 18th c. Italian Baroque masters. Giambattista Tiepolo's scenes from Roman history are outstanding.

The most important cabinets in this part of the gallery are:
Cabinet 2, with early works by Titian.
Cabinet 4, with works by Bassano.
Cabinet 10, with works by Velázquez and an altar-painting by Murillo originating in Seville and only acquired in 1987.

The Second Floor of the Museum houses the so-called "secondary galleries", where the exhibits are changed from time to time. However the famous Vienna townscape by Bernardo Belotto ("Canaletto") is permanently on display.

The Numismatic Collection, one of the largest and most important of its type, occupies three rooms.

Numismatic Collection/
Numismatic Cabinet
(Second Floor)

Room I: Development of money from natural forms of currency to modern forms of monetary transaction without cash. There is natural currency from Asia, Africa and America, stone currency from Yap Island, money in the form of bars and rings, minted currency and rare old versions of paper money.

Room II: Medals. Exhibition of the artistic and cultural history of medals from the Roman era to the present day.

Room III: Modern medals, insignia of Orders and honorific badges.

Künstlerhaus (art gallery) C4

Location
5 Karlsplatz, I

Underground station
Karlsplatz (U1, U2, U4)

Trams
1, 2, D, J, T

The Künstlerhaus (House of the Artists) is used for art shows, cultural events and art festivals. The most famous are the "Gschnas" festivals at carnival time.

The Vienna Artists' Society had this Neo-Renaissance building put up in 1865–68. The marble standing figures by the entrance represent Diego Velázquez, Raphael Santi, Leonardo da Vinci, Michelangelo Buonarroti, Albrecht Dürer, Titian, Bramante and Peter Paul Rubens.

Kupferstichkabinett

See Akademie der Bildenden Künste

Lainzer Tiergarten (wildlife park)

Location
Entrance Lainzer-Tor, XIII

Trams and Buses
Tram 60 or 62 to Speising
then bus 60B

Opening times
April–Nov. Wed.–Mon.
from 8 a.m. to dusk.
Hermes Villa Park
Wed.–Sun. 9 a.m.–4 p.m.

The Lainzer Wildlife Park occupies some 10 sq. miles (26 km^2) of almost unspoiled landscape. Here the Vienna Woods have remained almost untouched, with oaks and beeches, roe-deer and red deer, wild boars, moufflons, fallow deer and aurochs.

Once it was the hunting reserve of Emperor Joseph II and was fenced off with a stone wall 15½ miles (25 km) long. Since 1923 it has been open to the public, and it has been a nature sanctuary since 1941. In September a Hunters' Fair is held in honour of St Eustace, patron saint of the hunt. In the park there are 50 miles (80 km) of footpaths, almost half unfenced, with refreshment places and shelters, children's playgrounds and the Huburtuswarte observation tower. In July and August the Lipizzaner horses of the Spanish Riding School (see entry) spend their "summer holidays" in the Hermes Villa Park. The former hunting-lodge has been partially restored to its original condition and is now used for temporary exhibitions.

Landhaus (Provincial Government) B4

Location
13 Herrengasse, I

Underground stations
Schottentor (U2),
Stephansplatz (U1)

Bus
2A

Opening times
Tours if booked in
advance
Chapel: Sun. from 9 a.m.

The official seat of the Lower Austrian Provincial Government is in the "Palace of the Lower Austrian Estates". The Estates acquired the former "Liechtensteinisches Freihaus" in 1513. In the 16th c. the building was completely renovated, and in the 19th c. it was restored according to historical principles. The Renaissance rooms in which Beethoven, Liszt and Schubert performed and in which Abraham a Sancta Clara wrote his account of the plague in 1679 were restored in 1953. If a booking is made in advance it is possible to view the Hall of the Knights, the Hall of the Aldermen, the Hall of the Prelates, the great Debating Chamber and the parlours.

It was in the great Debating Chamber that the foundation of the Republic was approved in 1918.

In the courtyard of the Landhaus there is a 1571 tablet with an Imperial injunction that nobody should venture to scuffle or fight or cause a disturbance in front of or within the chartered Landhaus.

The Imperial peace was, however, broken, and in 1848 it was actually from the Landhaus that the Revolution started.

Laxenburg

The Court rode out to Laxenburg to seek refreshment when Vienna was hot in the summer. Three palaces stand in a delightful park. The Old Castle dates from the 14th c. It is historically important because it is here that Emperor Charles VI promulgated the "Pragmatic Sanction" which ensured the succession to the throne of his daughter Maria Theresa. The Franzensburg is an 18th and 19th c. copy of a Gothic castle. The New Castle (also called the Blue Castle) is a Late Baroque building which was the centre of the life of the Court in the time of Maria Theresa and during the Congress of Vienna.

The romantic Franzensburg which stands on an island in the Large Pool is now a museum. In the courtyard can be seen 37 busts of the Habsburgs.

Railway
from Wien-Mitte to Laxenburg-Biedermannsdorf (R61)

Distance
9½ miles (15 km) S

Franzensburg
Open: Easter to Oct. daily 10 a.m.–noon, 2–5 p.m.

*Lipizzaner   C4

Proudly called "Silver Stallions", the horses of the Spanish Riding School are a cross of Berber and Arabian stock with Spanish and Italian horses. The foals are born any shade between brown and mouse-grey; their coats turn white only when they are older, between four and ten years.

The horses were bred in Lipizza until 1918 when the stud was transferred to Piber in Styria. The stud which was partly moved to Czechoslovakia during the Second World War was saved from destruction by Colonel Podhajsky who was then head of the riding school (until 1956) as well as by the American horse-loving General Patton.

There still survive today six lines of stallions going back to their forefathers, Pluto (1765), Conversano (1767), Maestoso (1773), Neapolitano (1790), Favory (1799) and Siglavy (1810). The Spanish Riding School, which goes back to the "Spanischer Reitstall", founded in 1572, is now the only place in the world where "haute école" is still practised in the Classical style.

The stallions do not begin their long training until they are four years old. At about the age of seven they learn the so-called "ground exercises", which involve high-speed changes in gait, piaffes, passages and pirouettes. Then they graduate to the "aerial exercises", with pesades, levades, courbettes and caprioles.

Location
Winterreitschule, Hofburg, Stallburg, 1 Reitschulgasse, I

Underground stations
Stephansplatz (U1), Schottentor (U2)

Bus
2A

Stable visits
Wed. & Sat. 2–4 p.m., Sun. and public holidays 10 a.m.–noon, 1 July–31 Aug. daily 2–4 p.m., Sun. and public holidays 10 a.m.–noon

*Maria am Gestade (church)   B4

The Church of Maria am Gestade (Mary on the Strand) is popularly called the "Maria-Stiegen-Kirche" (Mary on the Steps). It is the Czech national church, and its entrancing pierced Gothic cupole is one of the characteristic sights of the N Old City.

Maria am Gestade, originally a wooden oratory dating from

Location
12 Salvatorgasse, I

Underground station
Schwedenplatz (U1, U4)
Bus
3A

the 9th c., used to stand on the steep slope up from the Danube. The present building, and its Gothic stained glass, was put up in the 14th c. The tower was rebuilt in the 16th c., and restoration was undertaken in 1817, 1890, 1930, 1946 and 1973.

The W front of the church is only some 30 ft (10 m) wide, but nearly 105 ft (33 m) high. The church looms above the old narrow lanes like the prow of a ship.

Inside there are two Gothic sandstone figures (by the second pillar on the E side of the nave) dating from the 14th c., and two 15th c. Gothic paintings in the chapel, dedicated to Clemens Maria Hofbauer, the Patron Saint of the city of Vienna. The organ-gallery and a stone Renaissance altar in the Johann Perger Chapel date from the 16th c. The other furnishings of the church are 19th c. work.

*Maria-Theresien-Platz and Memorial C4

Location
Burgring, I

Underground stations
Mariahilferstrasse,
Volkstheater (U2)

Buses
3A, 48A

Trams
1, 2, D, J

The monument to Empress Maria Theresa is one of the most impressive in all Vienna. It dominates the square of the same name but is surrounded by the Naturhistorisches Museum (see entry) and the Kunsthistorisches Museum (see entry). The square itself is laid out as a formal Baroque garden.

It was Franz Joseph who gave the commission to the sculptor Kaspar von Zumbusch, and his work was unveiled in 1887. The female monarch sits on her throne, holding the Pragmatic Sanction of 1713 in her left hand. She is surrounded by the major figures of her day: the standing figures are State Chancellor Kaunitz, Prince Liechtenstein, Count Haugwitz

Maria-Theresien-Platz with the memorial to the Empress

and her Physician, van Swieten, and Generals Daun, Laudon, Traun and Khevenhüller are on horseback.

The SW side of Maria-Theresien-Platz is formed by the Exhibition Palace. This 1,200 ft (360 m) long building was erected between 1723 and 1725 to plans by J. B. Fischer von Erlach and his son J. E. Fischer. Originally the Palace mews, it is now used for the Vienna International Fair.

The Tobacco Museum (entrance 2 Mariahilferstrasse) is housed in the side wing of the Exhibition Palace. Here there are 2,500 exhibits concerned with tobacco and smoking world-wide. In 1900 there were in Vienna 400 workers engaged in carving Meerschaum pipes; now there are only 2.

Opening times
Tues. 10 a.m.–7 p.m.
Wed.–Fri. 10 a.m.–3 p.m.
Sat., Sun. 9 a.m.–1 p.m.

*Michaelerkirche   B4

The Redemptorist Church of St Michael, (now also a cultural centre) used to be the Imperial Court's parish church, and it was also favoured for the interment of important Austrians. It stands directly opposite the Michaeler range of the Hofburg (see entry) on the E side of Michaelerplatz.

It is not known who was the founder of the church. It may have been the Crusader Archduke Leopold VI or else perhaps Ottokar Přemysl. The three-naved arcaded Late Romanesque basilica was built in the 13th c., in the same period as the "Alte Burg" (see Hofburg). The architects were connected with St Stephen's Cathedral. The basilica was enlarged in the 14th c. and restored in the Gothic style in the 16th c. The Baroque narthex with its portal was added in 1724–25 by A. Beduzzi. The W portal with the sculpture of the Fall of the Angels by

Location
1 Michaelerplatz, I

Underground station
Stephansplatz (U1)

Bus
2A

Guided Tours
Church and crypt daily
11 a.m.
Mon.–Sat. also 3 p.m.

Michaelerkirche, once the Imperial Court's parish church

99

Lorenzo Matielli dates from 1792, as does, too, the Classical façade.

Among the oldest treasures of the church are the remains of the once-famed Late Romanesque frescoes in the tower chapel, the "Man of Sorrows" (1430) in the Baptistery and the stone figures of 1350 in the Chapel of St Nicholas. Jean Baptiste d'Avrange designed the High Altar in 1781. The Chapel of St Nicholas, to the right of the choir, was founded by a ducal cook in about 1350 as a thank-offering when he was acquitted in a poisoning case.

Near the church, at the entry to Kohlmarkt, stands the Large Michaeler House; this, with its handsome inner courtyard, was built for the Barnabites in 1720.

The crypt was a burial place; the walls and floor are strewn with bones and there are 250 wood, metal and stone coffins.

---

*Minoritenkirche (officially the Snow Madonna Italian National Church) B4

Location
Minoritenplatz, I

Underground station
Schottentor (U2)

Bus
2A

Trams
1, 2, D, J (Ring)

The former Minorites' church has been called the Snow Madonna Italian National Church since 1786. It has been a Franciscan church since 1957.

The first church of the "Fratres Minores" in Vienna dates from 1230. It was a little chapel dedicated to the Holy Rood and twice burnt down. To replace it Duke Albrecht the Wise had the present Gothic aisle-less church built in the 14th c. It was altered in the 17th, 18th and 20th c.

The Gothic main portal is of architectural interest. It was created by Duke Albrecht's Confessor, Father Jacobus (1340–45). Inside may be seen Giacomo Raffaelli's copy in mosaic of Leonardo da Vinci's famous "Last Supper". It was commissioned by Napoleon because he wanted to take the Milan original to Paris and replace it by the Vienna copy.

After Napoleon's fall the Austrian Court agreed to purchase the copy at a cost of 400,000 guilders. Sight was lost of it when it was put in store at the Belvedere and only brought to the Minoritenkirche in 1845–47.

The picture above the High Altar by Chr. Unterberger is also a copy. The original "Snow Madonna" is an object of veneration in the Esquiline in Rome.

Museum Alte Backstube

See Josefstädter Bezirksmuseum

Österreichisches Museum für Angewandte Kunst B5

Location
5 Stubenring, I.

Underground and S-Bahn stations
Wien-Mitte (U4, S1, S2, S3, S7)

Buses
1A, 74A, 75A

The museum building, designed in Italian Renaissance style by Heinrich von Ferstel, was completed by an extension in Weisskirchnerstrasse in 1909.

The present Museum of Applied Art was founded in 1864 as the Austrian Museum for Art and Industry. In 1867 a School of Applied Arts was added. The museum is the oldest and one of the most important museums of applied art on the Continent. The trade and industrial development of Austria is in great measure attributable to it. Its comprehensive and varied collection from Late Antiquity (Coptic) to the present day are an eloquent testimony of artistic inspiration, not only in Europe but also in the Near and Far East. Especially renowned is the collection of Oriental carpets and other prominent exhibits including glassware, Viennese porcelain, ceramics, textiles, goldsmiths' work and furniture.

Trams
1, 2

Room I: Middle Ages (emphasis on textiles). The "Gösser Ornat" (c. 1260), the only complete altar frontal remaining from such an early date; three 15th c. tapestries with hunting scenes; folding chair (early 13th c.) from Admont Monastery; 12th c. chest.

Opening times
Thurs.–Mon. 10 a.m.–
6 p.m.

Room II: East Asian art work (especially from China). Examples from the Neolithic Age to the present day.

Room III: Dutch tapestries and Renaissance miniatures. Enamels from Limoges and Venice. Furniture and majolica from Urbino. The portal leading into Room V was originally in the Church of St Maria Novella in Florence.

Room IV: German Renaissance work. As well as goldsmiths' work, pewterware, vessels turned from ivory, and carved stone objects an attraction is an especially idiosyncratic carved Tyrol portal dating from about 1600.

Room V: Early Baroque furniture and miniatures. Meissen porcelain including a bear by J. G. Kirchner about 1730.

Room VI: 18th c. craft (especially French, German and Austrian furniture). Notable are two large intarsia wall decorations from the celebrated Röntgen workshop in Neuwied am Rhein.

Room VII: Biedermeier period. Viennese glass and porcelain; writing-desks and chairs.

Room VIII: Oriental carpets. The Vienna collection of Oriental carpets is notable for the so-called classical carpets from Persia, Egypt and Turkey which came from the former Austrian Imperial House. A silk hunting carpet and a rare silk Mameluke carpet (both 16th c.).

Room IX: Art Nouveau (especially Vienna at the turn of the century). Furniture, gold work, glass and ceramics. The star exhibit in the adjoining room is Klimt's cartoons for the dining-room frieze in the Palais Stoclet in Brussels (1911).

First Floor

The gallery of the pillared courtyard is used for small exhibitions. From a podium on the left there is a fine view of the Oriental carpets in Room VIII. Here can be found the library and art print collection; valuable old books and the most recent literature on art are available. The art print collection and the most valuable items in the so-called Baroque library can only be examined with prior permission.

Library
Opening times
Mon., Thur., Fri., Sun.
10 a.m.–6 p.m.

The rooms in the Baumann Building (3 Weisskirchnerstrasse) are reserved for exhibitions not only from the main collection but also for loans from all over the world.

Baumann Building

Museum mittelalterlicher österreichischer Kunst

See Belvedere-Schlösser

Museum für Völkerkunde (Museum of Ethnology)   C4

This museum developed from the Ethnographical Department of the Naturhistorisches Museum (see entry).
The collection is housed in the former "corps de logis" of the Neue Burg (see Hofburg). It comprises more than 150,000 objects pertaining to races that have not used writing.

Location
Neue Burg, Heldenplatz, I

Underground stations
Volkstheater
Mariahilferstrasse (U2)

Bus 3A	Because of shortage of space most of the collections can only be displayed in temporary exhibitions.
Trams 1, 2, D, J, 52, 58	Among the permanent exhibits are, on the ground floor, Benin bronzes with royal portrait busts going back to the 15th c. and the Mexico Collection which belonged to the Emperor Maximilian. It includes the famous feather head-
Opening times Mon., Thur., Fri., Sat. 10 a.m.–1 p.m.; Wed. 10 a.m.–5 p.m.; Sun. 9 a.m.–1 p.m. Film Shows (Oct.–June) Sun. 10 a.m. and noon	dress and feather shield of Montezuma, the Aztec ruler. In 1987 Aztecs tried to further their aim of recovering this exhibit by repeatedly staging demonstrations outside the museum, but until now these have had no effect. Here, too, are the collections made by the British seafarer James Cook which were purchased in London in 1806 at the Emperor's command. The most valued exhibits come from Polynesia.

Österreichisches Museum für Volkskunde   B3

Location 15–19 Laudongasse, VIII	The Folk Museum is housed in the former Schönborn Palais. The building was designed by J. L. von Hildebrandt, and the Classical façade was added in 1770, probably by Isidor Cane-
Underground station Rathaus (U2)	vale. The Museum was founded in 1895 by the Austrian Society for Folklore.
Bus 13A	Ground Floor: Models, pictures and plans illustrating types of houses and farms; interiors, country furniture and utensils;
Trams 5, 43, 44	farming and craftwork; food and clothing.
Opening times Tues.–Fri. 9 a.m.–4 p.m., Sat. 9 a.m.–noon, Sun. 9 a.m.–1 p.m.	Upper Floor: Life and traditions, including a collection of carved masks; popular music and dance; religious life and pilgrimages; social organisation (guilds); Christmas cribs.

Museum des 20. Jahrhunderts (see entry: Gartenpalais Liechtenstein)   D5

Location Schweitzergarten, III	The Austrian Pavilion at the 1958 Brussels World Fair was taken down and rebuilt in the Schweizergarten in Vienna. The Museum of Modern Art was housed here until it moved to the
Underground station Südtirolerplatz (U1)	Gartenpalais Liechtenstein (see entry). Since then the pavilion has served as the Museum of the 20th Century ("Zwanziger-
Trams 18, D, O	haus") as a venue for temporary exhibitions (open daily except Wed. 10 a.m.–6 p.m.). Next to it is a garden where Austrian and other sculpture is displayed.

*Musikvereinsgebäude (concert hall)   C4

Location 3 Dumbastrasse, I	It is in the famous "Golden Hall" of the Musikvereinsgebäude that the Vienna Philharmonic Orchestra gives its major con- certs. The New Year concert is broadcast world-wide from
Underground station Karlsplatz (U1, U2, U4)	here. The Gesellschaft der Musikfreunde (Music Lovers' Society)
Buses 4A, 59A	was founded in 1812. In 1867 it commissioned Theophil Han- sen to design this building. The terracotta statues are mainly by Franz Melnizki.
Trams 1, 2, D, J (Ring)	The "Golden Hall" was altered in 1911 when it was given its golden coffered ceiling. It can seat an audience of nearly 2,000; it is 165 ft (51·2 m) long, 63 ft (18·9 m) wide and 55 ft (17·6 m) high. There is room for 400 musicians, and it is

Museum of the 20th Century: sculpture garden

reckoned to be one of the world's best concert halls for acoustics.

The Musikfreunde possess a comprehensive collection of works on the history of music, an archive of musical scores and an excellent library (see Practical Information – Libraries).

Naschmarkt (market)   C4

The Naschmarkt is by far the largest and most interesting of the twenty or so markets of Vienna. The amount of produce on sale is enormous. At the S end of the Naschmarkt begins the Flea Market. Curios, valuables, new articles and rubbish are offered for sale.

In nearby Wienzeile there are two Jugendstil buildings by Otto Wagner. In 1973 the entire façade of No. 38 Linke Wienzeile was regilded. No. 40 has a façade entirely clad with majolica tiles decorated with plant motifs; on the frieze are sculpted lions' heads.

Location
Wienzeile, VI

Underground station
Kettenbrückengasse (U4)

Opening times
Naschmarkt
Mon.–Fri. 6 a.m.–6.30 p.m.,
Sat. 6 a.m.–1 p.m.
Flea Market
Sat. 8 a.m.–6 p.m.

Österreichische Nationalbibliothek (library)   C4

The Austrian National Library is housed in the commanding Baroque building on Josefsplatz (see entry). It was built during the reign of Charles VI to plans by Fischer von Erlach, father and son, between 1723 and 1726.

The Baroque building was originally free-standing, but it was linked by the Redouten range to the Hofburg (see entry) in 1750–60. The huge central section is crowned by a group of

Location
1 Josefsplatz, I

Underground station
Volkstheater (U2)

Buses
3A, 48A

Österreichische Nationalbibliothek

Austrian National Library: Hall of Honour

Trams
1, 2, D, J (Ring), 46, 49

All Departments closed
1–21 Sept.

statues representing the goddess Minerva with her chariot, drawn by four steeds. It is by L. Mattielli and dates from 1725. The National Library was formerly the Court Library, and it came into the possession of the State in 1920. Its collection goes back to the 14th c. The first Imperial Library Director was appointed in the 16th c. and in the 17th c. the collections were kept in the upper storey of the Reitschule (see Hofburg). By the 18th c. there was simply not enough space available in the Burg, and it was plain a new building must be provided.

The total collection of the National Library amounts at present to some 2½ million books. There are also the following special collections: printed materials, manuscripts, maps, papyri, portraits and picture archive, music and theatrical collections and an Esperanto Museum. The "New" building became far too small long ago, and it was necessary to expand into the S wing on Josefsplatz and into the Neue Burg (see Hofburg). Entry is from Josefsplatz: hall of honour, manuscript collection, map collection, reading room and administrative offices.

Hall of Honour

Opening times
Temporary exhibitions
From May to Oct. Mon.–Sat.
10 a.m.–4 p.m. otherwise
Mon.–Sat.
11 a.m.–noon.

The Hall of Honour is one of the most splendid of Baroque rooms. It was designed by Fischer von Erlach, father and son. It is 250 ft (77·7 m) long, 46 ft (14·3 m) wide and 65 ft (19·6 m) high. The paintings in the dome are by Daniel Gran, the life-size statues by Paul and Peter von Strudel. In the middle stand the 15,000 gold-stamped books from what was once Prince Eugene of Savoy's Library.

Manuscript Collection

The holdings amount to 43,000 manuscripts from the 6th c., 8,000 incunabula and some 240,000 holographs.

Among the most impressive manuscripts held are a Byzantine herbalist's treatise written about 512, the 6th c. "Vienna Genesis", and an 1160 St Peter's Antiphonary, the 16th c. Ambras Book of Heroes and a 15th c. Gutenberg Bible from Mainz. In the four showcases original material is on display throughout the year.

Opening times
Mon., Wed., Fri. 9 a.m.–
1 p.m., Tues., Thur.
1–6.45 p.m.

The Map Collection comprises at present about 240,000 sheets of maps and 280,000 geographical views. The most valuable objects are the copy of a 4th c. Roman map for travellers, the 46-volume Atlas by Blaeu, dating from the second half of the 17th c., and a map of the world made for Charles V in 1551.

Map Collection

Opening times
Reading Room Mon., Tues.,
Wed., Fri.
9 a.m.–3.45 p.m.

Of the 150 items in the Collection of Globes (open Mon.–Wed., Fri. 11 a.m.–noon; Thur. 2–3 p.m.) the two Mercator globes (*c.* 1550) and the 17th c. Coronelli globes are the most impressive.

The collections of the Nationalbibliothek in the Neue Burg amount to about 2½ million books which have been catalogued. There is also an open-shelf collection of about 56,000 volumes for ready reference.
The main reading-room is connected to the old buildings by teleprinter, pneumatic communication tube and telephone.

Printed Materials

Opening times
Reading Room Mon.–Fri.
9 a.m.–7.45 p.m.,
Sat. 9 a.m.–1 p.m.
(earlier closing in summer)

The Picture Archive and Collection of Portraits comprises about 1½ million articles and 120,000 volumes of specialist literature. It is the largest and most important institution for the scholarly collection of pictorial documentation in Austria and comprises negatives, graphics and photographs of every variety and produced by every kind of technique.

Picture Archive

Opening times
Mon. 9 a.m.–6.45 p.m.
Tues.–Fri. 9 a.m.–
3.45 p.m.; earlier closing in
summer

The Theatrical Collection is kept in the Michaelertrakt of the Hofburg (see entry), where the entrance is to be found. The Hugo Thimig Collection forms the basis of the collection. Among the most important recent acquisitions are the Hubert Marischka and the Albin Skoda Collections. There are more than 1 million printed items, holographs, theatrical manuscripts, drawings and prints.

Theatrical Collection

Opening times
Mon.–Wed., Fri.
9 a.m.–3.45 p.m.
Closed on each 1st and 3rd
Tues. in the month

The Papyrus Collection is housed in the buildings of the Albertina (see entry) at 1 Augustinerstrasse.
Most of the papyri (100,000) come from Egypt, and they date from the 15th c. B.C. to the 14th c. A.D., forming one of the world's finest papyrological collections. The most precious possessions are three Egyptian Books of the Dead (the oldest dating from the 15th c. B.C.), one of the oldest Greek papyri (4th c. B.C.) and the oldest example of Islamic writing.

Papyrus Collection

Opening times
Tues.–Fri. 9 a.m.–1 p.m.
Mon. 9 a.m.–6.45 p.m.;
earlier closing in summer

The Music Collection, too, is housed in the Albertina (see entry) at 1 Augustinerstrasse.
Among the holdings are precious manuscripts, including Mozart's Requiem, Beethoven's Violin Concerto, Franz Schubert holograms, some of the papers left by Anton Bruckner on his death and the score of Richard Strauss's "Rosenkavalier".

Music Collection

Opening times
Mon., Wed., Fri. 9 a.m.–
1 p.m., Tues. noon–
3.45 p.m., Thurs. noon–
6.45 p.m.; earlier closing
in summer

Naturhistorisches Museum   C4

The Natural History Museum is the counterpart of the Kunsthistorisches Museum (see entry) which is directly

Location
Maria-Theresien-Platz, I

Children's Room in the Natural History Museum

Donner Fountain on the Neuer Markt

opposite. It was designed, like the latter, by G. Semper and K. Hasenauer and was finished in 1881.

The objects are displayed in 39 galleries and a domed hall. The collection was founded by Francis I, the consort of Maria Theresa, who was interested in natural history. It was opened to the public by the Empress in 1765. The collections have been on show in the present buildings since 1889, and have been constantly extended and modernised.

Mineralogical and Petrographical Department (Raised Ground Floor).
Rooms I–V: The nucleus is the collection of minerals, with many examples from Austria.
In Room IV (precious stones) are the finest pieces of the collection (posy of precious stones of Maria Theresa, graduated emeralds, giant topaz weighing 258 lb (117 kg).
Room V is at present under rearrangement.

Geological and Palaeontological Collections (Raised Ground Floor)
Rooms VI–X: Fossils and petrified skeletons.
Rooms VI–IX are at present closed for reorganisation.
Room X houses dinosaurs.

Prehistory Collection (Raised Ground Floor)
Rooms XI–XV: Finds from excavations in Austria are displayed, from the Stone Ages to the La Tène culture. In Room XI the world-famous chalk figure of the "Willendorf Venus" can be seen. It dates from about 22000 B.C. (casting). In Rooms XIII and XIV can be seen the Hallstatt finds.

Anthropological Department (Raised Ground Floor)
Rooms XVI and XVII: Osteological collection with a great number of human skulls and skeletons from the Neo-Palaeolithic period to the present day. Somatological collection.

Children's Room (Raised Ground Floor)
Room XVIII: Microscopes, video recorders, dioramas, library.

Dome Hall (First Floor)
Skeleton of a giant lizard (extinct), giant crab, manatee.

Botanical Exhibition Gallery (First Floor)
Room XXI: Models of fungi and forms of spores.

Zoological Department (First Floor)
Rooms XXII–XXXIX: The collection illustrates in impressive fashion the long evolution from the single-cell organism to the anthropoid apes. – Bird collection. – Mammals.
Of interest are many extinct types (Moa, Dodo).

Underground station
Volkstheater (U2)

Bus
2A

Trams
1, 2, D, J

Opening times
Daily except Tues.
9 a.m.–6 p.m.

Neue Burg

See Hofburg

Neue Galerie in the Stallburg (art gallery)   B/C 4

The New Gallery is housed above the "Silver Stallions" on the second floor of the Stallburg (see Hofburg).
It was founded by Archduke Leopold William in 1656, enlarged by Emperor Charles VI in 1720, and in 1967 was

Location
2 Reitschulgasse, I

Underground station
Stephansplatz (U1)

Buses
2A, 3A

Opening times
Mon., Wed., Thur., Sat.,
Sun. 10 a.m.–4 p.m.

adapted to serve as the New Gallery of the Kunsthistorisches Museum (see entry).

The six rooms are devoted to 19th and 20th c. art by painters who are not of Austrian extraction. There are paintings representing all recent periods – Romanticism, Realism, Idealism, Impressionism and Expressionism.

Among the artists represented are Böcklin, Corot, Degas, Feuerbach, Van Gogh, Manet, Monet, Munch, Liebermann, Renoir, Spitzweg and Toulouse-Lautrec.

In the Stallburg's arcaded courtyard are statues, including Meunier's "The Carrier" and Renoir's "Vénus Victorieuse".

*Neuer Markt   C4

Location
Kärntnerstrasse, I

Underground station
Stephansplatz (U1)

This square is noisy and all bustle. In the afternoon rival gangs of youths often gather round the Fountain. From 1220 onwards the "New Viennese Market-place" served as a corn and vegetable market, as the site for tourneys, as an arena for mountebanks such as Hans Wurst, and as a place where the Court and nobility could come and skate. Today it is an important car park and feeder for the Kärntnerstrasse pedestrian zone (see entry).

The oldest houses remaining here are from the 18th c. No. 14 is a Baroque bourgeois house, No. 25 was the residence of the piano virtuoso Mayseder and No. 27 is the so-called "Herrnhuter House".

Joseph Haydn lived from 1795 to 1796 in the house where No. 2 now stands. It was there he wrote the Austrian Imperial Anthem.

*Donner Fountain (officially Providentia Fountain)

Underground station
Stephansplatz (U1)

In 1737–39 Georg Raphael Donner was commissioned by the city to create the Providentia Fountain which is better known in Vienna as the Donner Fountain.

The City Fathers desired that the central figure of Providentia should express the concept of the caring and wise government of the city. Donner decorated its plinth with four graceful naked putti. The figures on the edge of the fountain's basin symbolise the Rivers Enns, Traun, Ybbs and March.

Empress Maria Theresa objected to so much nakedness and had the figures removed. They were replaced only under Francis II in 1801. In 1873 the lead figures were so decayed they had to be replaced with bronze replicas. Donner's originals are on show in the Baroque Museum at the Belvedere (see entry).

Niederösterreichisches Landesmuseum   B4

Location
9 Herrengasse, I

Underground station
Schottentor (U2)

A former palace and its former Rococo apartments are the setting for the Niederösterreichisches Landesmuseum (the Museum of the State of Lower Austria).

On the second floor is the Department of Cultural History, the most important department of the Museum. Here a series of pictures lead the visitor into the past, from Kokoschka via

Gauermann, Waldmüller, Kupelweiser, Schnorr von Carolsfeld, Röttmayr, Maulbertsch, Altomonte and Kremser-Schmidt right back to 15th and 16th c. altar-pieces and woodcarvings (e.g. the Flachau Madonna of 1500).

Opening times
Tues.–Fri. 9 a.m.–5 p.m.,
Sat. 9 a.m.–2 p.m.,
Sun. and public holidays
9 a.m.–noon

Palais Liechtenstein   B4

Counts Kaunitz and Khevenhüller were previous owners of the building before it came into the possession in 1694 (completely rebuilt) of the Princes of Liechtenstein. The monumental gate with sculpture by Giuliani and a Triton fountain (1695) in the courtyard are worth seeing. The building is architecturally curious in having walls and floors that can be lowered and strange lift machinery. The summer seat of the Princes was the Gartenpalais Liechtenstein (see entry).

Location
4 Minoritenplatz/
9 Bankgasse. I

Underground station
Schottentor (U2)

Bus
1A

Palais Pálffy   C4

With its interior modernised and adapted the former Palais Pálffy is now available, under the title of "Osterreich-Haus", for cultural events. The Emperors' Austrian Chancellery stood on the site of the Palais Pálffy about 1500. It was converted into a nobleman's palace towards the end of the 16th c. The buildings were damaged by fire in the 18th c. and by bombs in the 20th c.; in each instance they were partially restored. Mozart produced his "Marriage of Figaro" for the first time before an audience of his friends in the room now called the "Figarosaal".

Location
6 Josefsplatz, I

Underground station
Stephansplatz (U1)

Bus
2A

Palais Schwarzenberg, once a summer residence, now an hotel

Parliament

Parliament, with its impressive architecture in Greek forms with . . .

. . . Pallas Athene Fountain and the bronze "Horse-tamer"

Palais Schwarzenberg   C5

Palais Schwarzenberg, now a hotel, was one of the first summer residences to be constructed outside the city walls. Its interior is particularly fine.

Prince Schwarzenberg settled in his own way the rivalry between the two great Baroque architects, J. B. Fischer von Erlach and L. von Hildebrandt. The first sketches were the work of Hildebrandt. In 1720 alterations were undertaken by Fischer von Erlach, and the magnificent Baroque gardens were laid out by Fischer von Erlach's son.

After the end of the war in 1945 the damaged palace was meticulously restored. It proved, however, impossible to save the frescoes by Daniel Gran.

Location
2 Rennweg, III

Underground station
Karlsplatz (U1, U2, U4)

Bus
4A

Trams
D, 71

*Parliament   B4

Since 1918 the meetings of the National and Federal Parliament have been held in these impressive buildings. They had been built between 1873 and 1883 by Theophil Hansen for the Imperial and Provincial delegacies which had been called into being by the 1861 Declaration and survived until 1918. It was in allusion to Greece, the land where democracy was invented, that he chose for the building Greek forms with Corinthian columns and rich decoration on the metopes and pediments. The debating chamber, which has been altered, has an area of 17,250 sq. yd (16,000 m²) and the building measures 450 ft (137 m) by 475 ft (145 m).

The building was severely damaged in 1945. Restoration was not completed until 1956.

The Pallas Athene Fountain was placed in front of the main portal in 1902. The 13 ft (4 m) high figure of Pallas Athene with gilded helmet and armed with a lance is the work of the sculptor Kundmann. The recumbent figures symbolise the Rivers Danube, Inn, Elbe and Moldau. Josef Lax's bronze "The Horse-tamer" keeps watch over the flight of steps. On the left are the seated marble figures of Herodotus, Polybius and Xenophon, while to the right are those of Sallust, Caesar, Tacitus and Livy. The granting by Franz Joseph I of a Constitution to the 17 peoples of Austria is represented in the triangular pediment above the portico. The attic is decorated with 76 marble statues and 66 reliefs.

On 11 November 1918 the Deputies debated the choice of a new name for their land which had undergone such great changes. Among the proposals were "Markomannien", "Teutheim", "Friedland" and "Hochdeutschland". It is recorded that finally they settled on "Deutsch-Osterreich" (German-Austria). On 12 November the House of Deputies of the Austrian part of the Empire went into dissolution.

Location
3 Dr-Karl-Renner-Ring, I

Underground station
Lerchenfelderstrasse (U2)

Bus
48A

Trams
1, 2, D, J

Tours
Mon.–Fri. at 11 a.m.
July and Aug. 11 a.m.,
2 p.m. and 3 p.m.

Pallas Athene Fountain

Pasqualatihaus (Beethoven and Stifter Museum)   B4

Beethoven came to live here several times in the period between 1804 and 1815. It was here he composed the Fourth, Fifth and Seventh Symphonies, the Fourth Piano Concerto, the Leonora overtures and the opera "Fidelio".

Location
8 Mölkertbastei, I

Underground station
Schottentor (U2)

Paulanerkirche

Trams
1, 2, D, T

Opening times
Tues.–Fri. 10 a.m.–4 p.m.,
Sat. 2–6 p.m., Sun. and
public holidays 9 a.m.–
1 p.m.

Although the memorial rooms are not actually those which Beethoven occupied they are in their close proximity. On show are furniture and articles used by Beethoven as well as drawings, lithographs and music.
The Adalbert Stifter Museum has also been housed here since 1979. On show are manuscripts and first editions by the author as well as more than half the surviving pictures which he painted.

Paulanerkirche (Church of the Holy Angels)   C4

Location
6 Wiedner Hauptstrasse/
Paulanergasse, IV

Underground station
Karlsplatz (U1, U2, U4)

Trams
62, 65

The Paulanites were summoned to Vienna by Emperor Ferdinand II who gave them their vineyards on the "Wieden" (meadows). The church is dedicated to the Guardian Angels and was built between 1627 and 1651. It was rebuilt after destruction in 1668 and restored in 1817. Inside the church there are some important oil-paintings: a Crucifixion (second altar) by J. M. Rottmayr, a portrait of the Founder of the Order (third altar) by J. J. Bendl and an Immaculate Virgin possibly by L. Kupelwieser (first altar). The fresco on the ceiling is ascribed to Carlo Carlone.

Pestsäule (Plague Pillar)

See Graben

*Peterskirche   B4

Location
Petersplatz, I

Underground station
Stephansplatz (U1)

Buses
1A, 2A, 3A

Perambulation

The Collegial and Parish Church of St Peter is modelled on St Peter's, Rome.
According to tradition, the site was originally occupied by a Late Romanesque church founded by Charlemagne in 792. The first documentary evidence for a church here, however, dates from 1137. That building was restored several times, but it was replaced early in the 18th c. by the present building which was probably completed by Lucas von Hildebrandt.

The church is built on an oval plan and is roofed with a massive dome (frescoes by J. M. Rottmayr). There are many artistic treasures to be seen.

Left-hand side
Going round the church in a clockwise direction visitors pass through Andreas Altomonte's magnificent portal and come to the Barbara Chapel. Franz Karl Remp's "Decollation of St Barbara" is especially noteworthy. The side-altar on the left has a reredos by Anton Schoonjans depicting the Martyrdom of St Sebastian. There is a painting by Altomonte in the Chapel of the Holy Family.

Choir
The choir lies just beyond the excessively richly carved Baroque pulpit. Beneath Antonio Bibiena's false dome stands the High Altar, a work by Santino Bussi. It has a reredos by Altomonte and a picture of the Immaculate Conception by Kupelwieser. The entrance to the crypt is also in the choir. At

Peterskirche, modelled on St Peter's, Rome ▶

the boat-houses, tennis at the WAC courts, and there is bowling, too.

The Prater was first mentioned in a document in 1403. Maximilian II had the area fenced off in the 16th c., so that he could use it as a personal hunting preserve, and it was not opened to the general public until 1766. The first Punch and Judy shows date from 1767, and the first firework displays from 1771. In 1791 Blanchard's first hot-air balloon rose into the sky; in 1840 Calafati first began to run a big roundabout here.

Planetarium and Prater Museum

Demonstrations
Sat., Sun., public holidays
3 and 5 p.m.; for children
Sun. 9.30 a.m.; closed Aug

The Planetarium, a gift from the Zeiss family in 1927, is situated in the main avenue. It also houses Professor Pemmer's private collection concerning the history of the Prater (open Sat., Sun. 2–6.30 p.m.; closed in Aug.). In the vicinity is the Lipburg spherical house ("Kugelmugel").

Ferris Wheel

Ferris Wheel: this giant pleasure wheel is an important landmark. It was built in 1896 by the English engineer Walter B. Basset for the World Exhibition of 1896. It was destroyed during the last war, but was rebuilt and has been once again in operation since 1946.

The giant wheel is 200 ft (61 m) in diameter. The weight supported by the 8 pylons is 160 tons (165·2 t); the total weight of the entire construction is 425 tons (430·05 t). It revolves at a speed of about 3 ft (0·75 m) per second.

Wurstelprater: the earliest shows were put on here in 1766. Basileo Calafati's famous roundabout dates from 1840; it has been guarded by "the great Chinaman" since 1854. Only 18 of the attractions on the Prater survived the war, but now there are all sorts of roundabouts, dodgem cars, race-tracks, swings and helter-skelters, shooting-galleries and electronic games. There are also stilt-walkers, mountebanks, sword-swallowers, ventriloquists and ponies.

Ziehrer Monument: this larger than life statue of the composer in Deutschmeister uniform was made by Robert Ullmann in 1960.

The Constantin Hill: this mound is man-made. It was formed from the spoil dug out when the buildings for the 1873 Vienna Exhibition were erected and was named after Franz Joseph's Chief Chamberlain, Constantin of Hohenlohe-Schillingsfürst. The miniature railway operates in the area near the main avenue. It stops at the Stadium swimming-pool.

Pleasure-House: the café-restaurant at the end of the main avenue was a pleasure-house out in the country 400 years ago. Emperor Joseph II had it rebuilt by Isidor Carnevale in 1783. Its greatest moment came in 1814 when during the Congress of Vienna the allied monarchs with their generals celebrated the anniversary of the Battle of Leipzig when Napoleon was crushingly defeated. 18,000 soldiers were given a meal on tables erected all round the building.

Maria-Grün Chapel: this little pilgrimage church stands on the site occupied once by a forest shrine. The "Maria-Grün" (Madonna in Green) picture above the High Altar is an object of veneration. A "Hubert" Mass for hunters is celebrated here in November.

E of the Wurstelprater (People's Park) lies the exhibition ground of the City of Vienna with pavilions and the 492 ft (150 m) high Mannesmann Tower.

Prater: the Wurstelprater with the Ferris Wheel

of Sorrows, is in fact the foundation-chapel, dating from 1699. The historic votive picture of "Our Lady of Malta" dates from the first half of the 15th c.

Of the other chapels, the most important by far is the Holy Cross Chapel, to the left of the choir. The picture of Christ on the Cross is by Maulbertsch and dates from 1772.

The votive picture of the Virgin over the High Altar is only a copy. The original is in Rome.

Porzellanmanufaktur

See Augarten

*Prater   B6

The Prater, the large natural park between the Danube and the right-hand Danube Canal, is almost a world apart. It is lively and gay by day, and something of a twilight zone by night. The park covers an area of some 3,200 acres (1,287 ha), stretching SE almost 6½ miles (10 km) from the Prater cross-roads through the former "Augebiet" to the end of the Prater. In the first section lies the so-called "Wurstel" or "Volk" Prater with eating-houses, dance-halls, shooting-galleries, round-abouts and other attractions.

Nearly every kind of sport is catered for in the Prater. There is riding in the Freudenau, trotting in the Krieau, swimming in the stadium pool, football in the large stadium, rowing from

Location
Vienna, II

Underground/S-Bahn station
Praterstern (U1, S7)

Bus
80A

Trams
1, N, O

the boat-houses, tennis at the WAC courts, and there is bowling, too.

The Prater was first mentioned in a document in 1403. Maximilian II had the area fenced off in the 16th c., so that he could use it as a personal hunting preserve, and it was not opened to the general public until 1766. The first Punch and Judy shows date from 1767, and the first firework displays from 1771. In 1791 Blanchard's first hot-air balloon rose into the sky; in 1840 Calafati first began to run a big roundabout here.

Planetarium and Prater Museum

The Planetarium, a gift from the Zeiss family in 1927, is situated in the main avenue. It also houses Professor Pemmer's private collection concerning the history of the Prater (open Sat., Sun. 2–6.30 p.m.; closed in Aug.). In the vicinity is the Lipburg spherical house ("Kugelmugel").

Demonstrations
Sat., Sun., public holidays
3 and 5 p.m.; for children
Sun. 9.30 a.m.; closed Aug

Ferris Wheel

Ferris Wheel: this giant pleasure wheel is an important landmark. It was built in 1896 by the English engineer Walter B. Basset for the World Exhibition of 1896. It was destroyed during the last war, but was rebuilt and has been once again in operation since 1946.

The giant wheel is 200 ft (61 m) in diameter. The weight supported by the 8 pylons is 160 tons (165·2 t); the total weight of the entire construction is 425 tons (430·05 t). It revolves at a speed of about 3 ft (0·75 m) per second.

Wurstelprater: the earliest shows were put on here in 1766. Basileo Calafati's famous roundabout dates from 1840; it has been guarded by "the great Chinaman" since 1854. Only 18 of the attractions on the Prater survived the war, but now there are all sorts of roundabouts, dodgem cars, race-tracks, swings and helter-skelters, shooting-galleries and electronic games. There are also stilt-walkers, mountebanks, sword-swallowers, ventriloquists and ponies.

Ziehrer Monument: this larger than life statue of the composer in Deutschmeister uniform was made by Robert Ullmann in 1960.

The Constantin Hill: this mound is man-made. It was formed from the spoil dug out when the buildings for the 1873 Vienna Exhibition were erected and was named after Franz Joseph's Chief Chamberlain, Constantin of Hohenlohe-Schillingsfürst. The miniature railway operates in the area near the main avenue. It stops at the Stadium swimming-pool.

Pleasure-House: the café-restaurant at the end of the main avenue was a pleasure-house out in the country 400 years ago. Emperor Joseph II had it rebuilt by Isidor Carnevale in 1783. Its greatest moment came in 1814 when during the Congress of Vienna the allied monarchs with their generals celebrated the anniversary of the Battle of Leipzig when Napoleon was crushingly defeated. 18,000 soldiers were given a meal on tables erected all round the building.

Maria-Grün Chapel: this little pilgrimage church stands on the site occupied once by a forest shrine. The "Maria-Grün" (Madonna in Green) picture above the High Altar is an object of veneration. A "Hubert" Mass for hunters is celebrated here in November.

E of the Wurstelprater (People's Park) lies the exhibition ground of the City of Vienna with pavilions and the 492 ft (150 m) high Mannesmann Tower.

Maria Treu, the church of the Patres Scholarum Piarum

Christmas every year the crib set up here attracts many to the church.

Right-hand side

The Johann von Nepomuk Altar is on the right-hand side, with a Madonna in Glory probably by Matthias Steinl. The Michael Chapel has a "Fall of the Angels" by Altomonte. In a glass coffin may be seen Benedict, the Saint of the catacombs. The reredos on the side-altar on the right is by Rottmayr. The Antony Chapel has works by Altomonte ("St Antony with the Virgin") and by Kupelwieser ("The Heart of the Madonna"). The Empress Elisabeth sometimes used to have herself locked in this church, so that she could pray in complete privacy.

Piaristenkirche Maria Treu   B3

Location
Jodok-Fink-Platz, VIII

Underground station
Rathaus (U2)

Bus
13A

The Piaristenkirche is a parish church and a church of the Order of the Piarists (Patres Scholarum Piarum).

When the Piarists came to Vienna in the 17th c., they first built themselves a little chapel. The present church is based on plans drawn up by Lucas von Hildebrandt in 1716. A number of changes were introduced, and the building was completed in the middle of the 18th c., probably by Kilian Ignaz Dientzenhofer. Further construction took place between 1751 and 1953. The church was consecrated in 1771, but the towers were not completed until 1858–60. The church is decorated with particularly beautiful frescoes by F. A. Maulbertsch. Dating 1752–53 they are the first major frescoes by this Master. The church has eight chapels. The oldest, the Chapel

Praterstrasse   B5

Praterstrasse no longer has the importance it used to have in the great days of the Prater. It lives on its memories now.
Josef Lanner used to give concerts with his band in No. 26 Zum Grünen Jäger (Green Huntsman's House). The office building at No. 3 occupies the site where once the famous Carl Theatre stood which made the figure of Kasperl immortal and had Johann Nestroy as its Manager.
No. 54, the house in which Johann Strauss wrote "The Blue Danube" in 1867, has become a museum. It is open daily, except Monday, 10 a.m.–12.15 p.m. and 1–4.30 p.m. and on Sundays from 9 a.m. to 1 p.m. Documents relating to the Waltz King's life are on show as well as personal mementoes.

Location
Vienna, II

Underground station
Praterstern,
Nestroyplatz (U1)

S-Bahn station
Praterstern (S7)

Trams
1, 5, O

Altes Rathaus (Old Town Hall; Museum of Austrian Resistance)   B4

The Old Town Hall, opposite the Böhmische Hofkanzlei (see entry), houses the archive of the Austrian Resistance Movement. In the Resistance Museum are exhibits illustrating the active revolt against Austrian Fascism (1934–38) and of the resistance and persecution under the National Socialists in Austria (1938–45). A memorial can be found at No. 6 Salztorgasse five minutes away.
Although the decision to set up the Museum of Austrian Resistance in the Old Town Hall had little to do with the history of the building, there are nevertheless parallels. The Old Town Hall was originally the house of a rebel, Otto Heimo. After Emperor Albrecht I was murdered in 1309 a number of influential Viennese citizens including Heimo resolved to resist the new Habsburg rulers. However the plot was discovered, the conspirators punished and their property confiscated. Duke Frederick the Fair gave Heimo's house to the municipality in 1316.
The building remained the town hall until 1885 and during this time was on several occasions altered, enlarged and partly rebuilt. It received its Baroque façade about 1700 and the portals with the sculptures of "Fides publica" and "Pietas" by Johann Martin Fischer are also 18th c. The Andromeda Fountain with a lead relief of Perseus and Andromeda in the courtyard is one of Raphael Donner's last works, dating from 1740 to 1741.

Location
6–8 Wipplingerstrasse, I
Staircase 3

Underground stations
Stephansplatz,
Schwedenplatz (U1, U4)

Bus
1A, 2A, 3A

Opening times
Mon., Wed., Thur. 8 a.m.–5 p.m. (Memorial room Mon., Wed., Thur. 9 a.m.–5 p.m.)

*Rathaus (Town Hall)   B4

The Town Hall is scarcely a hundred years old. The impressive Neo-Gothic building is the seat of the Vienna City and Provincial Assembly and is the administrative centre of the city. The huge building, occupying nearly 17,000 sq. yd (14,000 m^2) of the former Parade Ground, was erected during Franz Joseph I's reign by Friedrich von Schmidt, who was also responsible for the decoration and furnishings.
The symbol of the Town Hall is the "Rathausmann" on the top of the 320 ft (98 m) high tower. This banner-carrying figure is 10 ft (3·40 m) tall and weighs 4,000 lb (1,800 kg); it was the gift of the master locksmith, Wilhelm Ludwig. The arcaded court-

Location
Rathausplatz, I

Underground station
Rathaus (U1)

Trams
1, 2, D

Tours
Mon.–Fri. at 1 p.m. (except when Assembly is in session)

Old Town Hall

Town Hall

yard in the centre of the building, the largest of the seven courtyards, was originally intended for assemblies; the popular summer concerts (see Practical Information – Festivals) take place here.

The tour of the Rathaus interior begins in the Schmidthalle, the former "Community Vestibule" into which carriages could once drive. Today it houses the Civic Information Office. Proceeding up the two Grand Staircases we reach the official rooms: the Assembly Hall (233 ft (71 m) long; 66 ft (20 m) wide; 56 ft (17 m) high), two Heraldic Rooms, the City Senate Chamber and the "Roter Salon", the Mayor's reception room. The council chamber of the Vienna City and Provincial Assembly extends over two floors. Since 1922 Vienna, as the country's capital, has also had the status of a province and so the City Council is also a provincial body. Notable features are the coffered ceiling decorated with gold-leaf and the Art Nouveau candelabra, weighing 3·2 tonnes and lit by 260 lamps, also the work of Friedrich Schmidt.

*Ringstrasse   B/C4/5

Location
Vienna I

Underground stations
Karlsplatz (U1, U2, U4),
Schottentor,
Schottenring (U2),
Schwedenplatz (U1, U4)

The handsome Ringstrasse is a thoroughfare that runs right round the city centre of Vienna. It consists, going in a clockwise direction, of the following sections: Stubenring, Parkring, Schubertring, Kärntnerring, Opernring, Burgring, Dr-Karl-Renner-Ring, Dr-Karl-Lueger-Ring and Schottenring. The circle of the Ringstrasse is completed by the Franz-Josef-Quai along the Danube Canal.

The razing of the fortifications during Emperor Franz Joseph's reign made possible the laying-out of a tree-lined ceremonial way between 1858 and 1865. Many huge buildings were erected here in the second half of the 19th c., in the grandiose style that came to be called "Ringstrasse style".

The Ringstrasse is 2½ miles (4 km) long and 185 ft (57 m) wide. The ceremonial inauguration took place on 1 May 1865. Its finest hour was in 1879 when the painter Hans Makart mounted a parade with 10,000 participants in honour of the Imperial couple on the occasion of their Silver Wedding.

Trams
1, 2, D, J

Rohrau

Rohrau is Joseph Haydn's birthplace (house No. 60; mementoes; open Apr.–Oct. Tues.–Thur. 10 a.m.–5 p.m.). Here, too, is Count von Harrach's castle. The last great Viennese private nobleman's picture collection was brought here from the family mansion at Freyung (see entry) in 1970.

The gallery possesses some 200 paintings, including works by Rubens, Brueghel, Van Dyck, Jordaens, and Ruysdael.

Location
not far from Carnuntum

S-Bahn
to Petronell (S7), then by bus (1793, 1795)

Distance
30 miles (47 km) E
near Carnuntum

Roman Ruins

See Hoher Markt

Ruprechtskirche (officially St Ruprecht's Church)   B5

St Ruprecht's Church is the oldest church in Vienna. It stands on the N edge of the former Roman military settlement. It is supposed to have been built by Bishop Virgil of Salzburg, on the site of the subterranean Oratory of Cunard and Gisalrich, two apostles of the Faith. The church is first mentioned in documents in 1161.

There is evidence that the nave and the lower storeys of the tower were built in the 11th c. The tower was twice made higher, in the 12th and 13th c. A choir was added in the 13th c., as was a S side aisle in the 15th c. The church was thoroughly restored between 1934 and 1936 and between 1946 and 1948.

Its treasures include the oldest stained glass in Vienna (13th c.) in the central window in the choir, and the Altar of Our Lady of Loretto, the so-called "Black Madonna", whose aid was invoked when there was danger from the Turks or the plague.

Location
Ruprechtsplatz, I

Underground station
Schwedenplatz (U1, U4)

Trams
1, 2

Salvatorkapelle   B4

The Salvator Chapel was founded in 1301 by Otto Heimo, a famous conspirator. It formed part of the house which the authorities took over after the failure of the rebellion against Frederick the Fair and converted into the Altes Rathaus (see entry). Entry is through the Altes Rathaus.

On 10 October 1871 the church passed into the possession of the Old Catholics. After sustaining severe damage in the Second World War the building was fully restored in 1972–73.

Location
5 Salvatorgasse, I

Underground stations
Stephansplatz (U1),
Schwedenplatz (U1, U4)

Bus
3A

The magnificent Renaissance portal, dating from 1520 and one of the few Renaissance works in Vienna, is especially noteworthy. The statues of knights are copies; the originals are in the Vienna City Historisches Museum (see entry).

Sammlung alter Musikinstrumente (museum)   C4

Location
Neue Burg, Heldenplatz, I

Underground stations
Karlsplatz (U1, U2, U4),
Mariahilferstrasse (U2)

Bus
2A

Trams
1, 2, D, J

Opening times
Mon., Wed.–Fri. 10 a.m.–
4 p.m.,
Sat. and Sun. 9 a.m.–
4 p.m.

The Collection of Old Musical Instruments is housed in the middle section of the Neue Burg (see Hofburg). To form the collection the resources of the Archduke Ferdinand of Tyrol and of the Union of Viennese Music Lovers were pooled.

The greatest feature of the collection is the exceptionally fine stock of keyboard instruments from clavichords and cembaloes of the 16th c. down to modern pianos. The exhibits are arranged in such a way as to give a sense of general development, in the Marble Hall, the Keyboard Rooms, and in the rooms for stringed instruments, plucked instruments, for woodwind and brass. There is also a gallery.

The most valuable instruments are in the Marble Hall, together with those with the most interesting personal associations. There is a cembalo and a table piano which belonged to Joseph Haydn, a grand piano which Erard Frères of Paris presented to Beethoven, and a Viennese table piano at which Schubert composed his music.

Among the brass wind instruments are a richly ornamented trumpet made for Duke Ferdinand of Tyrol in 1581 and silver trumpets from Maria Theresa's Court Band. The woodwind collection includes the cornetti used by the City Waits. In the gallery there are wind instruments from the time of Mozart.

Sammlung Religiöser Volkskunst (museum)   C4

Location
8 Johannesgasse, I

Underground station
Stephansplatz (U1)

Opening times
Wed. 9 a.m.–4 p.m.,
Sun. 9 a.m.–1 p.m.

The Collection of Popular Religious Art is housed in the former Ursuline Convent. It is an offshoot of the Museum für Volkskunde (see entry). In its four rooms are exhibited examples of popular religious art from the 17th to the 19th c.

Room I: Adoration of Christ. Domestic altars, pictures on glass, wooden sculpture and wax figurines.

Room II: The old convent pharmacy with original furniture and equipment. A painting depicts Christ as the Apothecary.

Room III: The room is devoted to the cult of the Virgin. All the Marian pilgrimage centres are shown on maps.

Room IV: Material concerned with popular saints.

Schillerdenkmal (memorial)   C4

Location
Schillerplatz, I

Underground station
Karlsplatz (U1, U2, U4)

Bus
59A

The square in front of the Akademie der Bildendenkünste (see entry) used to be called the Kalkmarkt, but it was changed to Schillerplatz (Schiller Square) in 1876. At the same time the Schiller Memorial, the work of Johann Schilling from Dresden, was unveiled. The plinth is of red granite. The allegorical bronze figures represent the Four Ages of Man, and the reliefs portray Genius, Poetry, Truth and Learning.

Palace of Schönbrunn: the Gardens ▶

Trams
1, 2, D, J 62, 65

On the monument Schiller is shown standing, with Goethe sitting to one side. It is said that the admirers of Schiller were furious about this, but Franz Joseph I is supposed to have spoken in favour of portraying Goethe as sitting: "Let the old fellow be comfortable...."

Schloss Belvedere

See Belvedere-Schlösser

Schönbrunn (Palace and Park)   **D1**

Location
Schönbrunner
Schlossstrasse, XIII

Underground stations
Schönbrunn,
Hietzing (U4)

Bus
15A

Trams
10, 58

Opening times
State Apartments
Oct.–Apr. every day
9 a.m.–noon, 1–4 p.m.,
May–Sept. every day
9 a.m.–noon, 1–5 p.m.

Tours
May–Sept.
Tues.–Sun. 10 a.m.–5 p.m.,
Oct.–Apr.
Tues.–Sun. 10 a.m.–4 p.m.

After the glorious defeat of the Turks in 1683 Emperor Leopold I commissioned J. B. Fischer von Erlach to design an Imperial palace on the site of the little Palace of Katterburg which had been destroyed. For the Gloriette Hill Fischer planned a castle larger and more magnificent than the Palace of Versailles. The project was never carried out.

The more modest Baroque Palace of Schönbrunn with 1,441 rooms and apartments was built between 1696 and 1730. Nikolaus Pacassi was responsible for converting the palace into a residence for Maria Theresa. There were some alterations also between 1816 and 1819. Reconstruction of severe war damage was completed in 1952. Nowadays it is used for receptions given by the President of Austria.

After the time of Maria Theresa the most brilliant period for the palace was during the Congress of Vienna. It went into decline after the death of Franz Joseph I who was born in the palace and also died there. It was here, too, that Charles I renounced the Imperial Crown.

Victors have twice resided in the palace. Napoleon I occupied Maria Theresa's favourite rooms in 1805, and in 1945 the British High Commissioner set up his office in the room where the great Corsican had given his orders, much to the disgust of the French.

Palace Yard: The wrought-iron gate to the former parade ground (25,000 sq. yd (24,000 sq. m)) a magnificent example of Baroque layout, is flanked by two obelisks. Since 1809 these have been surmounted by French Imperial eagles. Austria's emperors were opposed to removing them after Napoleon's death. Franz Joseph I settled the matter: "They don't worry me," he said, "and folk seem to like them."

Palace (see p. 124)

Palace Theatre: The sole remaining Baroque theatre in Vienna was built in 1747 by Nikolaus Pacassi, Maria Theresa's favourite architect. Its Rococo decoration dates from 1767. Here in the "Habsburgs private theatre" concerts were given by Haydn and Mozart. Nowadays the Viennese Chamber Opera gives performances in July and August.

Mews: Historical coaches, sledges and sedan-chairs, with harness, etc. from the Imperial Palace are on show in the former Winter Riding School. The chief exhibits are the Viennese Court Imperial Coach, Napoleon's coach from Paris which was used for the coronation in Milan, the baby carriage, made in Paris for the Duke of Reichstadt (son of Napoleon I and Marie Louise), the Empress Caroline's Coronation Landau and the Emperor Franz Joseph's State Coach.

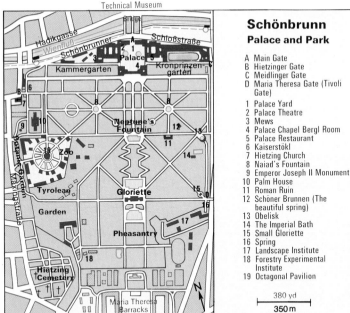

Schönbrunn
Palace and Park

A Main Gate
B Hietzinger Gate
C Meidlinger Gate
D Maria Theresa Gate (Tivoli Gate)

1 Palace Yard
2 Palace Theatre
3 Mews
4 Palace Chapel Bergl Room
5 Palace Restaurant
6 Kaiserstökl
7 Hietzing Church
8 Naiad's Fountain
9 Emperor Joseph II Monument
10 Palm House
11 Roman Ruin
12 Schöner Brunnen (The beautiful spring)
13 Obelisk
14 The Imperial Bath
15 Small Gloriette
16 Spring
17 Landscape Institute
18 Forestry Experimental Institute
19 Octagonal Pavilion

380 yd
350 m

The park round the palace covers an area of about 500 acres (2 km²). It is one of the most important Baroque gardens in the French style. It was laid out by Jean Trehet in 1705. In 1765 it was altered by Adrian von Steckhoven. By the paths on each side of the flower-beds stand 44 marble sculptures from the period about 1773.

Palace Park

Opening times
Daily from 6 a.m. until dusk

Neptune's Fountain: Neptune's Fountain forms the S boundary of the garden area. This fine ornamental fountain was designed by F. A. Zauner in 1780. The stone sculptures are based on themes from Greek mythology: Thetis implores Neptune's aid when her son Achilles sets out on a sea-voyage.

Schöner Brunnen (the Beautiful Fountain): The "Kaiserbrunnl" (Emperor's Spring), the old spring from which Emperor Joseph I had his drinking-water drawn, was turned into a grotto-like pavilion in 1799; the nymph Egeria pours out the water.

Roman ruins: The so-called Roman ruins are a Romantic folly with the appearance of a half-buried palace with Corinthian columns. It dates from 1778. J. F. Hetzendorf von Hohenberg who designed it wanted to symbolise the fall of Greece before the might of the Roman Empire.

Obelisk: This, too, was designed by Hetzendorf von Hohenberg and dates from 1777. It used to stand on top of a gilded turtle. The carved scenes depict the family history of the Habsburgs.

Schönbrunn

Small Gloriette: Once the Empress Maria Theresa used to take her breakfast here from time to time. Nowadays this little pavilion with its wall-paintings serves as a tea-room open to all.

Opening times
Daily May–Oct.
8 a.m.–6 p.m.

Gloriette: The park is crowned by the Classical Gloriette Arcade up on the top of the hill. J. F. Hetzendorf von Hohenberg built it in 1775 to close the prospect at the end of the park. The Gloriette commemorates the Battle of Kolin (1757), where Maria Theresa's troops defeated the Prussian army of Frederick the Great.

Tyrolean Garden: Archduke Johann introduced an Alpine note into the Schönbrunn Park by having the two Tyrolean timber houses erected here an an Alpine garden laid out.

Opening times
Daily
Summer 9 a.m.–6 p.m.
Winter 9 a.m.–4.30 p.m.

The origins of the Schönbrunn Zoo go back to Francis I's menagerie which he founded in 1752. It is the oldest zoo in Europe. At present some 750 species of animals live here, in special houses or running free in paddocks. In the middle of the zoo there is an octagonal pavilion which is now a café and restaurant; originally the Imperial family used to come there to watch their "pets".

Opening Times
May–Sept.
Mon.–Fri. 10 a.m.–6 p.m.,
Sat., Sun. 9 a.m.–7 p.m.
Oct.–Apr.
Mon.–Fri. 10 a.m.–4 p.m.,
Sat., Sun. 9 a.m.–4 p.m.

Interior of Palace

Palm House: This was the largest glasshouse in Europe and was built in 1883. There are three sections in which the numerous exotic plants are kept at various temperatures. At present it is possible to visit only the "Sunny" house. The Botanic Garden (see Botanischer Garten) which was founded by Francis I stands just to the S.

In the Palace 42 rooms are open to the public. They still have the character they had in Franz Joseph's day.
Rooms 1–15: The rooms used by the Emperor Franz Joseph and Empress Elisabeth.
Rooms 16–25: State Apartments.
Rooms 26–33: Guest Apartments.
Rooms 34–36: Suite for Grand Duke Charles with three antechambers.
Rooms 40–42: Reception Rooms.

▼ *The Gloriette with Neptune's Fountain in the foreground*

Palace of Schönbrunn

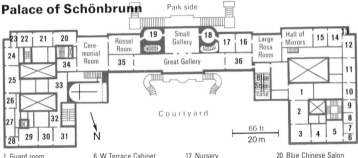

Park side

| | | | | Ceremonial Room | Rössel Room | 19 | Small Gallery | 18 | 17 | 16 | Large Rosa Room | Hall of Mirrors | 15 | 14 | 13 |
|23|22|21|20| | | | | | | | | | | | 12|

1 Guard room
2 Franz Joseph's Antechamber (Billiard Room)
3 Walnut Room
4 Franz Joseph's Writing-room
5 Franz Joseph's Bedroom
6 W Terrace Cabinet
7 Stair Cabinet
8 Dressing-room
9 Bedroom of Franz Joseph and Elisabeth
10 Empress Elisabeth's Salon
11 Marie-Antoinette Room
12 Nursery
13 Breakfast-room
14 Yellow Salon
15 Balcony Room
16 Small Rosa Room
17 Small Rosa Room
18 Chinese Round Cabinet
19 Oval Chinese Room
20 Blue Chinese Salon
21 Vieux Laque Room
22 Napoleon's Room
23 Porcelain Room
24 Million Room
25 Tapestry Room
26 Memento Room
27 Red Drawing-room
28 E Terrace Cabinet
29 Franz Joseph's Birth-room
30 Writing-room
31 Archduke Francis Charles's Drawing-room
32 Wild Boar Room
33 Passage Chamber
34 Machine Room
35 Carousel Room (Anteroom)
36 Lamp Room

Palace Chapel: This dates from about 1700. The painted ceiling is by Daniel Gran (1744), and the picture above the High Altar is by Paul Troger.

Bergl Rooms: Left of the entrance hall are the garden apartments which were furnished to Maria Theresa's taste. They were originally known as the "Indian Rooms" on account of their Romantic and exotic decoration which is the work of the Bohemian artist Johann Bergl. (Open: May–Sept. daily 9 a.m.–noon, 1–5 p.m.

The most handsome and important of the apartments: The Walnut Room: Emperor Franz Joseph's audience chamber takes its name from the walnut panelling dating from 1766. The candelabrum is carved out of wood covered with real gold.

Franz Joseph's Bedroom: It was in this simple soldier's bed that the Emperor died on 21 November 1916 after a reign of nearly 68 years.

Empress Elisabeth's Salon: On the walls of this reception-room hang pastel portraits by Jean-Etienne Liotard of Maria Theresa's children.

Marie-Antoinette's Room: On the left is F. Amerling's celebrated portrait of Francis I with the insignia of the Order of the Golden Fleece. A peculiarity of the picture is that the eyes of the Emperor seem to follow the spectator wherever he may go in the room.

Nursery: The Louis XVI cupboard in this panelled room belonged to Marie-Antoinette. There is a portrait of the future Queen of France on the left-hand side.

Breakfast-room: Maria Theresa used to take her breakfast in this room. The pictures of flowers embroidered in silks are said to be the work of the Empress's daughters.

Yellow Salon: The white marble clock which stands on the left-hand side was a gift of Napoleon III to Franz Joseph I. The salon takes its name from the yellow damask used for covering the chairs.

Hall of Mirrors: It was in this room the walls of which are covered with crystal mirrors in gilded Rococo frames, that Maria Theresa's Ministers used to swear their allegiance to her. Mozart performed here as a six-year-old prodigy.

Rosa Room: Joseph I's private apartments take their name from the landscape-paintings (1760–69) by the artist Josef Rosa.

Fountain of the Naiads in the Palace Park

Chinese Round Cabinet: It was here that Maria Theresa set up her "conspiracy headquarters" amid the East Asian lacquered screen panels under the dome with its stucco decoration. At that time State Chancellor Kaunitz was allowed to enter by way of a secret staircase. Meals were provided by means of a food lift; this meant there was no need to be disturbed by servants.

Small Gallery: It was in this 60 ft (18 m) long gallery that the Imperial Household ate its more intimate dinners. The painted ceiling is by Gregorio Guglielmi and dates from 1761. The huge windows offer a wonderful view out over the flower-beds in the park.

Ceremonial Room: Major weddings, baptisms and investitures (official inductions into certain high offices) took place here under the Habsburgs. The gold-framed paintings – School of van Meytens – depict the marriage of Joseph II to Isabella of Bourbon-Parma in 1760.

Blue Chinese Salon: Hand-painted Far Eastern wallpaper, blue and white Japanese vases and light blue silks form the setting in which the monarchy came to an end. It was in here that Charles I abdicated in 1918, and Austria became a Republic.

Vieux Laque Room: In the private apartment of the elderly Empress Maria Theresa East Asian art is combined with Viennese Rococo.

Napoleon's Room: Napoleon I lived in Maria Theresa's former bedroom in 1805. It was here, too, that his son, the Duke of Reichstadt, who had grown up in Schönbrunn, died in 1832. The room is furnished with valuable Brussels tapestries.

Porcelain Room: Blue and white wooden garlands look deceptively like decorations of genuine porcelain. Some of the 213 blue Indian ink sketches are by Maria Theresa's children who were artistically gifted.

Million Room: Maria Theresa's former private salon is panelled with precious rose wood, ornamented with gilt carvings. 260 precious Indian parchment miniatures have been set under glass in the panelling. Maria Theresa had them brought to Vienna from Constantinople. According to tradition the room cost "a million guilders".

Tapestry Room: The walls and furniture are covered with Brussels tapestries depicting Netherlandish folk scenes. The tapestry in the middle, "Port and Fish Market" is 280 sq. ft (26 m^2) in area.

Great Gallery: Glittering Imperial banquets used to take place in the Great Gallery under Gregorio Guglielmi's ceiling-paintings. Now the Republic has its grandest receptions here, too. One of the most important was when the State Treaty was signed.

Schönlaterngasse   B5

Schönlaterngasse, the winding lane in the oldest district of the inner city, takes its name from "The House with the fine lantern", which was built in 1680. The original "fine lantern" is now housed in the Historisches Museum (see entry). In 1971 a copy was placed on No. 6 Schönlaterngasse.

Location
Sonnenfelsgasse/
Postgasse, I

Schottenkirche

The Scots Church, built for Irish Benedictines

Underground stations
Stephansplatz (U1),
Schwedenplatz (U1, U4)

Opening times
Alte Schmiede Museum
Mon.–Fri. 9 a.m.–3 p.m.

In Schönlaterngasse the houses of the bourgeoisie and the traders are basically medieval with Baroque façades. They have all been thoroughly restored and renovated. Robert Schumann lived in No. 7a.
The Heiligkreuzerhof and the Basilikenhaus (see entries) and the old Jesuit House (No. 11), where the painter Kupelwieser lived, are notable. The Alte Schmiede (No. 9) was, until 1974, the workshop of Meister Schmirler who created the present "Schöner Laterne" and gave it to the city. The old smithy is now a cultural centre with an art gallery, a café and a literary rendezvous where readings and lectures are given.

*Schottenkirche (dedicated to the Virgin)   B4

Location
Freyung, I

Underground station
Schottentor (U2)

Bus
1A

In the 12th c. Irish monks were invited to come to Vienna from Regensburg. At the time Ireland was called "New Scotland", and this is why the church dedicated to Our Lady which was built for Irish Benedictines came to be called the Scots Church. It has been in the possession of the German Benedictines since 1418.
The Scots Monastery was founded by the Babenberg Duke Heinrich Jasomirgott in 1155, and work on the construction of the buildings began in 1177. The church was reconstructed in the Gothic style in the 14th and 15th c. It was altered and given a Baroque appearance by Andrea Allio and Carlo Carlone in the 17th c., and was restored again in the 19th c.
In the interior there are reredoses by Tobias Pock dating 1651–55, by Joachim Sandrart 1652–54, and August Eisen-

manger 1887–88. The finest is the "Apostles Departure" (near the Imperial Oratory). J. E. Fischer von Erlach designed the Baroque memorial, on the right behind the Penitents' Chapel, to Graf R. von Starhemberg who defended Vienna against the Turks.

The High Altar was the last work by Heinrich Ferstel, dating from 1883. The Lady Chapel Altar-piece has the oldest votive picture of the Virgin in Vienna. In the Crypt Chapel which was converted into vaults in 1960 lie the founder of the church, Heinrich II Jasomirgott, his consort Theodora and his daughter Agnes, Graf Rüdiger von Starhemberg who died in 1701, and the Baroque painter, Paul Troger, who died in 1762.

*Schottenstift (picture collection)   B4

The Schottenstift (Scots Foundation) on Freyung (see entry) is linked to the Schottenkirche (see entry) by the Schottenhof. It has a famous secondary school and an important picture gallery. The foundation Bull dates from 1161. The abbey was ceded to the German Benedictines in 1418.

The buildings date from the 12th c., but were extensively renovated in the 17th c. and enlarged in the 18th c. In 1832 they were rebuilt by Josef Kornhäusl in simple Classical style.

Among pupils of the school were the poet Bauernfeld, Nestroy, von Saar, Hamerling, the Waltz King Johann Strauss and the painter Moritz von Schwind. Austria's last Emperor, Charles I, also attended this school, as did the founder of Austrian Social Democracy, Viktor Adler. The collection of

Location
Freyung, I

Underground station
Schottentor (U2)

Bus
1A

Opening times
By appointment

Franz Schubert's birthplace, now a Schubert Museum

pictures here has been in existence for two and a half centuries. As well as works from the 16th c. to the 19th. c., there are in the chapter-house 19 pictures from the famous Late Gothic winged reredos of 1469–75. It was painted by two "Scottish Masters" and originally stood in the Schotten-kirche. The oldest surviving views of Vienna may be seen in the backgrounds of these pictures.

*Schubert Museum   A3

Location
Nussdorferstrasse, 54 IX

S-Bahn station
Nussdorferstrasse (G, GD)

Trams
D, 8, 42

Opening times
Tues.–Sun. 10 a.m.–
12.15 p.m. and 1–4.30 p.m.

On 31 January 1797 Franz Schubert was born in this little one-storey house – Zum roten Krebs (the red crab) in the Himmelpfort district.
The city of Vienna owns this house and has been able to preserve Schubert's birthplace virtually unaltered. A Schubert Museum has now been installed here, with manuscripts, pictures and everyday objects used by the composer. Not everything is entirely authentic, however, for when he was only four years old Schubert moved to a nearby house, No. 3 Saülengasse, where he lived for the next 17 years.

Schubertpark   A3

Location
Währingerstrasse, XVIII

S-Bahn station
Wahringerstrasse–
Volksoper (G, GD)

Trams
40, 41

A few gravestones and a Late Baroque cemetery cross indicate that Schubert Park was laid out on what used to be the Währinger Cemetery. On the E wall of the park are the two original graves of Schubert and Beethoven. Both composers were exhumed in 1808 and reburied in the Zentralfriedhof (see entry).
It was in the Währinger Cemetery that Franz Grillparzer pronounced his funeral oration over Beethoven. He said: "Beethoven withdrew from human society after he had given men all that he had and received nothing back in return."

*Secession (art gallery)   C4

Location
12 Friedrichstrasse, I

Underground station
Karlsplatz (U1, U2, U4)

Bus
59A

Trams
1, 2, D, J

Opening times
Tues.–Fri. 10 a.m.–6 p.m.,
Sat. and Sun. 10 a.m.–
4 p.m.

The exhibition gallery of the artists' union is easily recognised on account of its remarkable cupola in the form of an iron laurel bush. When the gilding was still visible the Viennese used to call it "the golden bunch". The building was designed by Josef Olbrich, a disciple of Otto Wagner's, in 1898. It was the first and epoch-making example of the Viennese Art Nouveau (called "Jugendstil" or sometimes "Secessionsstil"). It was damaged during the war and robbed of its treasures in 1945 but was restored and opened again in 1964. Reconstruction since 1986 has made it possible to put on musical and theatrical performances and video displays.
The need for the building arose after 1892 when the union of young artists under the leadership of the painter Gustav Klimt left – "seceded from" – the Künstlerhaus (see entry) group. In 1897 the still-surviving Artists' Union, called "Secession", came into being and created the artistic style that bears the same name.

Mark Antony group   *The Secession building*

The huge Mark Antony bronze group by Arthur Strasser on the E side is especially noteworthy. The Roman statesman's lion-drawn chariot was shown at the 1900 Universal Exhibition. Today in the Secession building can be seen Gustav Klimt's Beethoven frieze, a huge mural of some 270 sq. ft (70 m²) on the theme of Beethoven's Ninth Symphony. It was painted for the 14th exhibition of the Vienna Secession in 1902 and was purchased by the State in 1973 and restored from 1977.

*Servitenkirche   B4

The Servites' (or "Servants of our Lady") Church was founded by Field-Marshal Octavio Piccolomini, one of the leaders of the Wallenstein Conspiracy. Its dedication is to the Annunciation. It was built by Carlo Carnevale between 1651 and 1677. Dying in 1656, Piccolomini did not live to see the work completed.

The Servites' Church is the earliest building in Vienna based on a central oval form with its main space elliptical in shape. The traverse axis provides wide, rectangular chapels and in the diagonal corners there are small semicircular altar-niches. In the narthex there are two large 17th c. Baroque figures and a magnificent cast-iron trellis-work, dating from about 1670. There is rich stucco decoration by Giovanni Battista Barbarino (1669) and Giovanni Battista Bussi (1723– 24). Near the 19th c. High Altar is a late 15th c. wooden Crucifix from the "Raven Stone", the site of executions in days gone by. The carved figures of the Four Evangelists and the Three Virtues on the

Location
9 Servitengasse, IX

Underground station
Rosauer Lände (U4)

Tram
D

Display in the Spanish Riding School

pulpit of 1739 are by Balthasar Moll. Field-Marshal Octavio Piccolomini, who died in 1656, lies buried in front of the altar in the middle chapel on the left-hand side; there is no gravestone.

The Peregrini Chapel was built on to the middle chapel on the right; its fine Rococo ironwork and the frescoes in the dome are the work of Josef Mölk (1766).

The Tower Chapel on the right leads through to the little Chapel of the Poor; its altar-painting is attributed to Martin J. Schmidt. The left-hand Tower Chapel leads to the Lourdes-Grotto.

****Spanish Riding School** B4

Location
2 Reitschulgasse, I

Underground stations
Stephansplatz (U1),
Schottentor (U2)

Bus
2A

The displays in the Spanish Riding School (see Lipizzaner, Hofburg, Winterreitschule) are, as they always have been, performed in historical costume. The riders wear white buckskin breeches with high black boots, a brown jacket and a bicorn hat trimmed with gold. Deerskin saddles lie over the gold-trimmed red and blue saddle-cloths. At the start and end of each display the riders silently salute the picture of Charles VI who commissioned the building.

The Spanish Riding School is an inheritance from the Baroque era. The institution dates back to the time of Emperor Maximilian II. He it was who introduced the breeding of Spanish horses in Austria. The name "Spanish Riding School" is first mentioned in 1572.

Vienna State Opera House: the staircase ▶

The exterior of Vienna State Opera House

Demonstrations
Mar.–June, Sept.–Dec. Sun.
10.45 a.m.; Apr.–June,
Sept.–Oct. also Wed. 7 p.m.
Short programme
Sat. 9 a.m.
Morning exercise:
Mar.–June, Sept.–
mid Dec. Tues.–Sat.
10 a.m.–noon (also Mon.
in Feb.)

Stable Visits
See entry Lipizzaner

Since the time of Charles VI the prestigious riding displays have taken place in the Baroque Winter Riding School which was built by Joseph Emmanuel Fischer von Erlach between 1729 and 1735 in the Hofburg (see entry). This magnificent room was designed for the nobility to show their ability in riding skills and to compete together. It was later used for a variety of other purposes, but since 1894 it has been reserved exclusively for the training of the Lipizzaner horses and their displays.

---

*Spinnerin am Kreuz (officially Crispin's cross)   D4

Location
Triesterstrasse, X
(near No. 52)

Buses
15A, 65A

Tram
65

The Spinnerin am Kreuz is a 52 ft (16 m) high Gothic stone pillar in the form of a phial-shaped tabernacle. One of the landmarks of Old Vienna, it was designed by Hans Puschbaum, the architect of St Stephen's Cathedral and erected in 1452 to replace an older one which had been donated by Leopold III. According to legend a faithful wife sat here at her spinning-wheel, awaiting the return of her husband from a Crusade.

From 1311 to 1747 and from 1804 to 1868 the "gallows by the Spinnerin" was the site of public executions. Severin von Jaroszynski was hanged here in front of 30,000 spectators in 1827. He was a Polish aristocrat who had robbed and murdered a man in order to satisfy the excessive financial demands of the popular actress Therese Krone.

**Staatsoper   C4

The Vienna State Opera House is one of the world's three leading opera houses.

Operas have been performed in Vienna since 1688, first on the site of the present Nationalbibliothek (see entry), then in the Redoutensälen and in the old Burghtheater on Michaelerplatz, where Mozart's "Il seraglio" and "The Marriage of Figaro" were first performed, next in the Kärntnertor Theatre, where Weber's "Euryanthe" had its première. After that operas were performed in the Ring Theatre, which was subsequently destroyed by fire, and finally, from 1869, in the Hof Opera House. The vast Opera House with its clearly defined structure is designed in the French Early Renaissance style.

It was built between 1861 and 1869 to plans by August von Siccardsburg and Eduard van der Nüll. It was opened on 25 May 1869 with Mozart's "Don Giovanni" and a prologue spoken by Charlotte Wolter. Neither architect lived to see the day. The criticisms and cruel jokes of the Viennese while building was in progress drove van der Nüll to suicide, and Siccardsburg died just two months later, in 1868.

The Opera House was struck by bombs on 12 March 1945 and gutted by fire. Reconstruction was not completed until 1955. The second inauguration of the Opera House on the Ringstrasse took place on 5 November 1955 when Beethoven's "Fidelio" was performed.

The Opera House can accommodate an audience of 2,209, with 110 musicians. The area covered by the buildings is 8,650 sq. yd (9,000 m²). The main façade with its two-storey

Location
2 Opernring, I

Underground station
Karlsplatz (U1, U2, U4)

Trams
1, 2, D, J

Tours
July–Aug. daily 10 and 11 a.m., 1, 2 and 3 p.m.
May, June, Oct. daily 1, 2 and 3 p.m.
Nov.–Apr. daily 2.15 p.m.

City Park: the Strauss Monument

foyer opens on the Ringstrasse. The tripartite stage area covers an area of 1,450 sq. yd (1,500 m²); it is 175 ft (53 m) high and 165 ft (51 m) deep.

Inside a grand staircase leads up to the first floor. Immediately opposite is the "Schwind Foyer" which takes its name from the pictures by Martin Schwind of scenes from operas. The staircase, the foyer and the tea-room with its valuable tapestries were the only parts of the building left undamaged after the fire in 1945.

Every year on the last Thursday of Carnival the Opera Ball takes place here. It is one of the most elegant and famous balls in the world. The stage and the rows of seats in the auditorium which is decorated in cream, red and gold, are brought to the same level by means of a specially fitted floor. Thousands of carnations are flown in from the Riviera to decorate the boxes just for one night.

Stadtpark   C5

Location
Parkring, I

Underground station
Stadtpark (U4)

Trams
1, 2, J

The two parts of the City Park are linked by bridges of the River Wien. It covers an area of 28 acres (114,000 m²).

In 1857 Franz Joseph I instigated the creation of a garden where the old fortifications went down to the water, thinking the site "well suited to embellishment". The landscape-gardener Dr Siebeck carried through the plans drawn up by the landscape-painter Josef Szelleny. The gardens were opened in 1862, and the Pavilion in 1867.

In the part of the park nearest the city centre there are monuments to the painters Hans Canon, Emil Schindler, Hans Makart, and Friedrich von Amerling, to the composers Johann Strauss the Younger, Franz Schubert and Anton Bruckner, as well as to Anton Zelinka, the founding Mayor. The Donauweibchenbrunnen (The Spring with the Sprite of the Danube) is a copy; the original stands in the Historisches-Museum (see entry).

Stanislaus-Kostka-Kapelle (church)   B4

Location
6 Steindlgasse/
2 Kurrentgasse, I

Underground station
Stephansplatz (U1)

Bus
2A

There is gold and silver decoration in this chapel in the court-yard of the Jesuit presbytery.

Until 1582 the chapel was a single room in the house called "Zur goldenen Schlange" (The Golden Snake) where the Polish Jesuit Stanislaus Kostka lived. After the occurrence of two miracles, the room was converted into a chapel and given particularly rich ornamentation. Stanislaus Kostka was canonised in 1726.

The chapel was refurbished during Maria Theresa's reign, and Charles I served at the altar here while a schoolboy at the Schottengymnasiums.

**Stephansdom (St Stephen's Cathedral)   B4/5

Location
Stephansplatz, I

Underground station
Stephansplatz (U1)

Bus 1A

St Stephen's Cathedral with its 450 ft (137 m) high spire is not only the major sight in Vienna and the symbol of the city; it is also the most important Gothic building in Vienna. It has been the cathedral church of the archbishopric since 1722.

The cathedral has been the never-ending work of generations since the 12th c. It is an architectural representation of eight centuries of history. The original Romanesque church was replaced by a Late Romanesque one in the 13th c. All that remains of it are the massive gate and the Heiden (heathen) Towers. Next came reconstruction in the Gothic style in the 14th c. by Duke Rudolf IV von Habsburg, known as "The Donor".

The choir, and the Chapels of St Eligius, St Tirna and St Catherine were completed in the course of this century. The S tower, the nave and the Chapel of St Barbara belong to the 15th c. The N tower, which was not completed, was roofed over in the 16th c. Improvements and further construction followed in the 17th, 18th and 19th c.

The roof was destroyed by fire in the final days of the Second World War in 1945. The vaulting of the middle choir and the right-hand choir side of the choir collapsed, and the towers were gutted. Reconstruction and restoration went on from 1948 to 1962. It was a communal effort, involving all Austria. The new bell was paid for by Upper Austria, the new floor by Lower Austria, the pews by Vorarlberg, the windows by Tyrol, the candelabra by Carinthia, the Communion rail by Burgenland, the tabernacle by Salzburg, the roof by Vienna and the portals by Styria. Today atmospheric pollution is the danger. The cathedral buildings cover a surface of 4,186 sq. yd (3,500 m²). They are 350 ft (107 m) long and 128 ft (39 m) across. The height of the nave amounts to 90 ft (28 m). The Heiden Towers are 215 ft (66 m) high, the S tower 450 ft (137 m), and the uncompleted N tower 200 ft (61 m). The roof, whose apex is 200 ft (60 m) above ground-level, is covered with 230,000 glazed tiles.

Tours
Mon.–Sat. 10.30 a.m. and
3 p.m.; Sun. and holidays
3 p.m.
Evenings June–Sept.
Sat. 7 p.m.
July, Aug. also Fri. 7 p.m.

St Stephen's Cathedral

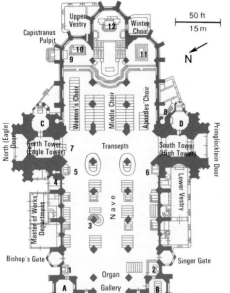

A Tirna Chapel (Holy Cross Chapel), burial-place of Prince Eugene (d. 1736); above it the Treasury Chapel
B Eligius Chapel
C Barbara Chapel
D Catherine Chapel

1 H. Prachatitz's altar canopy.
2 Canopy with Pötscher Madonna
3 A. Pilgram's pulpit with Peeping Tom on the pillar. On the pillar, the Servant's Madonna
4 Lift to Pummerin Bell
5 Organ-case by A. Pilgram (with Pilgram's self-portrait)
6 H. Puchsbaum's canopy
7 Entrance to catacombs
8 Tower stairs (313 steps)
9 Donor's gravestone
10 Wiener-Neustadt Altar (Frederick's reredos)
11 Emperor Frederick III's (d. 1493) raised sarcophagus
12 T. and J. J. Pock's High Altar

Dimensions: length, outside 350 ft (107 m), inside 300 ft (92 m). Width across transepts 230 ft (70 m) outside. Width across nave, inside, 130 ft (39 m). Height of nave, inside, 92 ft (28 m). Height of Heiden towers 215 ft (66 m), of N tower 200 ft (61 m), of S tower 450 ft (137 m).
Largest Bell: Pummerin – 20 tons (21 t); the original bell, dating from 1711, was recast in 1945

Stephansdom

Giant Gateway. The Late Romanesque Giant Gateway dates from 1230 and has uncommonly rich ornamentation. In earlier times it was opened only on festive occasions. In 1805 Napoleon's farewell proclamation hung down from its frieze with its dragons, birds, lions, monks and demons.

Heiden Towers: The Heiden Towers are part of the Romanesque church, and are mentioned in documents as early as 1295. Their name recalls the heathen shrine which is supposed to have occupied this site formerly. The towers are 215 ft (66 m) high. From the third storey upwards their shape alters from rectangular to octagonal.

Tirna Chapel: Prince Eugene is buried in the Tirna Chapel, which dates from 1359. The conqueror over the Turks is commemorated in a gravestone set in the floor. The Crucifix above the altar is 15th c. work. The beard of Christ is made of genuine human hair, and according to legend it is still growing.

Stone canopy: It is likely that the pierced stone Gothic canopy dating from about 1437 is the work of Hans von Prachatiz; the picture of the Sacred Heart beneath it, however, is 18th c. work.

Bishop's Gate: The gate – a counterpart to the Singer Gate – was the entry reserved for female visitors to the cathedral. Its figurative sculptures dating from about 1370 are examples of High Gothic Art. Among coats of arms may be seen the figures of Duke Albrecht III and his consort.

Pulpit: This is the most important work of art in the nave, a masterpiece of Late Gothic sculpture in sandstone. It was carved by Master Pilgram in about 1515 and is decorated with the figures of the Four Fathers of the Church. On the plinth Master Pilgram carved a representation of himself in the pose of a Peeping Tom.

The so-called Servant's Madonna, on the pillar by the pulpit, dates from 1340. According to legend, a maid employed by a Count turned to the Virgin for help when she was under suspicion of theft. The true miscreant was discovered, and the Count's lady paid for this figure in St Stephen's to commemorate the event.

Nave: The three-nave church is divided by rows of composite pillars which support the criss-crossing network of ribs in the vaulting overhead. On the pillars there are life-size statues of donors made of stone and clay. The most precious figure is that of St Christopher on the left-hand pillar by the choir; dating from 1470 it is probably the gift of Emperor Frederich II.

Organ-case: The organ itself was removed in 1720, and only the magnificent Late Gothic organ-case by Master Pilgram remains; the monogram indicates that it was made in 1513. The man with the compass and set square, again in the pose of a Peeping Tom, is Pilgram himself. The new organ which was installed in 1960 is, with its 10,000 pipes, one of the largest and most modern in the world.

Opening times
Tower and Pummerin, daily 9 a.m.–5.30 p.m. (lift)

North (Eagle) Tower: The reason why it remained uncompleted is according to legend as follows: Hans Puchsbaum who was in charge of construction made a pact with the Devil, but was cast down into the abyss by him because he ventured

St Stephen's Cathedral: chief sight and symbol of Vienna ▶

to pronounce a holy name. The new Pummerin bell was cast in 1951, and since 1957 it has been hanging in the Tower. It weighs 20 tons (21 t), and its diameter is 10 ft (3·14 m).

Catacombs: The entrance to the catacombs is through the chamber under the N Tower. They extend from under the cathedral choir out under Stephansplatz, and the bones of thousands of Viennese citizens are piled up in tiers (but this part is not open to the public). The major attraction is the Ducal Vault which Rudolf IV had constructed for members of the House of Habsburg in 1363. After the construction of the Imperial Vault in the Kapuzinerkirche (see entry) it became the custom to place here only copper urns containing the intestines of the members of the Ruling House, while their bodies were laid to rest in the Imperial Vault and their hearts in the Augustinerkirche (see entry). Since 1953 there has also been a vault in the catacombs for the Archbishops of Vienna.

Galilee/Adlertor: Master Puchsbaum is thought to be the builder of this part of the cathedral. The upper row of figures on the canopy which was set up in the 19th c. include Frederich III, Maximilian I, Franz Joseph I, with Elisabeth and Maria of Burgundy. The iron cylinder on the pillar to the left may be a medieval sanctuary knocker.

Barbara Chapel: Its plan is similar to that of the Catherine Chapel; it was designed by Master Puchsbaum.

Donor Memorial: Among these Early Gothic stone figures dating from before 1340 there is an especially fine Angel of the Annunciation and a statue of Our Lady the Protectress. They serve as ornamentation for the so-called "Women's Choir". Among the most important graves is the Donor grave of Rudolf IV (which is, in fact, empty).

The Wiener-Neustädter Altar: Frederick III was the donor of this winged reredos in 1447. It was only in 1884 that it was brought to Vienna from Wiener-Neustadt.

High Altar: This was constructed out of black marble between 1640 and 1660 by Tobias and Johann Jakob Pock. The statues round it represent the Patron Saints of the province, Leopold and Florian, and St Roch and St Sebastian, who were invoked in time of plague. Gothic stained glass has been preserved to the left and right of the High Altar.
Frederick III's raised sepulchre. The S choir is dominated by the huge raised sepulchre of Frederick III. It is made of red marble and has a larger than life-size statue of the Emperor which is surrounded by coats of arms. The design is by the Netherlandish painter Niclas Gerhaert van Leyden (1467–1513) who himself made the top of this Gothic grave.

Catherine Chapel: The marble font dates from 1481. The reliefs on the 14-sided basin depict Christ, John the Baptist and the Twelve Apostles. The Four Evangelists are on its plinth. The carved wooden font cover is particularly fine.

South Tower: The "Steffl" as the Viennese call it was begun in 1356. It is 450 ft (137 m) high, and is considered to rival the tower of Freiburg Minster as the most beautiful German Gothic tower.
It is possible to go up the tower as far as the watch room; that means climbing 343 stairs.

Nave of St Stephen's Cathedral with a view of the Organ ▶

Galilee and Primglöcklein Door: The porch between the two buttresses of the tower are 14th c., as are the sitting figures of the Apostles.

Canopy: The Late Gothic canopy over the Leopold Altar is presumed to be the work of Hans Puchsbaum. It was donated in 1448.

Singer Gate: This was the entry for male visitors to the cathedral. The nine Apostles and the legend of St Paul in the tympanum date from 1378.

The Pötscher Madonna: The Pötscher Madonna under its Late Gothic canopy has been an object of profound veneration in Austria and Hungary since the Battle of Zenta in 1697. According to legend, tears streamed from the eyes of the Madonna for a fortnight at the time of the battle against the Turks.

Eligius Chapel: It is also called the Dukes' Chapel and its statues count among the most important of the second half of the 14th c. The so-called "Hausmuttergottes" (the protective mother of god) from the former Himmelpfort Monastery was revered by the Empress Maria Theresa.

Stephansplatz (Square)   B4

Location
Stock-im-Eisen-Platz/
Rotenturmstrasse, I

Underground station
Stephansplatz (U1)

Bus
1A

Virgilian Chapel

Opening times
Daily except Mon.
10 a.m.–12.15 p.m.,
1–4.30 p.m.
Admission free

The square in front of St Stephen's Cathedral (see entry: Stephansdom) forms the centre of the inner city of Vienna and is now a bustling pedestrian precinct. After war damage and the building of an underground station, the entire open space was newly laid out.

Until 1732 Stephansplatz was a cemetery as is indicated by the tombstones incorporated in the external walls of the Cathedral and the Late Gothic column in which the eternal light burned for the dead. A copy can be seen at the W end of the S wall of the Cathedral. To the right of the Cathedral coloured stones mark the outline of the Chapel of Maria Magdalene which was burned down in 1781. When Stephansplatz Underground station was being constructed the Vigil Kapelle (Virgilian Chapel) was discovered beneath the crypt of Maria Magdalene. The Virgilian Chapel was probably planned as a mausoleum and was indeed used as such by the Chrannest family early in the 14th c. Later it became the meeting-place of religious societies and, finally, once again a place of burial.

Also of interest are the houses No. 2, Zur Weltkugel (The Globe), No. 3, Das Churhaus (Election House), No. 5, Domherrenhof (Prebendary's Court), No. 6, Zwettlerhof (Zwettler Court) and No. 7, the Archbishop's Palace.

Stock-im-Eisen-Platz (Square)   B4

Location
Stephansplatz-Graben, I

Underground station
Stephansplatz (U1)

Buses
1A, 2A, 3A

Stock-im-Eisen-Platz is a square next to Stephansplatz (see entry) and leading directly into Kärntnerstrasse (see entry). It takes its curious name from a tree-trunk into which many nails have been hammered. It stands in a niche of house number 3/4, at the corner of Graben and Kärntnerstrasse.

There is evidence the tree-trunk has been here since 1533. According to legend, every locksmith's apprentice who came to Vienna in the course of his wanderings had to hammer a nail into the tree-trunk.

Technical Museum for Industry and Trades

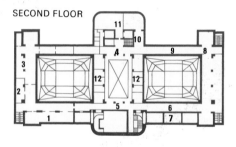

SECOND FLOOR

SECOND FLOOR
1 Posts and Telegraphs
2 Postage Stamps
3 Telecommunications
4 Photography
5 Bridge Building and Water Supply
6 Data handling
7 Administration
8 Türmer Room
9 Fire prevention
10 Music Technology
11 Organ
12 Offices

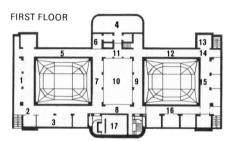

FIRST FLOOR

FIRST FLOOR
1 Textile Industries
2 Sewing-machines
3 Building Technology
4 Special Exhibitions
5 Printing
6 Typewriters
7 Stones and Earths
8 Weights and Measures
9 Aviation
10 Historic Aircraft
11 Paper Manufacture
12 Food Industries
13 Sugar Manufacture
14 Petrol and Natural Gas
15 Chemical Industries
16 Physics and Chemistry
17 Auditorium and Cinema

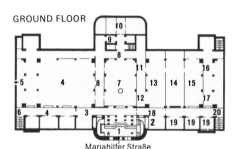

GROUND FLOOR

Mariahilfer Straße

GROUND FLOOR
1 Vestibule
2 Café
3 Seafaring
4 Railway Museum
5 Locomotives
6 Staircase to First Floor
7 Engine-building
8 Tram cars
9 Marcus car
10 Aviation
11 Gas Production and Distribution
12 Lighting
13 Electricity
14 Metalwork
15 Mining
16 Woodworking
17 Agriculture
18 Start of the Collections
19 Historic workshops
20 Stairway to coal-mine

143

On the site of No. 6 a new building is being erected (opening planned for autumn 1989). It comprises an exclusive shopping centre with a "Gourmet storey" (modelled on the Ka De We in Berlin) with offices and a roof terrace from which the view of Stephansplatz, Graben and the Stephansdom (see entries) may be enjoyed.

*Technisches Museum für Industrie und Gewerbe   D1

Location
212 Mariahilferstrasse, XIV

Underground station
Schönbrunn (U4)

Trams
10, 52, 58

Opening times
Tues.–Fri. and Sun.9 a.m.–4 p.m., Sat. and public holidays 9 a.m.–1 p.m.

Ground Floor

The Technical Museum of Industry and Trade occupies a site on the way to Schönbrunn (see entry). Emperor Franz Joseph laid the foundation-stone of the new museum in 1908, but it was ready for opening only in 1918, after his death.
The museum's collections go back as far as the 18th c. The Imperial "physical collection" evolved into an "industrial collection", which itself later became a "production collection". Finally this gave rise to the Technical Museum. On three floors are displayed collections which show a cross-section of the development of technology, business and industry with special reference to the Austrian contribution.

The Ground Floor houses the departments concerned with transport, machine-building, lighting, metalworking, electricity, mining, agriculture and woodworking. Among the exhibits are a Marcus car (1888), the original designs for Ressel's marine screw, an Ajax locomotive (1841), a horse-drawn railcar belonging to the Linz-Budweis Railway (also 1841), the first turbine (1919) and the first front-wheel drive car.

First Floor

The First Floor houses the collections concerned with the textile industries, sewing-machines and typewriters, graphic arts, construction, paper-making, measurement and surveying, aviation, physics and chemistry, the food industry, petrol and industrial chemistry. Among the most interesting exhibits are the model of a flying machine by Kress (1877), a Lilienthal glider (1894), the fine clock of Philippus Imsserus (1555), the calculating machine of Antonius Braun (early 18th c.), Negrelli's own sketches of cross-sections of the Suez Canal and the model of a space capsule.

Second Floor

The Second Floor houses the collections of the Postal and Telegraph Museum, together with exhibits concerning bridge construction, fire prevention and the technology of music. A section devoted to physics and atomic physics is being developed.
The most interesting objects on show are the world's first postcard (1869), Nussbauer's first device for the transmission of music by means of wireless which dates from 1904, the workshop of a 19th c. violin-maker and the writing-machine of Knaus (1760).

Theresianum   C4

Location
15 Favoritenstrasse, IV

Underground station
Taubstummengasse (U1)

The college for diplomats and the endowed Theresian Academy are housed in the Favorita, formerly an Imperial summer palace.
The Favorita was built between 1616 and 1625 and refurbished in the Baroque style in 1690. It was the favourite residence

Technical Museum: a Lilienthal glider

of Leopold I, Joseph I and Charles VI, who died here. The Empress Maria Theresa, however, preferred Schönbrunn (see entry) and handed the Favorita to the Jesuits, enjoining them with the provision of a "Collegium Theresianum" where the sons of the less well-off aristocracy could be trained as officials, as well as the Oriental Academy for the education of officials and diplomats.

In the large park of the Theresianum (Argentinier Strasse) stands Radio House, built by Clemens Holzmeister and others between 1936 and 1938. It is a building with a simple façade and a beautiful entrance hall.

Bus
13A

*Uhrenmuseum der Stadt Wien (Museum)   B4

The City of Vienna's Clock Museum has been housed since 1921 in the 300-year-old Obizzi Palace. It is the most important collection of clocks in the world.

Room 1: Mainly tower clocks, among them a tower clock from St Stephen's dated 1699 (Cat. No. 3043) and the oldest item in the collection, a 15th c. tower clock.

Room 2: Hand-made, weight-driven wall clocks. The *pièce de résistance* is an astronomical wall clock of 1663 (No. 794).

Room 3: Travelling, table and wall clocks. The four-poster-bed clock (No. 2472) was made in the mid 17th c.

Room 4: Pedestal clocks. One of the most valuable is a "Pendule" (No. 50) by Louis Monet of Paris; it is dated 1752.

Room 5: Part of Marie von Ebner-Eschenbach's Collection,

Location
2 Schulhof, I

Underground station
Stephansplatz (U1)

Bus
1A

Opening times
Daily (except Mon.)
9 a.m.–12.15 p.m. and
1–4.30 p.m.

including a Swiss gold pendant watch dated 1800 (Nos. 1490–92). Also valuable gold-enamelled clocks.

Room 6: Commode pedestal clocks and travelling clocks. The astronomical pedestal clock (No. 232) is of 1810 and comes from a Viennese workshop.

Room 7: Rare Japanese clocks, including unusual 18th c. pillar clocks (Nos. 799–802).

Room 8: Desk clocks and clocks in the form of figures. The "Rider's Clock" (No. 3064) is of Austrian manufacture and was produced about 1802.

Room 9: Empire grandfather clocks.

Following the reconstruction of the second and third floors further Empire and Biedermeier clocks are on show. On the third floor can be seen wall clocks with electric movements and compensation pendulums. The development of the wrist-watch is covered for the first time with elaborate watches from about 1850 through trench watches from the First World War, gentlemen's automatic watches from the 1930s to unusual modern creations.

Room 10: Seven clocks with pictures on them.

Room 11: Watches from the turn of the century in veneered wooden cases.

Room 12: Wall clocks, with a remarkable astronomical clock of 1863 (No. 326).

Room 13: Clocks from the turn of the century. Clock in the form of a bicycle.

Room 14: Clocks from the Black Forest and also a particularly fine Austrian carved cuckoo-clock (No. 3065).

Vienna University: its Italian Renaissance-style buildings

Room 15: Novelties, such as a night-light clock (No. 250) which was probably made in Switzerland.

Room 16: About 270 pocket watches and more than 170 wrist-watches dating form 1850 to the present day.

Room 17: Toy clocks, movements for automata.

Room 18: Clocks in the form of flutes, organs and harps.

Universität (University) B4

The University buildings were put up in the period when the Ringstrasse was being developed. The plans were by Heinrich Ferstel who took inspiration from the Italian Renaissance style. The buildings were opened in 1884 and renovated in 1953 and 1965.

In the arcaded central courtyard there are monuments to famous university teachers, among them Anton Bruckner, Gerhard van Swieten, Theodor von Billroth, Marie von Ebner-Eschenbach, Ludwig Boitzmann, Anton von Eiselsberg, Julius Wagner-Jauregg, I. Philipp Semmelweis, Sigmund Freud and the Nobel prize-winner Karl Landsteiner.

Location
1 Dr-Karl-Lueger-Ring, I

Underground station
Schottentor (U2)

Trams
1, 2, D

*UNO-City (officially Vienna International Centre)

The Vienna International Centre, bordering Donau Park (see entry), is also known as UNO-City. The idiosyncratic towering office-blocks were designed by Johann Staber and constructed between 1973 and 1976. They belong to the Austrian State and stand on land made available by the city of Vienna.

Location
Wagramerstrasse, II

UNO-City, officially Vienna International Centre

147

Danube Park
UNO-City

275 yds
250 m

Reichsbrücke   Lobau

— —O— —U- Bahn

The entire complex is, however, leased for a peppercorn rent of 1 schilling a year to the United Nations, several of whose important organisations are housed here: The International Atomic Energy Authority (IAEA) and the United Nations Industrial Development Organisation (UNIDO). Other UNO institutions which have been transferred to Vienna from Geneva and New York include the Centre for Social Development and Humanitarian Aims (CSDHA), the United Nations Commission for Infectious Diseases and the UN organisations associated with it (INCB and UNFDAC), the Department of the UN for International Commercial Law (UNCITRAL), and, in the summer of 1978, the headquarters of the UN Aid to Palestinian Refugees in the Middle East (UNRWA) and the High Commission for Refugees (UNHCR). Since 27 August 1979 the complex has been officially extra-territorial.

The office-blocks are between 177 ft (54 m) and 395 ft (120 m) high. The city has 43 passenger lifts and 15 goods lifts.

There are 24,000 windows, 6,000 doors, 80,000 fluorescent tubes and parking spaces for 2,500 cars. The electrical installations took 185 miles (300 km) of telephone wire and 155 miles (250 km) of high-tension cable. Twenty-seven of Austria's most renowned artists worked on the artistic embellishment of the interior. On UNO Plaza stands Joannis Avramidis's bronze "Polis" (The City). Inside may be seen pictures by Wolfgang Hollegha, Georg Eisler, Karl Korab, Kurt Regschek, Peter Pongratz, Friedensreich Hundertwasser as well as reliefs by Alfred Hrdlicka and Giselbert Hocke.

The Austria Centre Vienna adjoining UNO-City was opened in 1987. It is an ultra-modern centre for events and conferences and has the latest technical facilities. Until its completion the

Votivkirche: a fine example of historically inspired architecture ▶

148

mammoth project was strongly opposed. Nevertheless even when it is well used it still loses 600–1,000 million Austrian schillings a year.

Fourteen rooms of various sizes are available for concerts, dances, banquets, exhibitions and theatrical and TV shows, accommodating from 50 to more than 4,000 participants. The accommodation is on four floors and each has its own foyer and refreshment facilities, so that different events can be held at the same time. The floor space of the foyers totalling over a million square feet (9,390 m^2) can also be used for exhibitions. All the public rooms have the necessary technical provision for TV, film and slide projection, as well as for simultaneous translation in up to nine languages.

In addition there are offices and rooms for 10–70 people available for meetings. In the main centre conferences of UN size can be held (there are direct connections to the HQ of the United Nations). When laid out in parliamentary style it can accommodate 2,100 participants. In rows twice as many can be accommodated. There are, of course, in such a huge modern congress building a press centre and a radio station, a post office, bank, travel bureaux, restaurants, coffee-shops and a cocktail lounge.

Volksgarten (Park)   B4

Location
Dr-Karl-Renner-Ring, I

Underground station
Volkstheater (U1)

Bus
48A

Trams
1, 2, D

The Volksgarten lies between the Hofburg (see entry) and the Burgtheater (see entry). This, the second largest park in the City Centre, was opened in 1820 on the site of the fortifications which had been blown up by the French, and soon became a favourite place for the Viennese out for a Sunday-afternoon stroll.

In the middle of the gardens stands the Temple of Theseus which was built in 1823 for Antonio Canova's statue of Theseus. The order for this had originally been given by Napoleon I while he was in Vienna, but nothing came of it, for obvious political reasons, until Francis I sprang into the breach. Later, in 1890, the statue was removed from the Temple and placed in the staircase of the Kunsthistorisches Museum (see entry).

Notable monuments in the park include the Grillparzer Memorial with reliefs portraying scenes from six of his plays and the memorial to the Empress Elisabeth.

Votivkirche   B4

Location
Rooseveltplatz, IX

Underground station
Schottentor (U2)

Trams
1, 2, 37, 38, 40, 41, 42, 44, D

The prebendal church Zum Göttlichen Heiland (The Divine Saviour) was built as a votive offering after the failure of an attempt in 1853 to assassinate Emperor Franz Joseph I. Archduke Maximilian, Franz Joseph's brother, who was later to become Emperor of Mexico, led the way in providing the necessary finance.

Heinrich Ferstel chose the Neo-Gothic style, in imitation of the French Gothic cathedrals, and the chancel is one of the best examples of 19th c. historically inspired architecture. It was dedicated in 1879.

The church possesses several important works of art. There is Count Niklas Salm's Renaissance (1530–33) sepulchre with a recumbent figure of the Count surmounting it and 12 masterly reliefs on the sides in the Baptistery in the N transept; it comes from Loy Hering's Antwerp workshops. In the side-chapel in the S transept may be seen the Antwerp reredos, an important 15th c. carved altar with scenes from the Passion. In the S transept there is a copy of Our Lady of Guadelupe which recalls Emperor Maximilian of Mexico, the church's first protector. As a former garrison church, the building has many monuments to Austrian Army units.

*Waffensammlung (Museum)   C4

The first collectors were Archduke Ernst of Styria (15th c.) and Archduke Ferdinand of Tyrol (16th c.). It eventually became the most important collection of its type when in 1889 all the Habsburg armouries were combined. It was transferred from the Kunsthistorisches Museum (see entry) to the Neue Burg (see Hofburg) in 1935–36.

Nine Rooms and 6 galleries are filled with exhibits which visitors can examine in chronological order, going round the collection in counter-clockwise direction from Room 1.

Room 1: 500–1480. Archaeological finds, helmets, armour, including the armour of Frederick I of the Palatinate and a ceremonial sword belonging to Frederich III.

Room 2: 1480–1500. Late Gothic suits of armour, boy's armour, swords and Louis XII's crossbow.

Gallery A: Tournament armour, Maximilian I's jousting equipment, mainly from the Innsbruck Court workshops.

Room 3: 1500–1530. High Renaissance armour and ceremonial arms, with two suits of boy's armour made for Charles V.

Room 4: 1530–1545. Parade armour for Charles V, Philip II, King Ferdinand I and Francis I. Important examples of Milan craftsmanship and the earliest firearms.

Room 5: 1545–1560. The "Adlergarnitur" (Eagle armour), some of the finest armour; richly ornamented weapons.

Gallery B: Numerous examples of armour of Archduke Ferdinand of Tyrol including parade suits of armour and garments of the mid 16th c.

Room 6: 1550–1560. Ceremonial weapons, including Maximilian II's golden dagger of 1551; richly ornamented shields and helmets and 16th c. Ottoman weapons.

Room 7: 1560–1580. Richly decorated suits of armour, weapons for hunting and target practice, Maximilian II's "Rose Petal" armour and the "braided" armour of his sons.

Gallery C: 1560–1595. Papal gifts of Ferdinand II of Tyrol and Tyrolean armour of his sons.

Room 8: 1580–1610. Finely crafted weapons and Milanese parade armour.

Room 9: 1580–1620. Baroque armour and richly inlaid sporting weapons.

Arcaded Gallery: 17–19th. c. About a thousand weapons from the Court and hunting collections and from the armoury.

Hunt Room I: 1619–1657. Hunting weapons and equipment, including Archduke Leopold V's silver gun.

Location
Neue Burg, Heldenplatz, I

Underground station
Mariahilferstrasse (U2)

Bus
2A

Trams
1, 2, D, J, T

Opening times
Mon., Wed.–Fri.
10 a.m.–4 p.m.
Sat. and Sun 9 a.m.–
4 p.m.

Hunt Room II: 1667–1720. Fine hunting weapons and Turkish weapons seized as booty in the time of Leopold I.

Hunt Room III: 1720–1916. Imperial hunting weapons and equipment of the 18th and 19th c.

Wallfahrtskirche Maria Grün

See Prater

Wallfahrtskirche Maria Hilf (church)   C3

Location
65 Mariahilferstrasse, VI

Underground station
Mariahilferstrasse (U2)

Trams
52, 58

In the Maria Hilf pilgrimage church there are numerous sacred objects which pilgrims came to venerate. The "Gnadenbild" (Portrayal of Mercy) is a copy of the original in the Mariahilfberg at Passau.

After the destruction of the original chapel by the Turks, it was rebuilt in 1683, probably by Sebastiano Carlone. It underwent considerable alterations and was dedicated in 1730.

In a chapel built on to the church there is a monumental figure of Christ on the Cross. It comes from the "Malefizspitzbubenhaus", an ancient prison. It used to stand in Rauhensteingasse, and criminals used to be conveyed from there to the Hoher Markt (see entry) where they were executed.

**Wiener Sängerknaben (Vienna Boys' Choir)   A5

Location
Augarten-Palais II
(Boarding School of the
Vienna Boys' Choir)

Masses
In the Chapel of the
Wiener Hofburg: Jan.–
end June and mid
Sept.–Christmas Sun. and
Holy Days 9.15 a.m.

Nowadays there are four Vienna Boys' Choirs. Two are generally away touring, and one sings Mass on Sundays in the Chapel of the Hofburg (see entry). Each choir consists of 24 boys. After the boys' voices break they join the "Chor Viennensis".

The boys' choir to sing at church services for the Court was founded in 1498 under Maximilian I. For a long time the young choristers were paid out of the Emperor's Privy Purse. The most brilliant period for the Boys' Choir was the time of the Viennese classics when Mozart, Haydn and Beethoven wrote their incomparable Masses. Joseph Haydn was a chorister in the Court choir from 1740 to 1749, as was Franz Schubert from 1808 to 1813.

Winterpalais des Prinzen Eugen (palace)   C4

Location
3 Himmelpfortgasse, I

Underground station
Stephansplatz (U1)

Prince Eugene's town mansion has been occupied by the Ministry of Finance since 1848. There was almost an architectural tragedy when the conqueror of the Turks decided to change architects while construction was in progress. J. B. Fischer von Erlach was in charge from 1695 to 1698, but he was replaced by J. L. von Hildebrandt from 1702 to 1724.

Prince Eugene died here in 1736. He did not receive the final respects to which he was entitled. Emperor Charles VI was not present at his burial. In fact he went off to Laxenburg the day before "to pass the time". Prince Eugene's heiress, Anna Victoria of Savoy-Soissons, squandered the inheritance in a short while. In the end Maria Theresa purchased the palace for the State in 1752.

Visitors are allowed only into the vestibule with the Hercules Fountain and the famous ceremonial staircase.

Wotruba Kirche (Church of the Most Holy Trinity)

This church stands on St Georgenberg. It has no tower, no dome, no pillars and no gables; it gains its powerful effect by being constructed of 152 cast concrete cubic blocks piled one above another in an asymmetrical pattern. Designed by Fritz Wotruba (1907–75), one of the most famous Austrian sculptors, the church was dedicated in 1976. The building is intended to demonstrate that chaos can only be overcome by law and order.

Holy Trinity Church is a religious centre for the local community and also acts as a State school, an institute of home education and a school for the physically handicapped.

In the basement of the building which is 50 ft (15·5 m) high, 98 ft (30 m) long and 72 ft (22 m) wide, are meeting-rooms, an archive, a sacristy and a room for servers. The church itself can accommodate 250 worshippers. The altar consists of a marble block with a cross which is a replica of one which Wotruba made for the castle chapel of Bruchsal

Opening times: Sat. 2–8 p.m.; also Apr.–Sept. Mon.–Fri. 2–6 p.m., Sun. 9 a.m.–6 p.m.; Mar. and Oct. Tues.–Fri. 2–5 p.m., Sun. 9 a.m.–6 p.m.; Nov.–Feb. Tues.–Fri. 2.30–4.30 p.m., Sun. 9 a.m.–5 p.m.

Location
Mauer, corner of Georgsgasse/Rysergasse XXIII

Bus
60A (from S-/R-rail station Liesing)

Wotruba Kirche

*Zentralfriedhof (Cemetery)

Vienna's Central Cemetery was opened in 1874. It is the largest cemetery in Austria, with an area of 1 sq. mile (2·5 km^2). From the Main Gate (Gate Two) an avenue leads to the "graves of honour" reserved for famous personalities and the vault of the Austrian Federal President. The cemetery is open in spring and autumn from 7 a.m. to 6 p.m., in summer from 7 a.m. to 7 p.m., and in winter from 8 a.m. to 5 p.m. (entry up to 30 minutes before closing time).

The following musicians are among the many notable persons laid to rest here: Beethoven, Brahms, Gluck, Mozart (commemorative grave), Schubert, Johann Strauss (the Elder and Younger), Suppé and Wolf.

Location
234 Simmeringer Hauptstrasse, XI

S-Bahn station
Zentralfriedhof (S7)

Tram
71

Zum grünen Anker (restaurant)   B/C5

An aroma of Italian specialities hangs over it, for the Grüner Anker, where the Viennese first came to enjoy a glass of wine and later on a glass of beer, has specialised in Italian cooking since 1820. It was a favourite meeting-place for Schubert and his friends, and Grillparzer was a regular customer.

Close by the Grüner Anker stands the Kipfelhaus (The Croissant House) at 8 Grünargergasse. It was here that the famous Viennese delicacy started life, for here the first croissant was baked in 1683, probably as a joke at the expense of the Turkish crescent moon symbol.

Location
10 Grünangergasse, I

Underground station
Stephansplatz (U1)

Practical Information

During 1988 all telephone numbers in Vienna will be digitalised. Some numbers given in this guide may, therefore, be changed.

Advance booking

Theatre box-offices

The box-offices selling tickets in advance for the Staatsoper (State Opera), Burgtheater, Volksoper and Akademietheater are situated at Hanuschhof, I, entrance 3, Hanuschgasse, and 1 Goethegasse, tel. 53 24-0 (for information only).
Open: Mon.–Sat. 9 a.m.–5 p.m., Sun., public holidays 9 a.m.–noon.
Advance ticket sales always open four days before the date of the performance. For first nights or performances with famous guest artists theatre-lovers often start queueing up many hours – and sometimes through the night – before tickets go on sale.
All other theatres have their own box-offices. It is advisable to check by telephone whether tickets are available. Details of all theatre and cabaret programmes (together with box-office telephone numbers) are published in the "Kurier", the daily newspaper.

Postal bookings (from abroad)

All postal applications for tickets must arrive at the box-office at least 10 days before the performance. The address to write to is:

Österreichischer Bundestheaterverband
Bestellbüro
A 1010 Wien
1 Goethestrasse

Ticket Agencies

Tickets for all performances can be obtained through private agencies who normally charge a commission of up to 25% of the price of the ticket. Centrally located ticket agencies are:

Flamm, 3 Kärntner-Ring, I; tel. 52 42 25
E. Roessler, 33 Kärntnerstrasse, I; tel. 52 38 02
Weihburg, 3 Weihburggasse, I; tel. 52 84 34
Wiener Verkehrsbüro, 5 Opernring, I; tel. 5 60 00

Spanish Riding School

In order to avoid disappointment it is vital to reserve tickets for the Spanish Riding School well in advance. Performances are on Sunday mornings and Wednesday evenings. The Spanish Riding School (A 1010 Wien, Hofburg) accepts advance bookings for Sundays only and tickets for Wednesday displays and the short programmes can only be obtained through theatre ticket agencies and travel agencies.

American Express, 21–23 Kärntnerstrasse, I; tel. 5 51 40
Austria Reiseservice, 3 Himmelpfortgasse, I; tel. 5 12 05 95
Austrobus, Dr-Karl-Lueger-Ring, I; tel. 6 31 71 10
Cosmos, 15 Kärntner-Ring, I; tel. 5 15 33
Flamm, 3 Kärntner-Ring, I; tel. 52 42 25
Intropa, 38 Kärntnerstrasse, I; tel. 5 15 14

Niederösterreichisches Landesreisebüro, 2 Heidenschuss, I; tel. 63 47 73
Ruela Reisen, 1 Fleischmarkt, I; tel. 66 36 26
Wagons-lits-Reisebüro, 2 Kärntner-Ring, I; tel. 65 76 31

Seats for Sunday concerts of the Vienna Boys' Choir in the Burgkapelle must be booked at least eight weeks in advance at the Verwaltung der Hofmusikkapelle, A 1010 Wien. — Vienna Boys' Choir

Tickets may be collected on payment at the Burgkapelle on Fridays between 11 a.m. and noon or on Sundays by 9 a.m. at the latest. Only 2 tickets per person are allowed. Written applications may be made to Wiener Philharmoniker, 12 Bösendorferstrasse, A 1010 Wien.

Airlines

Austrian Airlines, 18 Kärntner-Ring A 1010 Wien, I; tel. (02 22) 65 57 57 and (reservations) 68 00
    608 Fifth Avenue, Suite 507, New York
    50 Conduit Street, London W1

British Airways, 10 Kärntner-Ring, A 1010 Wien, I; tel. (02 22) 65 76 91

Pan Am, Kärntner-Ring, A 1010 Wien, I; tel. (02 22) 52 66 46

TWA, c/o Austrian Airlines, 18 Kärtner-Ring, A 1010 Wien, I; tel. (02 22) 68 00

Canadian Pacific Airlines, c/o Hilton Centre, Am Stadtpark, A 1030 Wien; tel. (02 22) 75 75 76

Airport

Schwechat, Vienna's Airport, is 11 miles (17 km) SE of the city centre (Motorway). Its modern facilities include banks, restaurants, a supermarket, newspaper and souvenir shops, Duty Free shop, car hire kiosk, a free accommodation information service and a tourist information office (see Tourist Information).
Schwechat will soon have a "finger boarding system", so that passengers will be able to board and disembark along bridges.

There is a bus service between the airport and the City Air Terminal (3, Hotel Hilton/Stadtpark) from 6 a.m. to 7.20 p.m. every 20–30 minutes and from 7.20 to 10.10 p.m. every 40–70 minutes. There is also a shuttle service between the airport and the West and South stations. — Shuttle services
S-Bahn trains run hourly from the low-level station in the terminal building to Wien-Nord and Wien-Mitte stations.

Tel. 77 70 and 68 00. — Information

There are several flights each day by Austrian Airlines to Graz, Innsbruck, Klargenfurt and Salzburg and one flight daily to Linz. — Domestic flights

Antiques

Streets

A great many antique shops can be found in the narrow lanes S of the Graben including Bräunerstrasse, Stallburg-gasse, Dorotheergasse, Plankengasse, Spielgelgasse and Seilergasse.
There is also a smaller antiques district S of the Cathedral in Blutgasse, Wollzeile, Köllnerhofgasse and Schönlaterngasse. Items for sale span the range from medieval to Jugendstil (Art Nouveau) and the Viennese Workshops.

Flea Market

See A–Z, Naschmarkt

Auctions

See A–Z, Dorotheum

Auction rooms

Dorotheum

Out of interest or simply for their atmosphere it is worth paying a visit to an auction in one of the world's greatest salesrooms, the Dorotheum (see A–Z, Dorotheum) at 17 Dorotheergasse, I, tel. 52 85 65–0 (Underground station: Stephansplatz (U1)).
Auctions are held on Mon.–Fri. at 2 p.m. and Sat. at 10 a.m. Items are also on sale Mon.–Fri. 10 a.m.–6 p.m. and Sat. 8.30 a.m.–noon. At the auctions the emphasis on Monday is on table and decorative silver, Wednesday furniture and carpets, Thursday valuable jewellery and on Saturday decorative and practical items.

Banks

Opening times

Mon.–Fri. 8 a.m.–12.30 p.m. and 1.30 p.m.–3 p.m., Thurs. till 5.30 p.m., closed: Sat., Sun.

Eurocheques

Banks will cash Eurocheques and travellers' cheques.

Bureaux de change

Some bureaux de change are also open evenings and weekends in addition to the normal banking hours:
Westbahnhof, daily 7 a.m.–10 p.m.
Südbahnhof, daily, 6.30 a.m.–10 p.m.
Bahnhof Wien-Mitte, Mon.–Fri. 7.30 a.m.–7 p.m. Sat., Sun. 7.30 a.m.–1 p.m.
Airport, daily, 6.30 a.m.–11 p.m.
Air Terminal, daily, 8 a.m.–12.30 p.m. and 2–6 p.m.
Tourist Information, Opernpassage, daily 9 a.m.–7 p.m.

Boat trips

On the Danube

DDSG (Danube Steamship Company) operates regular services Vienna to Passau and Wachau as well as "Donaubus" round trips and excursions.

Departure times

Off season: Mon.–Sat. 1 and 3 p.m. (except Wed.). Sun. and public holidays 10 a.m., 1 and 3 p.m.
High season: daily 10 a.m., 1, 3 and 4.30 p.m., Thurs., Fri. and Sat. also 8.30 p.m.

Embarkation: Schwedenbrücke
Information: 265 Handelskai, II, tel. 26 65 36

ČPSD (Czech Danube Shipping Company) operates from Vienna to Bratislava, and Mahart, the Hungarian shipping line, from Vienna to Budapest. Journeys from Vienna to the Black Sea and Yalta are operated by the Soviet State Danube Shipping Company (SDP).

Information and bookings are obtainable at local travel agencies.

Embarkation

Breakdown service

Austrian Automobile and Touring Club (Österreichischer Automobil- Motorrad- und Touring-Club, ÖAMTC) tel. (02 22) 7 29 90; Breakdown service 120.

Driving, Motorcycling and Cycling Union of Austria (Auto-, Motor- und Radfahrerbund Österreichs, ARBÖ) tel. (02 22) 8 53 53 50; Breakdown service 123.

Automobile clubs

Calendar of events

1 January: New Year's Concert of the Vienna Philharmonic, New Year's Concert of the Vienna Symphony Orchestra

January

Last Thursday during "Fasching": Opera Ball

February

Spring Vienna International Trade Fair. (Exhibition grounds near the Prater and the Exhibition Hall.) Spring Flower Show in the Burggarten. Viennale Film Festival (in Urania)

March

Spring flower show in the Burggarten. The Prater opens. City Festival in the streets and squares of the inner city

April

Vienna Festival (Wiener Festwochen – end May to mid June). Danube Island Festival

May

Art auction in the Dorotheum. Musical Summer (until September). Folk Festival on the Danube Island

June

"Grüne Galerie" Exhibition in Stadtpark. World Youth Festival for music and visual arts. Vienna International College courses (until August). Summer courses of the "Verein Wiener Musikseminar". Spectaculum in the University Church

July

"Grüne Galerie" Exhibition in Stadtpark

August

Autumn Vienna International Trade Fair. Opening of the opera season. Austrian Film Festival. Folk Festival in the Prater

September

Theatre premières. Viennale in the Künstlerhaus Cinema

October

Art auction in the Dorotheum. Schubert Festival

November

Christ Child market on the Rathausplatz. Nativity cribs in the Peterskirche. Art Auction in the Dorotheum. Christmas exhibition in the Künstlerhaus. 31.12.: Fanfare from the loggia of the Rathaus. Imperial Ball in the Hofburg

December

Camp sites

Camp sites

There are five large camp sites within a 9 mile radius of the city.

Campingplatz Wien-West I (no reservation)
40 Hüttelbergstrasse, XIV, tel. 94 14 49
Tram 49, bus 52B
Open: Mid May to mid September

Campingplatz Wien-West II (no reservation)
80 Hüttelbergerstrasse, XIV, tel. 94 23 14
Tram 49, bus 52B
Open: April to October

Campingplatz Wien-Süd (no reservation)
269 Brietenfurterstrasse, XXIII, tel. 86 92 18
Tram 52, bus 62B
Open: May to mid September

Camping Wien-Süd (Rodaun)
Rodaun, XXIII, tel. 88 41 54
Tram 60
Open: End March to November

Campingplatz Schlosspark Laxenburg
Münchendorferstrasse Laxenburg, tel. 022 36–7 13 33
Bus from bus station Wien-Mitte
Open: April to October

Camping guide

Details of camp sites in and around Vienna, i.e. size of site and plots, facilities, location, opening times, directions how to get there, etc. are published in the annual ADAC and AA camping guides.

"Wild camping"

In Vienna it is not allowed to spend the night in a caravan or camper outside official camp sites. Offenders are liable to be fined. Outside the city three nights are permitted.

Car hire

Avis, 1 Opernring, I; tel. 5 87 35 95
Budget, Hilton Air Terminal, III; tel. 75 65 65
Europcar, 15 Mollardgasse, VI; tel. 5 97 16 75
Hertz, 17 Kärntner-Ring, I; tel. 5 12 86 77
InterRent, 9 Schubertring, VII; tel. 75 67 17

Cemeteries

Protestant Cemetery
Matzleinsdorferplatz, X
Bus 14A, trams 6, 18
The cemetery dates from 1856 and contains the graves of Friedrich Hebbel, Adele Sandrock and Heinrich Laube. The cemetery chapel is a brick building by Theophil von Hansen in the Byzantine style

Zentralfriedhof (Central Cemetery)
see A–Z, Zentralfriedhof

Hietzing Cemetery
15 Maxingstrasse, XIII
Bus 56B, tram 58, Underground station: Hietzing (U4)
Vienna's most beautiful cemetery lies on the edge of the
Schönbrunn Palace Park.
It has tombs of the Austrian aristocracy and many Empire and
Biedermeier tombstones. Here are the resting-places of Franz
Grillparzer, Gustav Klimt, Otto Wagner, Auer von Welsbach,
Field-Marshal Konrad von Hötzendorf and Chancellor Engel-
bert Dollfuss.

Chemists

Mon.–Fri. 8 a.m.–noon, 2–6 p.m., Sat. 8 a.m.–noon.   Opening times

Telephone 1550 to find out which chemists are open 24 hours   Emergency service
a day and on Sundays.

Internationale Apotheke (International Chemist) at 17   International chemist
Kärntner-Ring, I, stocks a wide range of foreign medicines.

Church services

In most of Vienna's Catholic churches services commence at   Catholic
6 a.m., on Saturdays at 6 p.m. On Sundays and public holi-
days there is also High Mass at 9 a.m. and 10 a.m. For information telephone 5 32 56 10

Old Catholic services   Old Catholic
6 Wipplingerstrasse, I, tel. 63 71 33
Service: Sun. 10 a.m.

Protestant services (Lutheran)   Protestant
18 Dorotheergasse, I, tel. 52 83 92
Service: Sun. 8 a.m. and 2 p.m.

Protestant services (Reformed)
16 Dorotheergasse, I, tel. 52 83 93
Service: Sun. 10 a.m.

Jewish services in the Synagogue ("City Temple")   Jewish
4 Seitenstettengasse, I, tel. 63 45 16
Services daily morning and evening.

Islamic prayer hours, Islamic Centre   Islamic
17–19 Am Hubertusdamm, II, tel. 30 13 89

Coffee houses (Kaffeehäuser)

The coffee house is just as much a part of the ambience of
Vienna as the Cathedral, but it was a Pole, Franz Georg Kolschitzky, who was the founder of these establishments. It is
said that he brought coffee back to Vienna from Turkey in
1683 as spoils of war and two years later was granted an
Imperial licence to serve the beverage. The triumphal progress of the coffee house began and it became an institution.
Newspapers and games, especially billiards became a funda-
mental feature of every good coffee house, and every good
citizen became a regular customer of his favourite rendezvous where he met his acquaintances, chatted, played

games, studied, brooded, wrote and observed for hours on end or even a whole day. Until 1840 the coffee house was exclusively for men and only with the advent of establishments with music during the Biedermeier period were ladies allowed in. At this time luxuriously appointed coffee houses came into being, especially the elegant ones in the Ring. The Vienna Kaffeehaus became part of Viennese culture, where literary figures, artists, scholars, politicians and journalists used to meet. When the Danubian monarchy came to an end the heyday of the coffee house was over, but there has recently been a renaissance of these establishments as meeting-places and centres of communication.

Commemorative locations

Gustinus-Ambrosi-Museum
1a Augarten/Scherzergasse, II
Open: Fri., Sun. 10 a.m.–4 p.m.

Bahr Memorial Room (National Library)
1 Josefsplatz, I
Open: Tues., Thur. 11 a.m.–noon on request; tel. 5 12 24 27

Bauernfeld Memorial Room
Villa Wertheimstein
96 Döblinger Hauptstrasse, XIX
Open: Sat. 3.30 p.m.–6 p.m., Sun. 10 a.m.–noon.

Beethoven Commemorative sites
(see A–Z Pasqualatihaus) also
22 Laimgrubengasse, VI
Open: May–Sept. Sun. 10 a.m.–noon

92 Döblinger Hauptstrasse, XIX
Open: Daily (except Mon.) 10 a.m.–12.15 p.m., 1–4.30 p.m.

Heimito-von-Doderer commemorative site
43 Währingerstrasse, IX
Open: Sun. 10 a.m.–noon

Commemorative site for the victims of the Austrian freedom struggle
see A–Z Altes Rathaus

Grillparzer Memorial Room in the Historical Museum of Vienna
see A–Z, Historisches Museum

Kálmán Memorial Room (National Library)
1 Josefsplatz, I
Open; Tues., Thur. 11 a.m.–noon on request; tel. 5 12 24 27

Reinhard Memorial Room (National Library)
1 Josefsplatz, I
Open: Tues., Thur. 11 a.m.–noon on request; tel. 5 12 24 27

Schubert, room in which he died,
6 Kettenbrückengasse, IV
Open: Daily (except Mon.) 10 a.m.–12.15 p.m., 1–4.30 p.m.

Johann-Strauss House
see A–Z Praterstrasse

Ziehrer Memorial Room (National Library)
1 Josefsplatz, I
Open: Tues., Thur. 10 a.m.–noon on request; tel. 5 12 24 27

Museums   See entry

Currency/currency regulations

The unit of currency is the Austrian schilling (öS) of 100 groschen.
There are banknotes for 20, 50, 100, 500 and 1000 schillings and coins in denominations of 10 and 50 groschen and 1, 5, 10, 25, 50, 100, 500 and 1000 schillings.

Currency

There are no limits on the amount of foreign currency that can be taken into Austria or brought out. Austrian currency can be taken in without limit on the amount, but no more than 50,000 schillings may be taken out without special permission.
It is advisable to carry money in the form of travellers' cheques or to take an international credit card such as Master-card, American Express, Visa, or Eurocard.

Currency regulations

Customs regulations

Visitors to Austria over the age of 17 can take in duty-free, for their own use, clothing, toilet articles and jewellery, together with other personal effects, including two cameras and a portable movie-camera, each with 10 films, a portable type-writer, binoculars, a portable radio, a portable television set, a tape-recorder, a record-player and 10 records, musical instru-ments, camping equipment and sports gear; also 1–2 days' supply of provisions for the journey (including tea and coffee). Visitors may also take in duty-free 200 cigarettes, 50 cigars, or 250 grammes of tobacco, 2 litres of wine and 1 litre of spirits.

On entry

Visitors, who take out purchased Austrian goods can have their VAT (18 or 30%) refunded if the amount of the purchase exceeds öS1000. The shop assistant will make out the receipt in the name of the purchaser, entering the tax separately from the total, and complete Form U34.
On departure both the merchandise and the receipt must be shown to Austrian Customs who then will confirm that the goods are being exported.
After export has been confirmed the receipts have to be returned to the shop which will in turn refund the VAT amount by cheque.

On departure

Motorists who purchase goods in a duty-free shop can get VAT refunded at the frontier customs office by producing the receipt and Form U34.

Doctors

In emergency call 141; the telephone is manned from Mon-day to Thursday from 7 p.m. to 7 a.m. and from 7 p.m. on Friday to 7 a.m. on Monday.

Doctors on call

The addresses of dentists on duty can be obtained by calling 52 95 04 or 55 46 46.

Dental emergencies

Embassies and consular offices

United Kingdom	Embassy: 40 Reisnerstrasse A 1030 Wien; tel. (02 22) 73 15 75–79 Consular Section: 8 Wallnerstrasse A 1010 Wien; tel. (02 22) 63 75 02
United States	Embassy: 16 Boltzmanngasse A 1091 Wien IX; tel. (02 22) 31 55 11
Canada	Embassy: 10 Dr-Karl-Lueger-Ring A 1010 Wien; tel. (02 22) 63 66 26–28

Emergency calls

For most important numbers see page 2

Fiacres

See A–Z, Fiaker Museum

Food and drink

Food

Viennese meals generally consist of soup, a meat dish and a sweet. The main meal of the day is usually the midday meal. Meals are served early, lunch between noon and 2 p.m. and evening meals from 6 to 9 p.m. Some restaurants do not serve hot meals after 10 p.m.

Drink

Apart from good beer (1 seidel=0·6 pint, 1 krügel=0·9 pint) the most popular beverage is wine. This is mostly from Lower Austria and Burgenland and is often drunk "g'spritzt", i.e. mixed with soda water.

The wines on offer include green Veltliner, Rhine Riesling, White Burgundy, Traminer Welschriesling, Muskat, Ottonel, Neuburger, Müller Thurgau, Zierfandler, Rotgipfler, Blaufränkischer, Blue Portuguese and Blue Burgundy.

An evening of wine-drinking is best spent at the "Heurige" (see entry) or cellar bars.

The ordering of coffee in a Vienna café is an art in itself: the customer is expected to specify exactly how he wants his coffee to be served. Visitors may find the following vocabulary useful.

The basis of every cup of Viennese coffee is **Mokka** (mocha). If you ask simply for "coffee" (*Kaffee*), you will usually get a "Brauner" (see below). Coffee is always accompanied by a glass of water.

Brauner (kleiner, grosser)	"brown" (small or large): with little milk
Dunkel	"dark": with little milk
Einspänner	hot coffee with whipped cream, served in a glass
Elskaffee	cold coffee, served in a glass with vanilla ice-cream, whipped cream and a wafer
Espresso *(Es)*	machine-made espresso
Fiaker	a "grosser Schwarzer", served in a glass
Gestreckt	diluted with water
Gold	a golden-brown "Melange"
Kaffee ohne Kaffee	"coffee without coffee" (caffeine-free)
Kaffee verkehrt	"coffee the wrong way round": little coffee but plenty of milk
Kaisermelange	"Schwarzer" with yolk of egg
Kapuziner	"Capuchin": dark-brown melange
Konsul	"Schwarzer" with a dash of cream
Kurz	"short": very strong
Licht	"light": with a lot of milk
Mazagran	a glass of cold coffee with maraschino, icecubes and a straw
Melange	"mixture": medium dark
Mokka	strong black Viennese coffee
Mokka gespritzt	coffee with a dash of brandy
Nusschwarzer	"nut-black": Mokka
Obers	cream
Obers gespritzt	cream with a dash of coffee
Portion Kaffee	coffee with a jug of milk, to be mixed according to taste
Schale	cup
Schlag(obers)	whipped cream
Schwarzer (kleiner, grosser)	black coffee (small or large)
Schwarzer gespritzt	coffee with a dash of rum
Teeschale	cup of milk
Teeschale Obers gespritzt	cup of cream with some coffee
Türkischer	Turkish coffee boiled in a small copper coffee-pot (along with sugar if taken)
natur	unfiltered
passiert	filtered
Weisser	"white": caffeine-free coffee

See Viennese Cuisine

Cuisine

Heuriger

The term "Heuriger" has two meanings; on the one hand it describes the wine and on the other the place where it is sold. Heuriger is the newest wine which is drawn from the barrel in spring and is on sale until the following year, when the next vintage is ready; then it is called "alter" (old).

Heurige also denotes inns where the vintner sells the wine which he has produced. In 1784 the Emperor Joseph II granted to vintners the privilege of selling their own wine for 300 days in the year in a "Buschenschank" (bush inn). The term refers to the bunch of spruce branches which is placed over the entrance to the establishment.

Nowadays many Heurige-restaurants are franchised businesses, some open throughout the year, others for only a few months generally early in the summer. In these restaurants food is served and music provided. In authentic Heurige, however, music is rarely heard and when it is, it is not loud and cheerful but quiet and sad. In summer many Heurige provide shady gardens for their customers.

The most famous district of Vienna for Heurige is Grinzing (see A–Z), but the characteristic bush sign can also be found in Sievering, Nussdorf, Neustift, Heiligenstadt, Stammersdorf and Oberlaa. A brochure called "Heurige in Wien", obtainable from the Verkehrsamt (tourist office), gives times of opening and facilities offered (garden, music, etc.).

Hotels (selection)

Reservations

Visitors are recommended to make and confirm reservations before departure.

Hotels are officially classified in five categories: 5 star = Luxury, 4 star = first-class, 3 star = good middle-class, 2 star = simple, 1 star = modest. A brochure of hotels is obtainable from the Vienna Tourist Association (Fremdenverkehrsverband) or from Tourist Information.

The prices given below in Austrian schillings are for accommodation (including breakfast, service and taxes). They are average prices, intended as a guide to price levels.

Category	Double room	Single room
*****	1500–2400	1000–1700
****	800–1100	600– 800
***	560– 650	400– 600
**	450– 530	250– 350
*	300– 360	240– 270

*****

Ambassador, 6 Neuer Markt, tel. 5 14 66, 176 b.
Bristol, 1 Kärntner-Ring, tel. 51 51 60, 270 b.
Clima Villenhotel, 2c Nussberggasse, tel. 37 15 16, 70 b.
De France, 3 Schottenring, tel. 34 35 40, 320 b.
Hilton Wien, Am Stadtpark, tel. 75 26 52, 1200 b.
Im Palais Schwarzenberg, 9 Schwarzenbergplatz, tel. 78 45 15, 75 b.
Imperial, 16 Kärntner-Ring, tel. 65 17 65, 275 b.
Inter-Continental Vienna, 28 Johannesgasse, tel. 7 50 50, 933 b.

Parkhotel Schönbrunn, 10–14 Hietzinger Hauptstrasse, tel.
82 26 76, 798 b.
Sacher, 4 Philharmonikerstrasse, tel. 5 14 56, 202 b.
SAS Palais Hotel, 32 Weihburggasse, tel. 51 51 70, 308 b.
Vienna Marriott, 12a Parkring, tel. 51 51 80, 608 b.

AEZ-Hotel Zentrum, 2a Landstrasser Hauptstrasse, tel. ****
72 21 16, 126 b.
Albatros, 89 Liechtensteinstrasse, tel. 34 35 08, 140 b.
Alpha, 8 Botzmanngasse, tel. 31 16 46, 112 b.
Am Parkring, 12 Parkring, tel. 52 65 24, 106 b.
Am Schubertring, 11 Schubertring, tel. 7 21 55 10, 73 b.
Astoria, 32 Kärntnerstrasse, tel. 51 57 70, 190 b.
Bellevue, 5 Althanstrasse., tel. 3 45 63 10, 320 b.
Biedermeier im Sünnhof, 28 Landstrasser Hauptstrasse, tel.
75 55 75, 420 b.
Bohemia, 9 Turnergasse, tel. 83 66 48, 203 b.
Capricorno, 3–4 Schwedenplatz, tel. 6 33 10 40, 79 b.
Clima Cityhotel, 21a Theresianum, tel. 65 16 96, 78 b.
Europa, 3 Neuer Markt, tel. 5 15 94, 150 b.
Graben, 3 Dorotheergasse, tel. 5 12 15 31, 86 b.
Hohe Warte, 7 Steinfeldgasse, tel. 37 32 12, 71 b.
Kaiserhof, 10 Frankenberggasse, tel. 65 17 01, 143 b.
Kaiserin Elisabeth, 3 Weihburggasse, tel. 51 52 60, 125 b.
König von Ungarn, 10 Schulerstrasse, tel. 5 26 52 00, 70 b.
Kummer, 71a Mariahilferstrasse, tel. 5 88 95, 165 b.
Mailbergerhof, 7 Annagasse, tel. 5 12 06 41, 80 b.
Maté, 34 Ottakringerstrasse, tel. 43 61 33, 233 b.
Modul, 78–80 Peter-Jordan-Strasse, tel. 4 71 58 40, 83 b.
Novotel Wien-West, Autobahnstation Auhof, tel. 97 25 42,
223 b.
Opernring, 11 Opernring, tel. 5 87 55 18, 70 b.
President, 23 Wallgasse, tel. 5 99 90, 160 b.
Prinz Eugen, 14 Wiedner Gürtel, tel. 65 17 41, 165 b.
Regina, 15 Rooseveltplatz, tel. 42 76 81, 232 b.
Ring, 1 Am Gestade, tel. 63 77 01, 50 b.
Römischer Kaiser, 16 Annagasse, tel. 5 12 77 51, 46 b.
Royal, 3 Singerstrasse, tel. 51 24 63 10, 162 b.
Stefanie, 12 Taborstrasse, tel. 24 24 12, 240 b.
Strudlhof, 1 Pasteurgasse, tel. 31 25 22, 100 b.
Tourhotel, (Oberlaa) 8 Kurbadstrasse, tel. 68 16 31, 520 b.
Tyrol, 15 Mariahilferstrasse, tel. 5 87 54 15, 68 b.

Austria, 3 Wolfengasse, tel. 5 15 23, 90 b. ***
Capri, 44–46 Praterstrasse, tel. 24 84 04, 80 b.
Ekazent, 22 Hietzinger Hauptstrasse, tel. 82 74 01, 64 b.
Fuchs, 138 Mariahilferstrasse, tel. 83 12 01, 120 b.
Kahlenberg, 1 Josefsdorf, tel. 32 12 51, 75 b.
Mariahilf, 121 Mariahilferstrasse, tel. 5 97 36 05, 120 b.
Mozart, 4 Julius-Tandler-Platz, tel. 34 15 37, 96 b.
Münchnerhof, 81 Mariahilferstrasse, tel. 5 88 25, 160 b.
Nordbahn, 72 Praterstrasse, tel. 24 54 33, 140 b.
Post, 24 Fleischmarkt, tel. 51 58 30, 180 b.
Wandl, 9 Petersplatz, tel. 63 63 17, 227 b.
Westbahn, 1 Pelzgasse, tel. 92 14 80, 100 b.
Wimberger, 34 Neubaugürtel, tel. 93 76 36, 173 b.
Zur Wiener Staatsoper, 11 Krugerstrasse, tel. 5 13 12 74, 50 b.

Altwienerhof, 6 Herklotzgasse, tel. 83 71 45, 37 b. **
Central, 8a Taborstrasse, tel. 24 24 05, 109 b.

Gabriel, 165 Landstrasser Hauptstrasse, tel. 72 67 54, 86 b.
Gloriette, 105 Linzerstrasse, tel. 92 11 46, 99 b.
Stadt Bamberg, 167 Marihilferstrasse, tel. 83 76 08, 95 b.
Steindl-Gasthof, 67 Triesterstrasse, tel. 6 04 12 78, 40 b.
Südbahn, 25 Weyringergasse, tel. 65 85 90, 50 b.
Wilhelmshof, 4 Kleine Stadtgutgasse, tel. 24 55 21, 75 b.

*

Fraanzenshof, 19 Grosse Stadtgutgasse, tel. 24 22 37, 74 b.
Hospiz, 15 Kenyongasse, tel. 93 13 04, 36 b.
Orient, 30–32 Tiefer Graben, tel. 63 73 07, 51 b.

There are many pensions which because of their family atmosphere are popular for longer stays, and also "season hotels" – students' accommodation is available during vacations.

Insurance

It is advisable to take out adequate medical insurance before leaving home. For nationals of the United Kingdom inpatient treatment in public hospitals is usually free (with a small charge for dependants), but other medical services must be paid for.
You are advised to apply to your local Social Security office, well before your date of departure, for a certificate of entitlement (Form E111).

Jazz

See Night life

Libraries, archives

Archives of the Vienna Philharmonic
12 Bösendorferstrasse, I
For specialists only, by prior appointment, tel. 6 55 09 72

Library of the Academy of Fine Art
See A–Z, Akademie der Bildenden Künste
Open Mon., Wed., Fri. 9 a.m.–4 p.m.; Tues., Thur., 9 a.m.–6 p.m., closed 15 July–14 August

Library of the Albertina
See A–Z, Albertina

Library of the Geologische Bundesanstalt (Federal Geological Institute)
23 Rasumofskygasse, III
For specialists only, open Mon. 1–4 p.m., Tues.–Fri. 8 a.m.–12.30 p.m.

Library of the Gesellschaft der Musikfreunde (Society of the Friends of Music)
12 Bösendorfstrasse, I
Open Mon., Wed., Fri. 9 a.m.–1 p.m.; closed 1 July–30 Sept.

Library of the Austrian Federal Railways
3 Praterstern, II
Open Mon.–Thurs. 9 a.m.–3 p.m., Fri. 9 a.m.–noon.

Library of the Austrian Museum for Applied Arts
See A–Z, Österreichisches Museum für angewandte Kunst
Open Mon., Thurs., Fri., Sun. 11 a.m.–6 p.m.

Library of the Austrian Folk Museum
See A–Z, Österreichisches Museum für Volkskunde

Library of Parliament
See A–Z, Parliament

Library of the Technical Museum for Industry and Trade
See A–Z, Technisches Museum für Industrie und Gewerbe

Library of the Museum of Art History
See A–Z, Kunsthistorisches Museum

Austrian National Library
See A–Z, Österreichische Nationalbibliothek

Journal reading room of the National Library
Neue Burg, Heldenplatz, middle entrance
Open Mon., Thurs. 9 a.m.–7.45 p.m., Tues., Wed., Fri.
9 a.m.–3.45 p.m., Sat. 9 a.m.–1 p.m.

University Library, 1 Dr-Karl-Lueger-Ring, I
For opening times of reading room tel. 4 30 00.

Vienna City and State Archives
2 Lichtenfelsgasse I, flight VI
Open Mon.–Fri. 8 a.m.–6 p.m.

Vienna City and State Library
2 Lichtenfelsgasse I, flight IV
Open Mon.–Thurs. 9 a.m.–6.30 p.m. Fri. 9 a.m.–4.30 p.m.

Lost property

22 Wasagasse, IX, tel. 3 16 61 10   Central lost property office
Underground station: Schottentor (U2)
Open Mon.–Fri. 8 a.m.–1 p.m.

The railway lost property office is: Zentralsammelstelle der
Österreichischen Bundesbahnen,
Westbahnhof, 2 Langauerstrasse
tel. 5 65 00 (S-Bahn stop: Westbahnhof)

Lost property found on trams or buses is collected at the
Vienna depots, tel. 65 93 00, and is sent to the Central lost
property office after three days.

Markets

Vienna's markets are at their most colourful in the morning
when there is the greatest selection of fruit, vegetables and
foodstuffs.
The following markets are not too far from the city centre:

Augustinermarkt
Landstrasser Hauptstrasse/Erdbergerstrasse, III
Station: Wien-Mitte, trams J and T

Naschmarkt
See A–Z, Naschmarkt

Schwendermarkt
Schwendergasse/Reichsapfelgasse, XV
Trams 52, 58

	Brunnenmarkt Brunnengasse, XVI Tram 44
Opening times	These markets are open Mon.–Fri. 6 a.m.–6.30 p.m. and Sat. 6 a.m.–1 p.m.

Museums

Admission to municipal museums marked "W" in the list below is free on Friday mornings; to national museums marked "St" it is free on the first Sunday in the month. By purchasing a collective ticket (14 coupons, obtainable in the museums) the admission for all municipal and national museums is reduced by up to 30%. There is no time limit for the collective ticket and it can be used by several persons in common.

Academy of Fine Arts (W)	See A–Z, Akademie der Bildenden Künste (Gemäldegalerie)
"Adler" Collection	See A–Z, Haarhof Heraldic and Genealogical exhibits
Albertina (St)	See A–Z, Albertina
Anatomica Plastica Collection	See A–Z, Josephinum
Art Gallery in the Stallburg	See A–Z, Neue Galerie in der Stallburg
Austrian Baroque Museum (St)	See A–Z, Belvedere-Schlösser, Österreichisches Barock-museum
Austrian Film Museum (St)	See A–Z, Albertina
Austrian Folk Museum	See A–Z, Österreichisches Museum für Volkskunde
Austrian Museum of Applied Art	See A–Z, Österreichisches Museum für Angewandte Kunst
Austrian Railway Museum (St)	See A–Z, Technisches Museum für Industrie und Gewerbe
Austrian Theatre Museum	See A–Z, Österreichische Nationalbibliothek
Carnuntum Open Air Museum	See A–Z, Carnuntum
Cathedral and Diocesan Museum	See A–Z, Dom- und Diözesanmuseum
Clock Museum (W)	See A–Z, Uhrenmuseum der Stadt Wien
Collection of Old Musical Instruments	See A–Z, Sammlung Alter Musikinstrumente
Collection of Popular Religious Art	See A–Z, Sammlung Religiöse Volkskunst
Collection of Weapons	See A–Z, Waffensammlung
Commemorative locations	See entry
Court Tableware and Silver Collection	See A–Z, Hofburg
Döblinger Regional Museum	Döblinger Bezirksmuseum 96 Döblinger Hauptstrasse, XIX Open Sat. 3.30–6 p.m., Sun. 10 a.m.–noon Biedermeier villa with commemorative rooms for Bauernfeld, the comic poet, and Ferdinand von Saar, the lyric poet. Also wine museum.
Ephesus Museum	See A–Z, Ephesos-Museum
Esperanto Museum	1 Josefsplatz, I (in the Austrian National Library) Open Mon., Wed., Fri. 9 a.m.–3.45 p.m.

On show at the Naschmarkt: fruit stalls . . .

. . . curios and heirlooms, bric-à-brac and objets d'art

Practical Information

Federal Pathological Anatomical Museum	2 Spitalgasse, IX (in "Narrenturm" General Hospital) Conducted tours Thur. 8–11 a.m. (closed in August)
Fiacre Museum	See A–Z, Fiakermuseum
Figaro House	See A–Z, Figarohaus
Film Museum (St)	See A–Z, Albertina
Fire Brigade Museum	Feuermuseum See A–Z, Am Hof
Freud Museum	19 Berggasse, IX Open Mon.–Fri. 9 a.m.–1 p.m., Sat., Sun. and public holidays 9 a.m.–3 p.m. Memorabilia of Sigmund Freud.
Funeral Museum	Bestattungsmuseum 19 Goldeggasse, IV, tel. 65 16 31–2 by prior appointment only Mon.–Fri. noon–3 p.m.
Gallery of Austrian Art of the 19th and 20th centuries (St)	See A–Z, Belvedere-Schlösser, Österreichische Gallerie des 19. und 20. Jahrhunderts
Gallery of the 19th c.	See A–Z, Neue Galerie in der Stallburg
Gallery of the 19th and 20th c.	See A–Z, Belvedere-Schlösser
Globe Museum	See A–Z, Osterreichische Nationalbibliothek
Haydn Museum	See A–Z, Haydn Museum
Hermes Villa	See A–Z, Lainzer Tiergarten (zoo)
Hernalser Regional Museum	Hernalser Bezirksmuseum 72–74 Hernalser Hauptstrasse, XVII Open Mon. 4–8 p.m. (closed July, Aug.) Collection illustrating the history of the Hernal District.
House of the Sea	Haus des Meeres (Vivarium Wien) Esterhàzypark, VI Open daily 9 a.m.–6 p.m. About 3,000 living animals; particularly impressive are the tropical and Mediterranean aquariums.
Josefstadt Regional Museum	See A–Z, Josefstädter Bezirksmuseum
Lehár Museum	Schikaneder-Schlössl 18 Hackhofer Gasse, XIX Open by arrangement for groups Late Baroque palace, home of Franz Lehár; museum
Leopoldstädter Regional Museum	Leopoldstädter Bezirksmuseum 9 Karmelitergasse, II Open Wed. 5.15–7 p.m., Sat. 2.30–5 p.m., Sun. 10 a.m.–noon Cultural history of the region
Mozart Museum	See A–Z, Figarohaus
Museum of Army History	See A–Z, Heeresgeschichtliches Museum
Museum of Art History	See A–Z, Kunsthistorisches Museum
Museum of Austrian Art of the Middle Ages	Museum mittelalterlicher österreichischer Kunst See A–Z, Belvedere Schlösser
Museum of the Austrian Freedom Struggle	See A–Z, Altes Rathaus
Museum of the Austrian Linguistic Enclave	Österreichisches Sprachinselmuseums 29 Semperstrasse, XVIII Open by arrangement; tel. 3 46 09 12 History of the language and culture of Austria and of the old Austrian linguistic enclave

Zirkus- und Clownmuseum 9 Karmelitergasse, II Open Wed. 5.30–7 p.m., Sat. 2.30–5 p.m., Sun. 9 a.m.–noon	Museum of Clowns and Circuses
See A–Z, Museum für Völkerkunde	Museum of Ethnology
Museum für Hufbeschlag, Beschirrung und Besattelung 11 Linke Bahngasse, III Open Mon.–Thur. 1.30–3.30 p.m. Educational collection and workshop	Museum of Farriery and Saddlery
See A–Z, Josephinum	Museum of the Institute of Medical History
See A–Z, Gartenpalais Liechtenstein	Museum of Modern Art (St)
See A–Z, Niederösterreichisches Landesmuseum	Museum of the State of Lower Austria
See A–Z, Museum des 20. Jahrhunderts (temporary exhibitions)	Museum of the 20th Century
See A–Z, Naturhistorisches Museum	Natural History Museum (St)
Neidharet-Fresken-Haus 19 Tuchlauben, I Open daily except Mon. 10 a.m.–12.15 p.m., 1–4.30 p.m. The frescoes, dating from about 1400, which were discovered in 1979 in a former reception room of an old Viennese mansion, were restored by 1982; they illustrate the songs of the Minnesänger Neidhart von Reuental (12th–13th c.).	Neidhart Frescoes
Alte Backstube (exhibition room) See A–Z, Josefstädter Bezirksmuseum (regional museum)	Old Bakehouse
Alte Schmiede (exhibition room) See A–Z, Schönlaterngasse	Old Smithy
See A–Z, Bundessammlung alter Stilmöbel	Period Furniture at the Federal Furniture Collection
Glockenmuseum (Glockensammlung Pfundner) 38 Troststrasse, X Open Wed. 2–5 p.m. Old church bells	Pfundner Bell Collection
See A–Z, Schottenstift	Picture Gallery of the Schottenstift
See A–Z, Prater	Planetarium
See A–Z, Technisches Museum für Industrie und Gewerbe	Post and Telegraphic Museum (St)
See A–Z, Prater	Prater Museum (St)
See A–Z, Am Hof	Roman Remains (W)
See A–Z, Schubert Museum	Schubert Museum
See A–Z, Secession	Secession (St)
See A–Z, Hofburg	Secular and Sacred Treasury
Sammlung Sobek See A–Z, Geymüller-Schlössl	Sobek Collection of Old Viennese Clocks
See A–Z, Pasqualatihaus	Stifter Museum
See A–Z, Technisches Museum für Industrie und Gewerbe	Technical Museum of Industry and Trade (St)
See A–Z, Maria-Theresien-Platz	Tobacco Museum
Schatzkammer des Deutschen Ordens See A–Z, Deutschordenshaus	Treasury of the German Order

Practical Information

Urania Observatory	1 Uraniastrasse, I Conducted tours Wed., Fri., Sat. 8 p.m. (9 p.m. Apr.–Sept.) on clear nights as well as Sun. mornings at 11 (closed in Aug.)
Vienna City Historical Museum	See A–Z, Historisches Museum der Stadt Wien
Vienna Tram Museum	Wiener Tramway Museum The Erdberg Depot of the Vienna Transport Undertaking 109 Erdbergstrasse, III Open: 31 May–26 Oct., Sat., Sun. and public holidays 9 a.m.–4 p.m. Trips by "Oldtimer tram" (31 May–26 Oct.) from Karlplatz; Sat. 2.30 p.m., Sun. and public holidays 10 a.m. The oldest exhibit is a horse-drawn tram of 1871
Virgilian Chapel (W)	See A–Z, Stephansplatz with collection of historical Viennese porcelain
Wine Museum	See Döblinger Regional Museum (above)

Music

Programme details	The Vienna Tourist Board (Wiener Fremdenverkehrsband) publishes monthly a free survey of musical events
Tickets	See Advance booking, except where otherwise stated
Opera/Ballet	See A–Z, Staatsoper Staatsoper im Künstlerhaus, 5 Karlsplatz, I Volksoper, 78 Währingerstrasse
Operetta/Musicals	Raimundtheater, 18–20 Wallgasse Theater an der Wien, 6 Linke Wienzeile VI Tickets for both theatres: written application to the Stadthalle, 14 Vogelweidplatz, tel. 4 28 00–208. Tickets can also be booked in advance at: 1. Zentralsparkasse, 2 Stephansplatz, I, and 2. Creditanstalt, 1 Kärntner-Ring, I, 6–8 Schottengasse and at other branches of the banks
Concert Halls	Funkhaus des Österreichischen Rundfunks (Austrian Radio headquarters), 30a Argentinerstrasse Broadcasts with an audience Tickets obtainable in advance from the above address or by telephone 65 95/881 Mon.–Fri. 4–7 p.m. Konzerthaus, 20 Lothringerstrasse, III Great Hall, Mozart Hall, Schubert Hall; orchestral concerts, soloists and chamber music. Tickets obtainable in advance by telephone, Mon.–Fri. 9 a.m.–6 p.m., Sat. 9 a.m.–1 p.m. Musikverein – see A–Z, Musikvereingebäude Sofiensäle, 17 Marzergasse, III, concerts on summer evenings. tel. 72 21 98/29 Bösendorfer Saal, 14 Graf Starhemberg-Gasse, IV, tel. 65 66 51

Haydn Haus, 19 Haydngasse, VI
Urania, Uraniastrasse, I, tel. 72 61 91

Burgkapelle, see A–Z, Hofburg; Burgkapelle   Church Music
Michaelerkirche, see A–Z; tickets: tel. 52 14 90
Augustinerkirche, Josefsplatz, I, tel. 52 33 38
Basilika Maria Treu, Jodok-Fink-Platz, VIII, tel. 42 04 25
Karlskirche, Karlsplatz, IV, tel. 65 61 87

See Night life   Jazz/Live music

See Festivals   Festivals

Night life

This is what the Viennese call the night-life quarter between   "Bermuda Triangle"
the Cathedral and the Danube, bounded by Schönlaterngasse
and Bäkkerstrasse (see entries) as far as St Ruprecht's Church.

Pets

In view of the stringent regulations regarding the prevention
of rabies you are strongly advised not to attempt to take pets
out of the U.K. or to bring them in when you return.

Police

Federal Police Headquarters of Vienna
(Bundespolizeidirekton Wien)
7–9 Schottenring
tel. 3 13 10

District Police Headquarters
(Bezirkspolizeikommissariat)
Inner City
3 Deutschmeisterplatz
tel. 31 76 01

Tel. 133 (24 hours a day)   Emergency

Postal services

Generally Mon.–Fri. 8 a.m.–noon, 2–6 p.m.   Opening times
The Head Post Office, 19 Fleischmarkt, I, and all the post
offices at stations are open 24 hours a day.

Letters up to 20 grammes within Austria 4 öS, to the United   Postal rates
Kingdom 6 öS, to the United States or Canada 8 öS (plus
1·5 öS per 5 grammes for airmail).

Postcards within Austria 2·50 öS, to the United Kingdom
5 öS, to the United States or Canada 7·50 öS.

Stamps can also be obtained from tobacconists and there are
vending machines in front of most post offices.

The central telegram office is at 1 Börseplatz, I.   Telegrams

Programme of events

The Vienna Tourist Board (Fremdenverkehrsverband für Wien) and the Vienna Municipal Office of Culture (Kulturamt der Stadt Wien) publish the forthcoming theatre and concert programmes in detail once a month.

Public holidays

1 January (New Year), 6 January (Epiphany), Easter, 1 May (Labour Day), Ascension Day, Whitsun, Corpus Christi, 15 August (Assumption), 26 October (national holiday), 1 November (All Saints' Day), 8 December (Annunciation), 25 and 26 December (Christmas).

Public transport

Local transport

Express, municipal and underground railways and trams and buses as well as routes operated by public and private undertakings which bear a "B" on the destination board, are incorporated in single network and tariff and can be used with the same tickets.

Information

Vienna Civic Undertakings – transport information service
Underground station Karlsplatz, tel. 5 87 31 86
Mon.–Fri. 7 a.m.–6 p.m., Sat., Sun. and public holidays 8.30 a.m.–4 p.m.
Underground station Stephansplatz, tel. 52 42 27
Mon.–Fri. 8 a.m.–6 p.m.; Sat., Sun. and public holidays 8.30 a.m.–4 p.m.
Underground station Praterstern, tel. 24 93 02
Mon.–Fri. 10 a.m.–6 p.m.

Buses

From the Wien-Mitte bus station (1b Landstrasser Hauptstrasse, III) regular services go to all the regions around Vienna (information tel. 75 01).

City buses

City buses operate on weekdays in the Inner City on four routes.
1A: Schottentor–Landstrasse (Wien-Mitte)–Schottentor
2A: Dr-Karl-Renner-Ring–Schwendenplatz–Dr-Karl-Renner-Ring
3A: Schottenring–Schwarzenbergplatz–Schottenring
4A: Karlsplatz–Rasmofskygasse–Karlsplatz

Night buses

In the nights of Fri.–Sat., Sat.–Sun. and the nights preceding public holidays night buses operate between 12.30 and 4 a.m. The central departure point is Schwedenplatz. Certain districts are covered in circular routes at intervals of 55 minutes; changing buses is permissible.

N1: II, XXII, XXI districts
N2: XX, XXI districts
N3: XI, XVIII, XIX districts
N4: IV, VII, XV, XIV, XVI, XVII districts
N5: IV, V, XII, XIII districts
N6: IV, V, XII, XXIII, X districts
N7: IV, V, X districts
N8: III, XI districts

Trams

The most important routes for visitors are:
31: Schottenring–Stammersdorf
38: Schottenring–Grinzing
46: Dr-Karl-Renner-Ring–Joachimsthalerplatz
58: Burgring–Unter-St-Veit
62: Karlsplatz–Lainz
67: Reumannplatz–Kurzentrum Oberlaa
D: Nussdorf–Schottenring–Südbahnhof
J: Ottakringerstrasse–Karlsplatz
N: Floridsdorferbrücke–Prater
O: Praterstern–Raxstrasse

At present the following lines are in operation:
U1: Zentrum Kagran–Reumannplatz
U2: Karlsplatz–Schottenring
U4: Heiligenstadt–Hütteldorf

U-Bahn (Underground)

The legendary S-bahn now operates on two routes only:
G: Heiligenstadt–Gumpendorferstrasse
GD: Friedensbrücke–Gumpendorferstrasse

S-Bahn (City railway)

The Schnellbahn links the SW of Vienna with the NE.
S1: Gänserdorf–Floridsdorf–Meidling–Baden–Wiener
Neustadt
S2: Mistelbach–Gerasdorf–Leopoldau–Südbahnhof–
Mödling
S3: Hollabrunn–Floridsdorf–Meidling
S7: Praterstern–Wolfsthal
S40: Franz-Josefs-Bahnhof–Tulln Stadt
S50: Westbahnhof–Neulengbach
S60: Südbahnhof–Neusiedl am See
S80: Südbahnhof–Hirschstetten-Aspern

Schnellbahn
(Express railway)

The "Vorortlinie" (suburban line) between the districts of
Hütteldorf and Döbling, which was reopened only in 1987 can
almost be called a "sight". Its bridges and tunnels, but
especially its stations were designed by Otto Wagner as an
architectural unity in pure Art Nouveau style.

For the local transport detailed above there is a single tariff
(changing possible; special regulations for children). It is
advisable to purchase tickets in advance (advance ticket
offices, tobacconists), since in the vehicles and at the ticket
machines only single tickets with a supplement are
obtainable.

Tariff

For tourists the following tickets are recommended: single
tickets (advance purchase in blocks of 5).

175

Special regulations for Underground, S-bahn and Schnell-bahn: For underground and S-bahn one can also use short journey tickets. For the Schnellbahn one can also use these tickets but changing trains is not permitted. Outside the boundaries of the common tariff the normal rail fare must be paid. On S-bahn lines one may also travel in ordinary trains. Tickets from automatic machines on the Underground and S-bahn are already cancelled. Other tickets must be placed in the cancelling machine at the entrance to the platform.

Special regulations for trams and buses: There are short journey tickets (not for buses with the addition of "B" to the number). Blue lettering on the destination board indicates no conductor, tickets are obtained from the driver (entry at front); tickets purchased in advance must be cancelled in the vehicle by the passenger.

Buses with the addition of "B" to the number: All tickets of the common tariff may be used but cannot be bought in the vehicle. There are no short journey tickets. Tickets for journeys not involving a change may be bought.

All trams and buses stop at red bus-stops but blue bus-stops are request stops only. In vehicles without a conductor passengers wishing to alight must press the stop-signal.

Children's fares

Children under 7 are carried free. Children between 7 and 16 may travel free on all Sundays and public holidays and during the school holidays. At other times they pay special children's fares (proof of age may be demanded).

Radio/TV

ORF (Austrian Radio/Television) currently broadcasts on two television channels and three radio stations.
Radio station: Ö1: 514 m, 584 kHz
Ö Regional: 203 m, 1475 kHz
Ö3: VHF 99.9 MHz
Vienna City Radio: VHF 90 and 95 daily 1–3 p.m.
Shortwave Ö: 49 m, 6155 MHz

Information on BBC overseas radio transmissions in English may be obtained from BBC External Services, PO Box 76, Bush House, London WC2B 4PH.

Television

The two television channels, FS1 and FS2, transmit the main news programme "Zeit im Bild" at 7.30 p.m.

Railway stations

Vienna has three major railway stations:

Westbahnhof

Mainline station for trains travelling West to W Austria, Germany, Switzerland, France, Belgium and the Netherlands. From Westbahnhof: City train connections for Meidling and Heiligenstadt, tram line from Mariahilferstrasse with lines 52 and 58 to the Ring (Inner City).

Mainline station for trains travelling South and East to S
Austria, Italy, Yugoslavia, Greece and Hungary.
From Südbahnhof: Underground 1 to Karlsplatz and
Stephensplatz, fast train to Meidling and Vienna Centre, tram-
line 18 serving the suburbs.

Südbahnhof/Ostbahnhof

Reorganised mainline station for trains travelling North to N
Austria, Czechoslovakia and East Berlin.
From Franz-Josefs-Bahnhof: Underground 4 (Friedensbrücke) for Schottenring and Heiligenstadt, City train for
suburbs and tramline D for city centre/Ring.

Franz-Josefs-Bahnhof

All stations have left-luggage lockers in the arrival hall. There
are not enough luggage trolleys and porters are in short
supply.

Lockers

Central train information: tel. 17 17
Western rail section: tel. 15 52
Southern rail section: tel. 15 53

Train information

Within Austria the intercity expresses are an excellent means
of transport. They leave Vienna every hour for Salzburg and
Graz and every two hours for Villach and Innsbruck.

Restaurants

There are many foreign restaurants also inns, "beiseln"
(typically Viennese eating-places with plain cooking, good
beer and local wine), snack-bars, wine-cellars, "heurigen-
schänken (wine-shops, with music, selling new wine), café-
restaurants, cafés and "konditoreien" (cake-shops).

Austrian Cuisine

Altwienerhof, 6 Herklotzgasse, XV, tel. 83 71 45
Belvedere-Stöckl, 25 Prinz-Eugen-Strasse, III, tel. 78 41 98
Gottfried, 45 Untere Viaduktgasse/3 Marxergasse, III, tel.
73 82 56
Kervansaray Hummerbar, 9 Mahlerstrasse, I, tel. 5 12 88 43
Korso, 2 Mahlerstrasse, I, tel. 51 51 65 46
Kupferdachl, 7 Schottengasse, I, tel. 63 93 81
Palais Schwarzenberg, 9 Schwarzenbergplatz, III, tel. 78 45 15
Schubertstüberl'n, 4–6 Schreyvogelgasse, I, tel. 63 71 87
Steirereck, 2 Rasumofskygasse, III, tel. 73 31 68

Luxury restaurants

Alter Rathauskeller, 8 Wipplingerstrasse, I, tel, 66 33 36
Altes Fassl, 37 Ziegelofengasse, V, tel. 55 42 98
Amon, 13 Schlachthausgasse, III, tel. 78 81 66
Bayrischer Hof, 5 Obere Augartenstrasse, II, tel. 35 51 10
Bierhof, 13 Naglergasse (entrance in the Haarhof), I, tel.
63 44 28
Brezlg'wölb, 9 Ledererhof, I, tel. 63 88 11
Butterfass, 122 Prater Hauptallee, II, tel. 24 41 05
Domicil, 2 Rudolfsplatz, I, tel. 63 94 60
D'Rauchkuchl, 37 Schweglerstrasse, XV, tel. 92 13 81
Eckel, 46 Sieveringerstrasse, XIX, tel. 32 32 18
Fischerbräu, 17 Billrothstrasse, XIX, tel. 31 62 64
Frackerl, 11 Brückengasse, VI, tel. 5 97 38 40
Glacis-Beisl, 1 Messeplatz, VII, tel. 96 16 58
Gulaschmuseum, 20 Schulerstrasse, I, tel. 5 12 10 17

Restaurants and Beisln

Hedrich, 2 Stubenring, tel. 52 95 88
Himmelpforte, 24 Himmelpfortgasse, I, tel. 5 13 19 67
Holzdackl, 8 Naglergasse, I, tel. 63 89 07
Korso, 2 Mahlerstrasse, I, tel. 5 15 16/5 46
Leupold–Zum Schottentor, 7 Schottengasse, I, tel. 63 93 81
Ma Pitom, 5 Seitenstettengasse, I, tel. 66 43 13
Marienhof, 9 Josefstädterstrasse, VIII, tel. 43 22 25
Meierei Holzdorfer, 3 Prater Hauptallee, II, tel. 23 31 51
Motto, 30 Schönbrunnerstrasse, V, tel. 5 87 06 72
Niki Ziegler, 76 Woedner Hauptstrasse, tel. 5 87 62 03
Ofenloch, 8 Kurrentgasse, I, tel. 63 88 44
Oswald & Kalb, 14 Bäckerstrasse, I, tel. 52 13 71
Peters Beisl, 98 Arnethgasse, XVI, tel. 46 53 75
Pfudl, 22 Bäckerstrasse, I, tel. 52 67 05
Piaristenkeller, 45 Piaristengasse, VIII, tel. 42 91 52
Rheintaler, 5 Gluckgasse, I, tel. 52 33 66
Salzamt, 1 Ruprelchtsplatz, I, tel. 63 53 32
Silberwirt, 21 Schlossgasse, V, tel. 55 49 07
Steinerne Eule, 30 Halbgasse, VI, tel. 93 22 50
Ubl-Zum guten Hirten, 26 Pressgasse, IV, tel. 5 87 64 37
Vincent, 7 Grosse Pfarrgasse, II, tel. 33 23 29
Wien-Comptoir, 6 Bäckerstrasse, I, tel. 5 12 17 60
Zauberlehrling, 2 Lazaristengasse, XVIII, tel. 34 51 35
Zum Herkner, 123 Dornbacherstrasse, XVII, tel. 4 61 05 54
Zum Hirschen, 6 Hirschengasse, VI, tel. 5 75 00 25
Zur Stadt Krems, 37 Zieglergasse, VII, tel. 93 72 00

Fist restaurants	Landhaus Winter, 262 Alberner Hafenzufahrtsstrasse, XI, tel. 76 23 17 Scampi, 11 Mahlerstrasse, I, tel. 5 12 22 97
Vegetarian restaurants	Siddharta, 16 Fleischmarkt, I, tel. 5 13 11 97 Wrenkh, 9 Hollergasse, XV, tel. 83 41 28
Snack bars	Do & Co, 3 Akademiestrasse, I, tel. 5 12 64 74 Trzseniewski, 1 Dorotheergasse, I, tel. 52 32 91
Heurige	See Heuriger
Coffee Houses	See Coffee Houses

Foreign Cuisine

Balkan	Balkan Grill, 13 Brunnengasse, XVI, tel. 92 14 94
Chinese	Pan Asia, 22 Praterstrasse, II, tel. 24 73 82 Soho, 20 Stubenring, I, tel. 5 12 94 04
French	Chez Robert, 4 Gertrudplatz, XVIII, tel. 43 25 44 Creperie Spittelberg, 12 Spittelberggasse, VI, tel. 96 15 70 Franchi's, 3 Schwarzenbergplatz, I, tel. 75 53 34
Greek	Athen grüsst Wien, 56 Alserstrasse, IX, tel. 42 62 04 Janis, 56 Prinz-Eugen-Strasse, IV, tel. 65 18 21 Mykonos, 7 Annagasse, I, tel. 5 12 02 43 Orpheus, 10 Spiegelgasse, I, tel. 52 38 53
Indian	Kwality, 73 Schottenfeldgasse, VII, tel. 93 23 39
Italian	Castellamare, 32 Ratschkygasse, XII, tel. 8 37 73 52 La Strada, 90 Hütteldorferstrasse, XV, tel. 92 22 47 Rimini, 23 Hauslabgasse, V, tel. 55 43 56 Valentino, 6 Berggasse, IX, tel. 31 42 62

Sapporo Inn, 9 Heumarkt, III, tel. 73 11 99   Japanese

Seoul, 116–118 Neustiftgasse, VII, tel. 93 34 28   Korean
Senara, 4 Schwarzenbergstrasse, I, tel. 5 12 99 83

Casa Do Manuel, 23b Stolbergasse, V, tel. 54 38 39   Portuguese

Levante, 14 Josefstädterstrasse, VIII, tel. 48 53 06   Turkish

Sightseeing

Vienna Sightseeing Tours, 4 Stelzhamergasse, III, tel. 7 51 14   By coach
20 and 71 24 68 30
Cityrama Sightseeing I Börsegasse/25 Tiefer Graben, I, tel.
33 36 75

For all these tours visitors can be collected from their hotels; it
is also possible to book tours through the hotels.

Special Tours, 6 Millöckergasse, VI (booking through travel
agents).

The City of Vienna organises tours on various themes which
take in the city's latest buildings, engineering projects, etc.
Departure: Rathaus, entrance Friedrich-Schmidt-Platz, I
Information: Rathausinformation, tel. 4 28 00/29 50.

A comfortable and nostaligic way of getting to know Vienna is   By "Fiaker"
to go for a ride in a "Fiaker", the famous Viennese horse-cab.
There are ranks in Kohlmarkt, Josefsplatz and Heldenplatz,
outside the Albertina and at the Cathedral.

In high season (31 May–26 Oct.) by "Oldtimer-tram". $2\frac{1}{2}$ By tram
hours through the city; every Sat. 2.30 p.m.; Sun. and public
holidays 10 a.m. from Otto Wagner Pavilion, Karlsplatz. For
information tel. 25 87 31 86.

In fine weather there are flights (15 minutes) over Vienna on   By plane
most days from Schwechat Airport between 9 a.m. and 5 p.m.
(summer 9 a.m. and 6 p.m.).
For information tel. 67 94 54.

See entry   Boat trips

Souvenirs and Shopping

Viennese craft products, following old traditions of crafts-   Viennese craft
manship, are valued for their beauty and quality. Particularly
popular are petit-point work, hand-painted Augarten porcelain, jewellery and goldsmith's work, hand-made dolls, fine
ceramic ware, enamel and wrought iron, and leather goods of
all kinds.

Smart, exclusive shops of all kinds can be found in the inner   Shopping streets
city close to and around the Cathedral: Kärntnerstrasse,
Graben, Kohlmarkt, Tuchlauben, Wollzeile, Spiegelgasse and
Neuer Markt. Another good area for shopping is the Mariahilferstrasse where large stores can also be found.

Sports

Fitness Centres	Budo-Zentrum, 9 Gutheil-Schoder-Gasse, X, tel. 62 52 89 Crocodile, 13 Waldgasse, X, tel. 6 27 21 22 Donau-Fitness-Center in the Stadtpark, 1 Parkring, I, tel. 75 77 75 Fit & Fun, 2a Landstrasser Hauptstrasse, III, tel. 73 61 65 Fitnesscenter, 73 Ober Donaustrasse, II, tel. 33 73 99 Olympic, 97 Davidgasse, X, tel. 78 33 95
Football stadiums	Praterstadium, Krieau, II (90,000 capacity) Stadion Hohe Warte, First Vienna Football Club, Hohe Warte, XIX
Golf course	Golf Course Freudenau, 2a Freudenau, II, tel. 74 17 86
Ice-rinks	Donauparkhalle, 1 Wagramerstrasse, XXII Kunsteisbahn Engelmann, 6–8 Syringgasse, XVII Eisring Süd, 2 Windtenstrasse, X Stadthalle, 15 Vogelweidplatz, XV
Horse-racing	Trotting: Krieau racetrack, Pratergelände, II Underground; Praterstern (U4); Tram 1 Season: September–June The major events on the Austrian racing calendar include the Austrian trotting Derby at the end of May and the International Count-Kálmán-Hunyady-Commemorative Race on the second Sunday in October. Flat racing: Freudenau racetrack, Pratergelände, II Information: Wiener Rennverein, 5 Josefsplatz, tel. 52 25 38 Bus 81A Season: Spring and Autumn
Squash	Fit & Fun, 2a Landstrasser Hauptstrasse, III, tel. 73 61 65 Squash-Haus Penzing, 183 Linzerstrasse, XIV, tel. 94 85 51 STS (Squash-Tennis-Sauna), 83 Baumgasse, III, tel. 78 82 01 Squash-Sportanlagen, 13 Hernalser Hauptstrasse, XVII, tel. 43 86 27
Tennis	Isfo-Tennis-Center, 1 Heubergstättenstrasse, X, tel. 67 97 73 La Villa, 5 Kirchfeldgasse, XXIII, tel. 64 67 37 Tenniszentrum Herzig, 82 Leberstrasse, XI, tel. 74 34 40 Tennisplätze, 1 Arsenalstrasse, III, tel. 78 21 32

Swimming-pools (selection)

Outdoor pools	Angelibad, An der oberen Alter Donau, XXI Bundesbad Schönbrunn, Schönbrunner Schlosspark, XIII Freibad Baumgarten, 26a Hackingerstrasse, XIV Freibad Donaustadt, 36 Portnergasse, XXII (with covered bath) Freibad Grossfeldsiedlung, 44 Oswald-Redlich-Strasse, XXI (with covered bath) Freibad Hadersdorf-Weidlungau, 412 Hauptstrasse, XIV Freibad Hietzing, 14 Atzgersdorferstrasse, XIII (with covered bath) Gänsehäufel, 21 Moissigasse, XXII Hohe-Warte-Bad, 8 Hohe Warte, XIX Kongressbad, 7a Julius-Meinl-Gasse, XVI

Krapfenwaldbad, 65–73 Krapfenwaldgasse, XIX
Laaer-Berg-Bad, 14–16 Perchtoldsdorferstrasse, XXIII
Neuwaldegger Bad, 58 Promenadegasse, XVII
Ottakringer Bad, 11 Johann-Staud-Strasse, XVI (with covered bath)
Satzgerbad, Am Satzberg, 100 Steinböckengasse, XIV
Schafbergbad, 2 Josef-Redl-Gasse, XVIII
Schwimmbad Pratersauna, 135 Waldsteingartenstrasse, II
Strandbad Alte Donau, 91 Arbeiterstrandbadstrasse, XXII
Strandbad Stadlau, Am Mühlwasser, XXII
Theresienbad, 3 Hufelandgasse, XII (with covered bath)

Amalienbad, 23 Reumannplatz, X (beautifully restored Art Nouveau building)
Dianabad, 7–9 Lilienbrunnengasse, II
Hallenbad Döbling, 6 Geweygasse, XIX
Hallenbad Floridsdorf, 22 Franklinstrasse, XXI
Hallenbad Simmering, 5 Florian-Hedorfer-Strasse, XI
Jörgerbad, 42–44 Jörgerstrasse, XVII
Stadt des Kindes, 7 Mühlbergstrasse, XIV (entrance Hofjägerstrasse)
Stadthallenbad, 15 Vogelweidplatz, XV
Thermalbad Oberlaa, 14 Kurbadstrasse, X

Indoor pools

Taxis

Taxis in Vienna operate from taxi ranks from which they can also be summoned by telephone. Although officially they are not allowed to ply for hire ("frei" on their illuminated sign means that they are available) it is possible to hail a taxi on streets away from the main thoroughfares.

Numbers to call radio taxis in Vienna:
31 30, 62 82, 43 69, 91 01, 31 25 11 (Airport and out of town).

Telephone numbers

Main taxi ranks in the City Centre: Corner of Opernring/Operngasse, tel. 56 52 05, Babenbergerstrasse-Burgring, tel. 93 23 55, Hoher Markt/Marc Aurel-Strasse, tel. 63 04 98. 14 Dr-Karl-Lueger-Ring, tel. 5 33 12 60, Stubenring, tel. 52 32 36.

Taxi ranks

Other ranks (without telephone): Kärntnerstrasse/corner of Mahlerstrasse (on the left near the Opera House), Philharmonikerstrasse (in front of the Sacher Hotel), Am Hof, Rathausplatz, Hoher Markt, Neuer Markt.

The fare is made up of a minimum charge plus a mileage supplement and a small surcharge for inflation, which is only a few schillings and does not appear on the meter.

Fares

Telephone

All Post Offices have kiosks for long-distance calls and coin-operated telephones and there are coin-operated telephones in the stations and at sites throughout the city.

One-schilling coins are required for local calls and 10-schilling coins for long-distance calls.

Local calls

A telephone call to the United Kingdom costs 14 öS per minute; to the United States or Canada 40.50 öS per minute. After 6 p.m. and at week-ends from Saturday noon long-distance calls are from 30 to 40% cheaper.

Long-distance calls

Practical Information

Dialling codes		
	From the United States or Canada to Vienna	011 43 222
	From the United Kingdom to Vienna	010 43 222
	From Vienna to the United States or Canada	0 1
	From Vienna to the United Kingdom	0 44

In dialling an international call the zero prefixed to the local dialling code should be omitted.

Theatres

Programme details
: The Vienna Tourist Board issues a free leaflet giving details of current programmes (see Programme of Events).

Tickets
: See Advance Booking or obtainable direct from the theatre.

Federal theatres
: Akademietheater
1 Lisztstrasse, III
Burgtheater company

Burgtheater
See AZ, Burgtheater

International Theatre
8 Porzellangasse/Müllnergasse, I, tel. 31 62 72

Kammerspiele
20 Rotenturmstrasse, XI, tel. 5 33 28 33
Comedies, satire with the Josefstadt Theatre Company

Kleine Komödie in the Theater am Kärntnertor
4 Walfischgasse, I, tel. 52 42 80
Contemporary boulevard theatre

Theater in der Josefstadt
26 Josefstädterstrasse, VIII, tel. 42 76 31
Contemporary light plays

Vienna's English Theatre
12 Josefgasse, VIII, tel 42 12 60
Plays in English

Volkstheater
1 Neustiftgasse, VII, tel 93 35 01
Plays, mainly contemporary, and sometimes avant-garde pieces

Little theatres (selection)
: Ateliertheater am Naschmarkt
4 Linke Wienzeile, VI, tel. 5 87 82 14

Drachengasse 2/Courage
2 Drachengasse, I, tel. 5 13 14 44

Experiment am Lichtenwerd
132 Liechtensteinstrasse, IX, tel. 31 41 08

Freie Bühnen Wieden
60b Wiedner Hauptstrasse, IV, tel. 5 86 21 22

Intime Bühne
29 Franz-Josefs-Kai, I, tel. 5 33 24 34

Jura Soyfer Theater
94B Steigenteschgasse, tel. 93 24 58

Kunst-Theater Wien
7 Börseplatz, I, tel. 63 93 69

Die Komödianten
5 Karlsplatz, I, tel. 5 87 05 04
theatre in the Künstlerhaus

Original Pradler Ritterspiele
2 Biberstrasse, I, tel. 52 54 00
plays of chivalry

Schauspielhaus
19 Porzellangasse, IX, tel. 34 01 01

Schönbrunner Schlosstheater
Schloss Schönbrunn, XIII, tel. 82 94 65/34

Serapions Theater
6 Wallsteinplatz, XX, tel. 33 42 31

Theater am Schwedenplatz
21 Franz-Josefs-Kai, I, tel. 6 32 09 73

Theater beim Auersperg
17 Auerspergstrasse, VIII, tel. 43 07 07

Theater Brett
2 Münzwardeingasse, VI, tel. 5 87 06 63

Theater "Die Tribüne" in Café Landtmann
4 Dr-Karl-Lueger-Ring, I, tel. 63 84 85

Theater-Forum
50 Porzellangasse, IX, tel. 31 54 21

Theatergruppe 80
67 Gumpendorferstrasse, VI, tel. 5 87 47 87

Theater Spielraum
8 Palmgasse, XV, tel. 87 35 25

Treffpunkt Petersplatz
1 Petersplatz, I, tel. 5 35 32 00

Cabaret Fledermaus   Cabarets
2 Spiegelgasse, I, tel. 5 12 84 38

Hernalser Stadttheater (Metropol)
50 Geblergasse, XVII, tel. 43 35 43

Kabarett & Komödie am Naschmarkt
4 Linke Wienzeile, VI, tel. 5 87 22 75

Kabarett Niedermair
1a Lenaugasse, VIII, tel, 48 44 92

Spektakel
14 Hamburgerstrasse, V, tel. 5 87 06 53

Tabor Brettl
5 Obere Augartenstrasse, II, tel. 35 51 10

Theater Kabarett Simpl
36 Wollzeile, I, tel. 52 47 42

See Music   Opera, ballet, concerts

Time

Austria observes Central European Time (one hour ahead of
Greenwich Mean Time; six hours ahead of New York time).
From April to September summer time (two hours ahead of
GMT; seven hours ahead of New York time) is in force.

Times of opening

Shops open as a rule Mon.–Fri. 9 a.m.–6 p.m. and until noon   Shops
on Saturdays. Shops outside the city centre close in the lunch-
hour from noon till 2 or 3 p.m.

Foodshops often open before 8 a.m. and close at 6.30 p.m.,
with lunchtime closing usually from 12.30 to 3 p.m.

Practical Information

Late-night and Sunday opening	Outside official business hours it is possible to shop for some items in the evening and on Sundays.
Banks	See entry
Post offices	See Postal Services
Museum, galleries	There are no fixed times of opening for museums and galleries. See A–Z Museums/galleries under the appropriate heading. The times given for Sunday opening apply in general also to public holidays, but most museums and collections remain closed on 1 January, Good Friday, Easter Sunday, 1 May, Whitsunday, Corpus Christi, 1 and 2 November and on 25 and 26 December.

Tipping

The usual tip for waiters, hotel maids, taxi-drivers, hairdressers, etc. is 10 to 15% of the bill. A tip is customary even when, as in restaurants, service is already included in the bill.

Do not tip the self-styled "parking attendants" who hang around the car parks used by tourists.

Tourist information

Austrian National Tourist Office (ÖsterreichInformation)

United Kingdom	30 St George Street, London W1R 9FA; tel. (01) 629 0461
United States	545 Fifth Avenue, New York, NY 10017–3642; tel. (212) 697 0651
	Standard Oil Building 200 E. Randolph Drive, Suite 7023 Chicago, IL 60601 tel. (312) 861 0100–02
	3440 Wilshire Boulevard, Suite 906, Los Angeles, CA 90010; tel. (213) 380 3309
	1007 NW 24th Avenue Portland, OR 97210; tel. (503) 224 6000
Canada	2 Bloor Street East, Suite 3330, Toronto, Ontario M4W 1A8; tel. (416) 967 3380
	1010 Sherbrooke Street West, Suite 1410 Montreal, P.Q. H3A 2R7; tel. (514) 849 3709
	Suite 1220–1223, Vancouver Block 736 Granville Street, Vancouver, B.C. V6Z 1J2; tel. (604) 683 5808-09

Austrian National Tourist Office (Österreich-Information)
1 Margaretenstrasse,
A 1040 Wien IV;
tel. (02 22) 58 86 60
Open Mon.–Fri. 9 a.m.–5 pm.

In Vienna

Fremdenverkehrsverband für Wien
5 Kinderspitalgasse,
A 1095 Wien IX;
tel. (02 22) 43 16 08

Tourist Information
Opernpassage, I, tel. (02 22) 43 16 08
Open Mon.–Sat. 9 a.m.–7 p.m.

Stadtinformation,
Rathaus, Friedrich-Schmidt-Platz, I;
tel. 43 89 89
Open Mon.–Fri. 10 a.m.–noon, 1–6 p.m.

Tourist information and room reservation:

For motorists

On W motorway (A1) entry to Vienna (Wien-Auhof)
Open Nov.–Mar. daily 10 a.m.–6 p.m., Apr.–Oct. daily
8 a.m.–10 p.m.

On S motorway (A2) entry to Vienna (Triesterstrasse)
Open Apr., May, June, Oct. daily 10 a.m.–6 p.m., July–Sept.
8 a.m.–10 p.m.

At Westbahnhof, tel. 83 51 85 (open daily 6.15 a.m.–11 p.m.)
At Südbahnhof, tel. 65 21 26 (open daily 6.30 a.m.–10 p.m.)

For rail travellers

Tourist information at the airport (Arrivals concourse)
Open June–Sept. daily 9 a.m.–11 p.m., Oct.–May 9 a.m.–
10 p.m.

For air travellers

Official Tourist Information DDSG, Schiffsstation
Reichsbrücke.
May–Sept. daily 7.30–9 p.m.

For boat passengers

Traffic

The Highway Code here is broadly similar to that of other countries where they drive on the right and, unless otherwise indicated, traffic coming from the right has priority.

Highway Code

On motorways the speed limit is 130 km p.h./80 m.p.h. for private cars (70 km p.h./43 m.p.h. if towing).
On ordinary roads the speed limit is 100 km p.h./62 m.p.h. for private cars (60 km p.h./37 m.p.h. if towing).
In built-up areas the speed limit is 50 km p.h./31 m.p.h.

Speed limits

The wearing of seat-belts in the front seats is compulsory and in the rear seats if fitted. Failure to comply is subject to a fine of 100 öS. Children under 12 are not allowed to ride in the front seat.

Seat-belts

Drivers are warned that there are severe penalties for exceeding the permitted level of alcohol.

Drinking and Driving

Motorcyclists must use dipped headlights at all times.

Motorcycles

Studded tyres may be used from the beginning of November to the end of April. Vehicles fitted with such tyres may not exceed a speed of 80 km p.h./50 m.p.h. on ordinary roads or 100 km p.h./62 m.p.h. on motorways and must display an appropriate sign on the rear of the vehicle. A total ban on studded tyres is planned.

Studded tyres

Practical Information

Parking

From 15 December to 30 March there is a general ban on parking in Vienna from 8 p.m. to 5 a.m. in any street where there are tramlines, in order to facilitate clearance of heavy snowfall. Where short-term parking is designated (city centre, Mariahilferstrasse, Rathaus, outside stations and the airport), parking on weekdays between 8 a.m. and 6 p.m. is only permitted with parking discs for a maximum of 1½ hours. Parking discs are for 30, 60 and 90 minutes and can be obtained from Vienna's public transport ticket offices, at petrol stations, tobacconists and a number of banks, etc. Once used, the discs are stamped with the time and the date. Bear in mind that constant checks are made to ensure that the discs in use are valid.

Compulsory equipment

All motorists are required by law to carry a first-aid kit and a warning triangle.

Vehicles towed away

Vehicles obstructing the traffic are towed away. A motorist finding that a vehicle is no longer where he left it will probably find it at Eibisbrunnergasse in the XII district. The vehicle can be recovered from Mon. to Fri. between 8 a.m. and 3 p.m. (at other times application must be made to the Magistrates' Department 48, 3 Einsiedlergasse, V).

Travel documents

Passport

Visitors to Austria from the United Kingdom and the United States and Commonwealth countries require only a passport to enter the country. No visa is required unless the visit exceeds three months or the visitor proposes to work in Austria.

Driving licence, etc.

National driving licences and car registration documents from these countries are recognised in Austria. Foreign vehicles must carry an oval *nationality plate*. Third-party insurance is obligatory in Austria, and it is advisable to have an *international insurance certificate* ("green card").

Travelling to Vienna

By car

The usual approach for British visitors to Vienna is from Calais, Ostende and Zeebrugge, via Belgium to Aachen to join the German Autobahn network, then onwards via Köln (Cologne), Frankfurt, Nürnberg, Passau and Linz. The distance from Calais to Vienna is just over 800 miles and usually requires two night stops.

By motorail

There are motorail services from Brussels (Schaerbeek) and 's-Hertogenbosch to Salzburg. Information from Sealink Travel Ltd, PO Box 29, London SW1V 1JX, British Rail travel centres or appointed travel agents.

By rail

It is advisable to travel by international trains and reserve a seat in advance. There is an excellent network of fast intercity trains within Austria. These depart from Vienna from 7 a.m. onwards at 1- or 2-hourly intervals.

Foreign tourists can purchase a network ticket covering 9 or 16 days or 1 month and young people under 26 years of age can buy for 1000 öS the 9-day "Austria Ticket"; both tickets are valid on all Austrian trains and the buses operated by Austrian Railways and the Postal Services.

There are numerous package tours by coach, either going direct to Vienna or including Vienna in a longer circuit. For information apply to any travel agent.

By bus

Vienna's Schwechat Airport (see Airport) is served by flights from 45 European and 15 non-European airports. There are direct services daily between London and Vienna and less frequently between Manchester and Vienna (British Airways and Austrian Airlines).

By air

During November and December flights can be delayed by fog so it is advisable during these months to book on late morning or early afternoon flights.

Within Austria there are daily flights from Vienna to Graz and Innsbruck and flights 5–6 times a week to Klagenfurt and 6 times a week to Linz and Salzburg.

From May to September DDSG (Donau-Dampschiffarts-Gesellschaft-Danube Steamer Company) operates a fast service between Passau and Vienna. The trip takes 15 hours downstream and about 22 hours travelling upstream (with overnight stay in Linz).

By boat

Travellers with international railway tickets or travel agency tickets can also opt to travel by DDSG vessels if their rail ticket covers the stretches to Vienna from Passau, Linz and Melk. Vouchers, on which a supplement is payable, for the transfer from rail to river travel can only be obtained from the DDSG offices at points of embarkation.

Viennese cuisine

The key to the success of the Viennese cuisine lies in its variety, owing as it does a great deal to Bohemian, Hungarian, Croatian, Slovene and Italian influences. Neither light in texture nor low in calories, it nevertheless makes use of many natural ingredients. It covers an astonishing range of freshwater fish and, during the October/November season, game dishes are extraordinarily good.

The "New Viennese Cuisine" is modelled on the French "nouvelle cuisine" but is only to be found in a small number of restaurants.

Beef broth (Rindsuppe), garnished with various types of pastry (Friatten, Schöberl, Backerbsen), dumplings and noodles (Markknödel, Griessnockerl, Lungenstrudel, Milzschnitten), and pea or vegetable soup with fish roe (Fischbeuschelsuppe).

Soups

Carp in garlic butter (Wurzelkarpfen), fillet of pike-perch (Zander) fried in bacon fat or grilled (Fogosch) with paprika sauce, steamed sheathfish (Wels) and fish pie (Zwiebelfisch).

Fish

Schnitzel-style chicken (Backhendel), chicken paprika (Paprikahendel), stuffed breast of goose (Ganselbrust), capon (Kapaun) in anchovy sauce, pheasant (Fasan) roast in bacon, woodcock (Schnepfen).

Poultry, game-birds

Practical Information

Game	Wild boar (Wildschwein) in cream sauce with dumplings, venison as a ragout (Hirschragout) with chives or as a pot-au-feu (Rehrücken in Wurzelwerkbeize), jugged hare (Hasenrücken).
Meat	Wiener Schnitzel, i.e. veal cutlet coated with breadcrumbs, cuts of beef (Tafelspitz, Beinfleisch, Esterhazy-Rostbraten), larded veal (Kalbsvogerl), Viennese roast pork (Wiener Schweinebraten), stewed pork with horse radish (Krenfleisch), salted meat (Selchfleisch), sucking pig (Spanferkel), roast loin (Nierenbraten), goulash (Gulasch) and dishes made from kidneys, liver, sweetbreads, etc. (Salonbeuschl, Kavaliersbries).
Pancakes, puddings, etc.	Stuffed pancakes (Topfenpalatschinken, Kaiserschmarren), yeast dumplings with fruit, etc. (Topfenknödel, Germknödel, Marillenknödel, Zwetschenknödel, Buchtein), mille-feuille (Millirahmstrudel) with vanilla sauce, plum purée (Powideltascherin) and apple strudel (Apfelstrudel).
Cakes	Sachertorte, Dobostorte.
Food and drink	See entry
Restaurants	See entry

Youth hostels

Jugendherberge der Stadt Wien
8 Schlossberggasse, tel. 82 15 01
Open all year, 273 b.

Jugendgästehaus Brigittenau
24 Friedrich-Engels-Platz, tel. 3 38 29 40
Open all year, 282 b.

Jugendherberge Myrthengasse
7 Myrthengasse, tel. 93 63 16
Open all year, 123 b.

Jugendherberge Lechnerstrasse
12 Lechnerstrasse, tel. 73 14 94
Open 1 Mar.–30 Nov., 52 b., young men only

Jugendherberge Ruthensteiner
24 Robert-Hamerling-Gasse, tel. 83 46 93
Open all year, 77 b.

Information
Osterreichischer Jugendherbergsverband
28 Schottenring

Osterreichisches Jugendherbergswerk
6 Freyung, tel. 6 31 83 30

Notes

Notes

Baedeker's Travel Guides

"The maps and illustrations are lavish. The arrangement of information (alphabetically by city) makes it easy to use the book."
—*San Francisco Examiner-Chronicle*

What's there to do and see in foreign countries? Travelers who rely on Baedeker, one of the oldest names in travel literature, will miss nothing. Baedeker's bright red, internationally recognized covers open up to reveal fascinating A-Z directories of cities, towns and regions, complete with their sights, museums, monuments, cathedrals, castles, gardens and ancestral homes—an approach that gives the traveler a quick and easy way to plan a vacation itinerary.

And Baedekers are filled with over 200 full color photos and detailed maps, including a full-size, fold-out roadmap for easy vacation driving. Baedeker—the premier name in travel for over 150 years.

Please send me the books checked below:

☐ **Austria** $17.95
0–13–056127–4

☐ **Caribbean.** $17.95
0–13–056143–6

☐ **Costa Brava** $12.95
0–13–055880–X

☐ **Denmark.** $17.95
0–13–058124–0

☐ **Egypt.** $17.95
0–13–056358–7

☐ **France** $17.95
0–13–055814–1

☐ **Germany.** $17.95
0–13–055830–3

☐ **Great Britain** $17.95
0–13–055855–9

☐ **Greece** $17.95
0–13–056002–2

☐ **Greek Islands.** $12.95
0–13–058132–1

☐ **Ireland** $17.95
0–13–058140–2

☐ **Israel** $17.95
0–13–056176–2

☐ **Italy** $17.95
0–13–055897–4

☐ **Japan.** $17.95
0–13–056382–X

☐ **Loire.** $12.95
0–13–056375–7

☐ **Mediterranean Islands** . . $17.95
0–13–056862–7

☐ **Mexico.** $17.95
0–13–056069–3

☐ **Netherlands, Belgium and Luxembourg** $17.95
0–13–056028–6

☐ **Portugal** $17.95
0–13–056135–5

☐ **Provence/Côte d'Azur** . . . $12.95
0–13–056938–0

☐ **Rail Guide to Europe** $17.95
0–13–055971–7

☐ **Rhine** $12.95
0–13–056466–4

☐ **Scandinavia.** $17.95
0–13–056085–5

☐ **Spain** $17.95
0–13–055913–X

☐ **Switzerland** $17.95
0–13–056044–8

☐ **Turkish Coast.** $12.95
0–13–058173–9

☐ **Tuscany** $12.95
0–13–056482–6

☐ **Yugoslavia** $17.95
0–13–056184–3

Please turn the page for an order form and a list of additional Baedeker Guides.

A series of city guides filled with color photographs and detailed maps and floor plans from one of the oldest names in travel publishing:

Please send me the books checked below:

☐ **Amsterdam** $12.95 0–13–057969–6		☐ **London** $12.95 0–13–058025–2
☐ **Athens** $12.95 0–13–057977–7		☐ **Madrid** $12.95 0–13–058033–3
☐ **Bangkok** $12.95 0–13–057985–8		☐ **Moscow** $12.95 0–13–058041–4
☐ **Berlin** $12.95 0–13–367996–9		☐ **Munich** $12.95 0–13–370370–3
☐ **Brussels** $12.95 0–13–368788–0		☐ **New York** $12.95 0–13–058058–9
☐ **Budapest** $12.95 0–13–058199–2		☐ **Paris** $12.95 0–13–058066–X
☐ **Colgne** $12.95 0–13–058181–X		☐ **Prague** $12.95 0–13–058215–8
☐ **Copenhagen** $12.95 0–13–057993–9		☐ **Rome** $12.95 0–13–058074–0
☐ **Florence** $12.95 0–13–369505–0		☐ **San Francisco** $12.95 0–13–058082–1
☐ **Frankfurt** $12.95 0–13–369570–0		☐ **Singapore** $12.95 0–13–058090–2
☐ **Hamburg** $12.95 0–13–369687–1		☐ **Stuttgart** $12.95 0–13–058223–9
☐ **Hong Kong** $12.95 0–13–058009–0		☐ **Tokyo** $12.95 0–13–058108–9
☐ **Istanbul** $12.95 0–13–058207–7		☐ **Venice** $12.95 0–13–058116–X
☐ **Jerusalem** $12.95 0–13–058017–1		☐ **Vienna** $12.95 0–13–371303–2

PRENTICE HALL PRESS
Order Department—Travel Books
200 Old Tappan Road
Old Tappan, New Jersey 07675
In U.S. include $1 postage and handling for 1st book, 25¢ each additional book.
Outside U.S. $2 and 50¢ respectively.

Enclosed is my check or money order for $_____

NAME_____

ADDRESS_____

CITY_____STATE_____ZIP_____